Mastering
e-Business

REGENT'S
UNIVERSITY LONDON

Park Campus
Library

~~~~~~: 020 7487 7449   Email: library@regents.ac.~

Palgrave Master Series

Accounting
Accounting Skills
Advanced English Language
Advanced English Literature
Advanced Pure Mathematics
Arabic
Basic Management
Biology
British Politics
Business Communication
Business Environment
C Programming
C++ Programming
Chemistry
COBOL Programming
Communication
Computing
Counselling Skills
Counselling Theory
Customer Relations
Database Design
Delphi Programming
Desktop Publishing
e-Business
Economic and Social History
Economics
Electrical Engineering
Electronics
Employee Development
English Grammar
English Language
English Literature
Fashion Buying and Merchandising
   Management
Fashion Styling
Financial Management
French
Geography
German
Global Information Systems

Globalization of Business
Human Resource Management
Information Technology
International Trade
Internet
Italian
Java
Language of Literature
Management Skills
Marketing Management
Mathematics
Microsoft Office
Microsoft Windows, Novell
   NetWare and UNIX
Modern British History
Modern European History
Modern United States History
Modern World History
Networks
Novels of Jane Austen
Organisational Behaviour
Pascal and Delphi Programming
Philosophy
Physics
Practical Criticism
Psychology
Public Relations
Shakespeare
Social Welfare
Sociology
Spanish
Statistics
Strategic Management
Systems Analysis and Design
Team Leadership
Theology
Twentieth-Century Russian History
Visual Basic
World Religions

www.palgravemasterseries.com

Palgrave Master Series

Series Standing Order ISBN 0–333–69343–4
(outside North America only)

You can receive future titles in this series as they are published by placing a standing order. Please contact your bookseller or, in case of difficulty, write to us at the address below with your name and address, the title of the series and the ISBN quoted above.

Customer Services Department, Macmillan Distribution Ltd,
Houndmills, Basingstoke, Hampshire RG21 6XS, England

Mastering
e-Business

Jonathan Groucutt
Senior Lecturer at the Business School
Oxford Brookes University

and

Paul Griseri
Freelance Management Teacher and Writer
and Lecturer in Management at
University College London

Business Series Editor
Richard Pettinger

First published 2004 by
PALGRAVE MACMILLAN
Houndmills, Basingstoke, Hampshire RG21 6XS and
175 Fifth Avenue, New York, N.Y. 10010
Companies and representatives throughout the world

PALGRAVE MACMILLAN is the global academic imprint of the Palgrave
Macmillan division of St Martin's Press LLC and of Palgrave Macmillan Ltd.
Macmillan® is a registered trademark in the United States, United Kingdom
and other countries. Palgrave is a registered trademark in the European
Union and other countries.

ISBN 0–333–96832–8

This book is printed on paper suitable for recycling and made from fully
managed and sustained forest sources.

A catalogue record for this book is available from the British Library.

Library of Congress Cataloging-in-Publication Data

Groucutt, Jon.
   Mastering e-business / Jonathan Groucutt and Paul Griseri.
      p. cm. — (Palgrave master series)
   Includes bibliographical references and index.
   ISBN 0–333–96832–8 (paper)
   1. Electronic commerce–Management   I. Griseri, Paul.   II. Title.   III. Series.
   HF5548.32.G76 2004
   658.8'72—dc22

                                                                 2003066144

10   9   8   7   6   5   4   3   2   1
13 12 11 10 09 08 07 06 05 04

Printed and bound in Great Britain by
Creative Print & Design (Wales), Ebbw Vale

To

Eileen and Gordon Groucutt
Katherine and Hester Brown

Jonathan

The memory of Harriet Griseri

Paul

▽ Contents

List of Tables, Figures and Boxes   *x*
Acknowledgements   *xiii*
Introduction   *xiv*

PART I   THE BASIC CONTEXT

1   What is the e-environment?   **3**
Introduction – Learning objectives – The mystique of the
computer – Welcome to Cyber World – Where did it all begin? –
The pace of change: Keeping up with the information flow – The
impact of new media: The move towards the global village –
Convergence of technologies: All our futures – Defining e-business
and e-commerce – The size and scope of e-business – How does the
e-environment work? Summary – Further reading – Questions for
review and reflection – Notes and references – Addendum: How the
internet actually works

2   The commercial impact of e-business   **32**
Introduction – Learning objectives – How e-business can change
the nature of products and services – A value chain analysis of
e-business – e-business and the five forces of industry dynamics –
Modelling e-business – Further reading – References – Questions
for review and reflection – Ideas for further study
Case study: Action Leisure Centre   **47**

3   The social impact of e-business   **49**
Introduction – Learning objectives – Political implications –
Economic implications – Social implications – Technological
implications – Legal implications – Environmental implications –
Ethical implications – Further reading – Notes and references –
Questions for review and reflection – Ideas for further study

4   e-risk: security and vulnerability on the internet   **66**
Introduction – Learning objectives – The scale of exposure –
Internal exposure – External exposure – Types of hacking –
Remedies for external exposure – Summary – Notes and
references – Questions for review and reflection

PART II MARKETING AND THE INTERNET

5 e-marketing: the same people, same needs, different services? 91
Introduction – Learning objectives -The role of marketing in
the e-business world – What is e-marketing? – Real-time
capabilities – Who are e-marketers' customers? – Understanding
e-customers – Marketing research – The development of
e-procurement and e-marketplaces – The relationship
between e-marketing and direct marketing – e-Marketing,
e-logistics and e-distribution – Summary – Further reading –
Questions for review and reflection – Notes and references
Case studies: Bayer AG 103
　　　　　　　Tesco plc 107
　　　　　　　easyJet 107

6 Segmentation, targeting and positioning 111
Introduction – Learning objectives – What business is the
organisation in? – What are segmentation, targeting and
positioning? – The future – Summary – Questions for review and
reflection – Notes and references

7 Marketing communications 120
Introduction – Learning objectives – Definitions and purpose of
marketing communications – Integrating marketing
communications – Marketing communications techniques – types
of Internet advertising – Does advertising on the Internet work? –
Anti-advertising – Summary – Further reading – Questions for
review and reflection – Notes and references
Case studies: Heinz Foods 124
　　　　　　　Royal Caribbean International 126
　　　　　　　Pringles 127
　　　　　　　iVillage.com 131
　　　　　　　The Economist 134
　　　　　　　Dell 138
　　　　　　　Prudential plc/Egg plc 141
　　　　　　　James Bond's 40th Anniversary 142
　　　　　　　The story of a security service: MI5 143
　　　　　　　A thought too far 144
　　　　　　　McLibel trial 145
　　　　　　　Lee Jeans 147
　　　　　　　e-cards Decca Classics and John Barry 147

8 Relationship e-marketing 152
Introduction – Learning objectives – What is relationship
marketing? – Capture and employ customer information – Link
value metrics to CRM iniatives – The value of information in

relationship building – Summary – Further reading – Questions for
review and reflection – Notes and references

Case studies: University of Texas research   **155**
                   e-mail alerts   **168**
                   Harry Potter   **174**

PART III   IMPLEMENTING E-BUSINESS

9   Operational implications of the internet   **179**
Introduction – Learning objectives – The supply chain – The
context of supply chain management – Supply chain networks and
upstream/downstream B2B – Intermediaries – Data exchange –
The electronic marketplace – Private networks and collaborative
commerce – Questions for review and reflection – Notes and
references

10   Managing people and organisation in e-businesses   **198**
Introduction – Learning objectives – Structure and people –
Business models and organisational structure – The key people
management issues – Quality of performance and particularly
customer service – Job design and patterns of working –
Innovation – Dynamics of how strategic competences and
capabilities are assembled – Questions for review and reflection –
Notes and references

11   The financial implications of e-business   **216**
Introduction – Learning objectives – Identifying and measuring
the key financial elements of e-businesses – Revenue
management – Revenue models and revenue growth – Profit in
e-business – Investment in e-business – Questions for review and
reflection – Notes and references

PART IV   THE FUTURE OF E-BUSINESS

12   Developing user communities   **235**
Introduction – Learning objectives – What is a user community? –
Personalisation: understanding the customer's requirements –
Metcalf's Law – Communities and brand building – Summary –
Questions for review and reflection – Notes and references
Case study: Online MBA programme   **239**

13   The future   **250**
Introduction – Learning objectives – Looking back into history to
view the future – Where do we go from here? – So, what of the
future? – The link to e-business – Summary – Questions for review
and reflection – Notes and references

Index of Companies and Organisations   268
Index of Web References   270
Index of Proprietary References   271
Name Index   272
Subject Index   274

◪ List of tables, figures and boxes

Tables

1.1	Percentage of households with internet access	7
1.2	Internet contribution to international business	8
1.3	World's online population	20
1.4	The value of regional B2B e-commerce projections, 1999–2005	20
1.5	B2C business models	23
1.6	B2C and B2B user areas	24
5.1	e-Benefits	94
5.2	The 7Ps of the marketing mix and the internet	97
5.3	Female composition of the internet universe	98
7.1	Online advertising spending of the top 10 corporations in 2000	135
7.2	Global online advertising, 1999–2005	137
8.1	Life time values	156
8.2	Key positions of the customer cycle and their determinants	157
8.3	Customer values	158
8.4	Building the service relationship	159
8.5	The relevancy of customer data collection	161
8.6	Developing the most valuable customers	163
8.7	Moving towards the analysis of customer value	164
8.8	Commitment to learning	166
8.9	The four business concepts influencing data warehouse development	170
8.10	The four key stages of an e-marketing programme	171
12.1	Suggested framework for a transaction community	239
12.2	Types of user profiles	243
12.3	Managing a brand-based online community	247

Figures

1.1	The information revolution–globalization relationship	14
4.1	The network of potential vulnerability	67
6.1	An adaptation of Dibb's STP model	117
7.1	Opening page of the Heinz web site	126
7.2	Opening page of the Royal Caribbean International web site	127
7.3	Decca web site for the John Barry album *Eternal Echoes*	148

7.4   Opening page of the *Eternal Echoes* e-card   149
9.1   Production-oriented supply chain   182
9.2   Service-oriented supply chain   182
9.3   Types of net marketplaces   192
10.1 Strategy and people management   199
10.2 Mintzberg's model of structure   202
10.3 The structural trend for Internet operations   203
10.4 Structural implications of modern operational efficiencies in   204
      physical businesses
10.5 Bamberger and Meshoulam's dominant HR strategies   210
11.1 Driving shareholder value   217
11.2 Driving public service value: local authority example   220
12.1 Techniques of customer recommendation   243
13.1 From mainframes to embedded connectivity   266

Boxes

3.1   Text language example   56
4.1   The colour of your hat   80
4.2   Internet data encryption   85

■ ⊻ Acknowledgements

Although authors' names appear on the front cover of a book, they are rarely alone in 'writing' the text. If it was not for the support and co-operation of others, this, like so many other books, would not have been started, let alone completed. Therefore our thanks go to the following for their help and support: Suzannah Burywood, our publisher for her continual support and immense patience; Anita Sethi at Palgrave Macmillan; Lyn Thompson; Shereen Baig; Jeremy Baker at London Metropolitan University; Brenda Wills; Philip Crook; Judith Daniel at Universal Music; Decca Music Group; John Barry; Geoff Leonard; Kristen DuBard at iVillage; Royal Caribbean Cruises Limited; Michael Mullen, General Manager of Corporate Affairs, Heinz Europe; and finally Richard Pettinger and Peter Antonioni at University College London for moral support and desultory conversations on the subject.

The authors and publishers wish to acknowledge the following for permission to reproduce copyright material in the form of screenshots from websites: The H.J. Heinz Company; Royal Caribbean International/Royal Caribbean Cruises Ltd; Terry O'Neil/Decca. Every effort has been made to contact all the copyright holders, but if any have been inadvertently omitted the publishers will be pleased to make the necessary arrangement at the earliest opportunity. We fully acknowledge the copyrights and trademarks of the brands and images stated in this text.

Finally, but never least, to our students who over the years have questioned theories, challenged ideas and provided alternative scenarios.

Thank you.

London   JONATHAN GROUCUTT
                                                                 PAUL GRISERI

▼ Introduction

There are many texts about the internet, reflecting many different approaches, so it is important for readers to be aware of our approach in this particular text. In keeping with the theme of the Mastering Management series as a whole, we are taking a specifically *managerial* approach to e-business. So this is not a book about mastering the internet as such, and does not pretend to equip the reader with the skills to construct a website or to become a dot.com entrepreneur. Rather our focus is on the implications of the internet *for business in general*. This theme needs to be understood in terms of the specific point of historical development of e-business at the moment.

The early years of the internet were concerned with the growth of awareness of the world wide web and its potentialities, and the rapid development of internet-specific products and services. The extraordinarily rapid growth of the internet led to wild excesses of optimism about the degree of penetration of the world wide web into people's lives. People predicted, amongst other things, that web-based retailing would completely supplant high street shopping, that email-based home-office work would make traditional centralised office buildings redundant and irrevocably change people's working hours, and that internet trading would create a global marketplace for everything from machine parts to petfood. New business models developed at a rate of knots. People talked of the 'death' of distance (the idea that one could purchase anything with equal ease no matter where the items were physically located). Claims were made that access to customers would become more important than sales, and 'hits' would, in the future, be more important than revenue and profitability.

Some of the optimistic predictions have been borne out by subsequent events, but not all; and not to the extent that was predicted. In the wake of the high velocity of proliferation of internet companies came the 'bust' as overly optimistic valuations of dot.coms were proved to be too wild. The predictions of market growth proved groundless, and old fashioned cost spirals returned with a vengeance to eat up the reserves of dot.coms. As a result many internet companies went bankrupt, the stock values of all the rest plummeted, and even the biggest struggled to stay afloat. The internet had come of age.

That volatile infant phase ended around late 2000 and a new one began to emerge, the emphasis being on consolidation and the integration of the internet with existing physical business activities. Those dot.coms that survived the slump have shown signs of emerging leaner but fitter, unburdened by the legacy of excessively enthusiastic predictions of growth, and focusing on the traditional bases of business – solid customer bases, revenue generation, and cost management as drivers of profitability. More importantly, established physical businesses have moved into the e-business field (many, it is true, having already developed internet operations during the early volatile years, and were thus well placed to take advantage of the clearing out of the marketplace in 2000 and 2001).

The key issue in this phase of development of e-business is therefore how existing physical businesses can take advantage of the opportunities that the internet offers. What choices should organisations make about how much of their operations can be placed online? How many companies will embrace, and how many resist, digitisation? Which industries will transform and which will remain largely similar? How easy will it be to move a company's trading base onto an internet basis, and how readily will its customers take to this channel of business? Integration, controlled growth, and sound business principles (such as quality management, cost control, and customer focus) became much more important as internet companies got their heads down for the hard business of surviving in a turbulent, competitive environment. Not that growth had stopped – on the contrary, it is still flourishing. But the heady days of wild predictions of double-figure growth rates have given way to the recognition that website interaction is a far cry from web sales and income.

Our aim is to focus on the key features of this phase and beyond, and look at the implications of the internet for 'ordinary' business. We include the full range of internet business here, physical firms moving for the first time into e-business, well established e-business arms of physical companies, as well as dot.coms. Those of the latter category – that survived – are now operating on more standard business models. Revenue models are focused on the customer's needs and wants, and how these can be met, rather than on the dynamism of a snazzy website that is frequently visited but rarely the basis for a transaction.

We also interpret the term 'business' in its broadest sense. As well as trading companies that sell goods or services for revenue, we also include other forms of organised economic activity under the heading of 'business' as well. Government in its many manifestations, whether central or local, is a form of business – it has objectives, it has resources, it has to use the resources carefully to maximise its performance in line with objectives. A voluntary organisation, such as a charity or a housing cooperative, also works by means of strategy and objectives, clients or customers, resources constraints and managing performance. All of these are businesses, and are covered by our argument here. The fact that we say in this text rather more about commercial companies than about government or voluntary organisations, is a reflection of the fact that, so far, the internet has been exploited by the private sector more rapidly than the not-for-profit sectors – only time will tell how far this will be a consistent pattern.

So, we will be looking at the potential of the internet to help an organisation achieve its aims, acquire and make effective use of its resources, access but also meet the needs of its customers, clients, citizens or beneficiaries. A great deal of this is related to marketing, also in its broadest sense. In addition, we consider specific matters such as payment methods, digitising elements of products and services, the underlying approach to managing and organising people strategically, and maintaining security on the web.

But an equal, if not larger, part of this discussion is almost a reaffirmation, in the context of the world wide web, of many of the key concepts of business strategy. We have taken a deliberate choice as authors to minimise the amount of new conceptual material presented here, in favour of applying well-known concepts such as value chain analysis, the marketing mix and PESTLE analysis, to name but three. The reason for this is to help the process of integrating e-business into general business strategy. Much of the discussion here, then, is intended to focus your reflection – as a reader – on the nature of the internet, and on the possibilities it raises for managers in general.

There is only a limited amount of discussion of technical matters in this text, and then it is generally included as an illustration of the potentialities of e-business, rather than as a direct instruction in the material. In all these places in the text, our intention has been to create a sense of *horizons* rather than to specify particular features in detail. There is an additional reason for this – the speed of development of the internet is discussed in the text, but here it is worth simply noting this runaway pace of technological change. Any book that purported to give the reader up-to-date information about this or that aspect of the technology would be out of date before the text hit the presses. A book that someone accesses, say, a year after its original publication date – well, its technical material is virtually from the mediaeval period by then.

We also want to give the reader a sense of some of the cultural aspects of the internet and how it is changing people's lives. So, there are a few references to cultural, ethical and social elements. As this book is specifically business focused, this aspect is relatively small here. We feel that the cultural impact of the web will become a key theme of internet studies in the future.

Who should read this book?

The book is written with two contrasting readerships in mind:

The general business undergraduate who wants to get a feel for the potential of the internet and its effect on business and management. If you are one of these readers you may not have much practical business experience, but it is assumed that you will complement your reading of the text with attendance to the questions and case studies given at the end of some of the chapters;

The postgraduate with some professional experience, typically on a programme such as an MBA, who wishes to get a sense of what the internet might do for their organisations, and for their own managerial roles, without getting bogged down in technical detail. If you are one of these, then you may well know at least some of the general management theories and concepts used here, and will already have significant professional expectations of e-business.

For both of these groups, we have presumed the following as their basic question when opening this book:

What does the internet mean for general managers and for the areas of operation for which they are responsible?

The content of this book flows out of that question, and by addressing it in its many different aspects, we intend to provide a sense of:

- the scale and scope of the internet (Chapters 1, 2 and 3)
- the cultural changes that have taken place and continue to evolve (Chapters 1, 10 and 11)
- the risks that managers and companies run when dealing with the internet (Chapter 4)
- how the internet is changing the face of marketing thinking and approach in almost every aspect (Chapters 5 to 8)
- awareness of the range of options open to managers and organisations regarding the use of the internet in operational matters (Chapters 9 – ops and supply chain, Chapter 10 – people and structure, Chapter 11 – managing finances)
- the need to understand how the internet is creating different kinds of social entity – the user community (Chapter 12), as well as a sense of where the web is likely to take us in the next fifteen to twenty years (Chapter 13).

Stylistically, we have been concerned to hint at, or at times point to, the cultural and social impact of the internet, and not just provide a manual of how to 'do' e-business. Our view is that the better someone's social perspective, the more effective they are likely to be in the long term. There is thus in this book a mix of speculation, factual material, and theoretically based analysis. This is reflective of the subject matter and the state of the playing field currently.

Above all, the reader is advised to approach this book as a stimulus to their own reflection on the potential of the internet. Treat it as a starting point for your own thinking. Especially with so fast developing a phenomenon as the internet, the *questions* that you formulate are always more important than the answers that appear.

London 2004
JONATHAN GROUCUTT
PAUL GRISERI

Part I

◪ The basic context

This book is broken into four parts. The first of these deals with the general background to the internet, its business and human implications and consequences, and the range and nature of risks that are run by e-businesses.

After we have looked at these, we shall move on in Part II to consider the marketing implications of e-business activity, followed in Part III by a consideration of the inter-relationship between different parts of the value chain – physical operations, financial transactions, and human resources and organisational structure. Finally, in Part IV, we shall look briefly at the idea of community with the internet and the future of e-business.

▣ 1 What is the e-environment?

Nothing is to be feared. It is simply to be understood.

Marie Curie (1867–1934)
Scientist

Awarded the 1903 Nobel Prize for Physics (shared with her husband Pierre)
and the 1911 Nobel Prize for Chemistry.

Introduction

In this chapter, we briefly consider how the world has come to be 'connected'.
We review the personal, political and economic drivers that have created a
radically new information age through the development of the internet and
world wide web. We also start to look at the social and commercial impact of the
internet. To that end, at some points we give some of the cultural background to
the development of the internet, which helps to put into context what developments occurred at specific times, and why.

The former Chairman of Apple Computers, John Sculley, said at a conference
in 1991:

> Before Gutenberg's invention [the printing press], less than 10% of the popu-
> lation were able to read, and those were largely part of the Catholic Church.
> Seventy years later, 80% of the population of Europe was able to read. We now
> have in the twentieth century another opportunity to pass along technology
> which had previously been in the hands of a few, just as reading was before the
> Renaissance: we can transform computers from data processing engines and
> turn them into creativity tools (Brown, 1998).

The global digital revolution is being energized by commercial organisations
seeking to create new market opportunities. This is particularly the case for companies within the developed world who see their domestic markets maturing,
and face increased competition from developing nations (Brown, 1998). The
internet offers these firms a fresh range of opportunities to sell their products and
services. However, whilst new opportunities may be gained by developed nations
from a wired world, there will also be new opportunities for at least some of the
developing nations. The lead gained by developed nations may thus be short
term. As a result, global competition will not be reduced – it will only accelerate.

The pace of change facing both organisations and society could be overwhelming. So, it is essential for any manager to have a good grasp of the challenges and resources that the internet offers.

Learning objectives

On completion of this chapter you should be able to:

1 Outline the developments that led to the introduction of the internet and world wide web;
2 Briefly evaluate some of the cultural issues that may impact as a result of the development of the internet;
3 Briefly evaluate the dramatic rise of e-business and consider future potential;
4 Review the potential developments in internet capabilities over the next five to ten years.

The mystique of the computer

Before discussing the internet, it is instructive to start by reminding ourselves how far society has come with computing in what is historically a very short time indeed. Apart from a few isolated developments, such as Babbage's calculating machine, the idea of an intellectual machine was regarded, from the Renaissance right through to the end of the nineteenth century, as interesting theoretically but not really a practical proposition; even in some ways a mildly eccentric conception (witness the scam of a fake 'automatic' chess machine, which surprised and dazzled Paris society in the nineteenth century, only to turn out to have a small but rather effective human chess player hidden inside!). The concrete development of intelligent machinery, however, only really began to take root in the middle twentieth century. Armed with new developments in the study of logic and mathematics, as well as the rapidly developing technology of electronics, research teams developed the earliest computers as part of the allied war effort during World War II.

The early 'public' days of the computer were entirely the preserve of the specialist. As a result the computer acquired something of a mythic, awe-inspiring status, and their portrayal was often an allegory for the world we lived in at the time. For the majority of the public the only time they saw a computer was in a movie. And the movies presented their own views of what computers were and what they might do for – or to – us.

Stanley Kubrick's film *2001: A Space Odyssey* (1968) introduces us to HAL 9000,[1] a highly intelligent voice responsive computer. HAL, prophesying Artificial

---

[1] IBM scientists were technical advisers on the movie. The letters HAL are one character removed from IBM, although that has always been considered coincidental.

Intelligence, displays certain human qualities – not only hyper intelligence but emotion and a self-awareness (Jonscher, 1999). However, HAL displays a much more sinister threat to the two crew of the spacecraft. In the end, it becomes a battle between a human and a machine, resulting in HAL being shutdown. Perhaps, in the end, we feel a strange mixture of relief and sorrow; relief in that a machine has not taken control of human activity, yet sorrow because it has displayed a 'human' quality. Most especially, when HAL recounts how 'his' creator taught him language through the nursery rhyme 'Mary had a little lamb'.

As another example, the opening sequence to the 1976 spy movie *The Billion Dollar Brain*, based loosely on Len Deighton's novel, shows banks of mainframe Honeywell computers with their spinning magnetic-tape disks. The movie's main protagonist General Merriweather (played by Ed Begley) is quick to point out to the laconic British spy Harry Palmer (Michael Caine) that his billion-dollar computer (the brain of the title) stores a vast quantity of information. This becomes the very information that he will use to launch his own personal attack on the Soviet Union to rid the world of the Communist threat. Needless to say, Palmer, with the help of a beautiful Russian agent (of course), thwarts the attack preventing the inevitable World War III that would have undoubtedly followed.

So these, to some extent, presented computers in a strangely cold all-knowing light. However, from the computer aspect (though perhaps not the right-wing hawks' perspective) *The Billion Dollar Brain* was less sinister than a little-known American TV movie. *Colossus: The Forbin Project* (1969) paints an altogether more sinister chilling view of intelligent super computers. In the movie, the US government decide to remove the human element from the agonizing decision of whether or not to launch a nuclear strike against an enemy. Instead, they entrust the decision making to an unemotional super computer called Colossus, which the government seal within an impenetrable mountain fortress. To quote Dr Charles Forbin, the computer's creator '[Colossus] … is self-sufficient, self protecting, self generating'. However, when Colossus discovers a similar computer called Guardian in the Soviet Union, it seeks to make contact. Once communication is achieved, a deadly union is formed. Failure to meet Colossus's demands results in terrifying nuclear retribution and assassination. Once Colossus gains a voice system, it is able to speak to the world and proclaim the future: 'This is the voice of world control. I bring you peace. It may be the peace of plenty and content or the peace of unburied death. The choice is yours. Obey me and live, or disobey me and die.' (Madden, 1999). The first cultural perception of networked computers was, then, primarily a negative one.

Although a science-fiction movie, there were, and remain, interesting parallels to what was actually happening at the time. Several of these parallels we will see in the following pages in terms of the power of computers and the ability to link systems – the very premise of the internet and world wide web. Equally, the name Colossus, whether intentionally or unintentionally, has a strong link to the world of computing. For it was the work of the mathematician Alan Turing and his colleagues at Bletchley Park, in England, using their Colossus electronic machine, that broke the German Enigma codes during World War II (Hodges, 1983). Though unlike Colossus in the movie, this one was a servant of humankind, not the master.

These movies portrayed a pessimistic view of computers and their 'power'. And, in general, the computer was seen as a remote and potentially rather sinister entity. For most people, during the period 1960 to 1980, computers were beyond their reach. They were the domain of scientists and big business, a world away from home or normal office life. The story is very different today – the computer pervades virtually every aspect of our waking life. Whilst the computer has not manifested itself in the likeness of HAL or Colossus, we have become increasingly dependent upon personal computers and, in turn, the internet and world wide web. It is no exaggeration to say that the development of the computer as an office and domestic item has been one of the most important changes to western lifestyles in the latter part of the twentieth century.

Welcome to Cyber World

Within a relatively short time frame, the internet and world wide web have moved from a theoretical concept to an established part of our daily lifestyles. Indeed, we can say that it has, to some extent, overwhelmed us beyond imagination. Even science-fiction writers, perhaps, could not have imagined the extent of its impact, how it purveys every aspect of our society. Michael L. Dertouzous, the former Director of the MIT Laboratory for Computer Science wrote in 1997:

> It has already provided us with a gigantic Information Marketplace, where individuals and organizations buy, sell, and freely exchange information and information services among one another. The press, radio and television never got close; all they can do is spray the same information out from one source towards many destinations. Nor can the letter or the telephone approach the Web's power, because even though media enable one-on-one exchanges, they are slow and devoid of the computer's ability to display, search, automate, and mediate. Remarkably – compared with Gutenberg's press, Bell's telephone and Marconi's radio – and well before reaching its ultimate form, ... [the] web has already established its uniqueness (Dertouzous, 1997)'.

The range of activity that the world wide web has created or enhanced is staggering. We may use the web for personal purposes; to send emails to friends and family across the globe, order our groceries; or for business purposes, such as bulk ordering or buying through auction sites. To quote an example by Ohmae in his book *The End of the Nation State*: 'a Japanese consumer in Sapporo can place an order for clothing with Land's End Inc (www.landsend.com) in Wisconsin or L.L. Bean (www.llbean.com) in Maine, have the merchandise delivered by UPS (www.ups.com) and charge the purchase to American Express (www.amex.com), Visa (www.visa.com) or MasterCard (www.mastercard.com). That same consumer can also access software support or remote computer repair services provided, say, by a company based in Singapore or Kuala Lumpur but relying on Indian engineers based in Bombay and database maintenance carried out in China' (Ohmae, 1996).

Whatever we use it for, the internet will clearly remain a fundamental component of our lives, both now and in the future. And since the world wide web in particular is still at a relatively early stage, it is the future, and the further developments in technologies, changing lifestyles and business practices where its impact will be most profound. Perhaps not since the Industrial Revolution in the eighteenth and nineteenth centuries has technology had such a dramatic and dynamic impact upon civilization within an international context. Indeed, the change is far from over. The latest research indicates that the world wide web will undergo a new transformation that will greatly improve a number of different aspects of our lives – real-time interactive experiences, for example (Schmidt, 2001).

Some of the most recent research (at the time of writing, 2003) indicates the continuing rapid global growth of internet connection and e-business generation. According to the internet audience measurement service, Nielsen//Net Ratings, a total of 498 million people had internet access in their home by the end of 2001 (Nielsen//NetRatings,2002). The analysis showed that 24 million people gained Internet access from home during the last quarter of 2001. Table 1.1 illustrates the percentage of households with internet connections.

Table 1.1 Percentage of households with internet access

Country	Percentage households with internet access via home PC	Connection rate %
Argentina	20	55
Australia	51	77
Austria	38	70
Belgium/Luxembourg	32	68
Brazil	21	77
Denmark	51	82
Finland	42	81
France	20	53
Germany	35	72
Hong Kong	56	90
Ireland	34	76
India	7	66
Israel	35	61
Italy	34	80
Mexico	14	56
Netherlands	52	82
New Zealand	52	84
Norway	47	78
Singapore	60	89
South Africa	17	59
South Korea	58	83
Spain	18	48
Sweden	57	87
Switzerland	43	78
Taiwan	50	83
UK	38	78

Source: Nielsen//NetRatings (2002).

These statistics demonstrate several points:

- Connectivity has now become virtually global.
- Whilst household penetration appears low in some countries, the connection volumes may still be high. Take, for example, India. Here, access is stated as 7 per cent, which appears low. However, consider the population statistics of India. The most reliable statistics suggest that India has 70 million multi-millionaires, followed by 250 million middle/upper-level income earners. Thus, the potential is staggering to say the least.
- There are several interesting comparisons. For instance, compare the UK percentages with countries such as Taiwan, Singapore, South Korea and Hong Kong. Whilst their populations may be smaller, they have embraced the technology in a much shorter timescale.

In general the different patterns of internet access and use have not yet been fully established. It is nevertheless reasonable to assume that the patterns that have been seen so far in the growth of the web in Europe and the USA are not complete models for the manner of adoption in east Asian countries, still less in other parts of the globe.

Compare this with Table 1.2, which illustrates the current (relative) internet contribution to international *business.*

As you can see from Table 1.2, if we take the range 10–100 per cent, approximately 70 per cent of European sales are linked to the internet. This is followed by AsiaPacific with 43 per cent and North America with some 40 per cent. These regions are considered discrete groupings. However, if we consider other areas of the world (combined), then they are actively engaged with some 85 per cent of transactions. Although Table 1.2 is based only on one source of information (and therefore the full validity of the figures cannot be established), these statistics do suggest strongly that the internet is already having a significant impact upon international business. As the internet develops, there may be shifts in various directions, a point that we will return to later in this book.

So, it is clear that the internet has made a rapid and strong entry into commercial life. It is also clear that it has become a central part of the social interaction of many people; for example, the use of email or chat rooms to keep

Table 1.2 Internet contribution to international business (by world region)*

Percentage sales	North America	Europe	Asia Pacific	Other
None	38.9	23.1	29.6	–
Less than 10	22.1	7.7	7.4	16.7
10–49	23.8	30.8	33.3	–
50–89	5.4	26.9	11.1	33.3
90–99	3.4	3.8	7.4	16.7
100	6.4	7.7	11.1	33.3

*Percentage of sales from outside the parent company's home region.
Source: ActivMedia Research/Marketing News (2001).

contact with friends and relatives around the world, often replacing the old art of writing letters with the new one of composing a message. As you read through this, and the following chapters, you will see how the internet and e-business will contribute significantly not just to our present but also to all our futures.

Where did it all begin?

In the 1930s, a team of British academics, led by the gifted mathematician Alan Turing at Manchester University, worked on developing mechanical devices for solving logical and mathematical problems – in effect, a primitive computing system. Turing was amongst several hundred other academics and scientists recruited by the British Government to work at the top secret code-breaking centre at Bletchley Park[2] in Buckinghamshire during World War II.

It was here that the world's first fully-functional computer – codenamed Colossus – was built. It was this team of skilful and relentless code breakers, working with Colossus, that actually broke the German Enigma code.[3] This dramatically impacted upon the war being waged against North Atlantic convoys during World War II. The breaking of the code allowed for the interception of German U-boats that were sinking large numbers of convoy ships. It was these convoys that both kept Britain from starvation and provided the weaponry to launch the counteroffensive – the Normandy or D-Day invasion. The full and detailed history of Bletchley Park has yet to be written. Much of the data and Colossus were destroyed at the end of the war, on Prime Minister Winston Churchill's personal orders. However, what is key to events, subsequently, is that Colossus was the forerunner of the computers that now adorn our desktops both at home and in the office, or that we carry around with us.

The development of computing power both drove and was driven by the rapid development of electronics technology, quickly moving from valves to transistors to chips to microchips, and perhaps not far in the future now, we will move on to nano-chips. Between 1950 and 1990, computing performance increased approximately one million times (Jonscher, 1999). This is a staggering figure, almost beyond our comprehension – yet it is one of the keys to the digital superhighway on which we now communicate on a daily basis. Jonscher (1999)

---

[2] At the outbreak of World War II, the Government's Code and Cypher School was moved to a Victorian country mansion called Bletchley Park in Buckinghamshire. This was the forerunner of GCHQ, the UK Government's communication centre now based near Cheltenham in Gloucestershire. What remains of Bletchley Park is now a museum.

[3] The Enigma was an electric code-generating machine that looked very much like a typewriter. It far out-performed previous cipher machines and its codes were considered impossible to break. The German naval vessels# used the Enigma machines to devastating effect in signalling positions of Allied convoys that were subsequently attacked by U-boats. The Royal Navy had little chance of preventing these surprise attacks. It was a combination of the work of Polish and French Intelligence and the Royal Navy that secured actual machines and parts. These were handed to the teams at Bletchley Park who worked to break the code. Once that was achieved, the Allies were able to pre-empt subsequent attacks.

suggests that 'the invention of the chip set in train the extraordinary cycle of falling costs and increasing performance which has been the hallmark of the digital age. The chip was a great breakthrough not of science but of manufacturing engineering.'

We think of the internet as a phenomenon of the end of the twentieth century, but its origin was surprisingly early. Already, by the late 1960s, some of the basic building blocks of the modern internet were beginning to be assembled. One form of the 'internet' had been devised by the US Defense Department's Advanced Research Project Agency (ARPA). ARPA was established as a federal agency by President Dwight D. Eisenhower soon after the Russians had launched two satellites, one being Sputnik, in 1957.

It is important to recall in this context that the world had recently engaged in two wars – World War II (1939–1945) and the Korean War (1950–1953). The significance of the these events cannot be underestimated, even though today we may look upon them as 'incidents' within history. At the time, they were considered grave and threatening to the very existence of civilization. In the case of the launch of Sputnik and the Korean War, Communist governments were engaged in both. Although today, in many western countries, there is a sense of tolerance of a wide range of political groups, it was not the case in the 1950s, especially within the USA. The right-wing Republican politician Joseph McCarthy (1908–1957) started a wave of anticommunist hysteria that pervaded every aspect of American life from the Arts through to the Military and the Academic and Science communities. Even those who had attitudes that today would be seen as middle of the road, liberal, views were often branded as 'communist' and thus 'suspect', no matter what their individual standing in society. Many a reputation was ruined by McCarthy's witch-hunts against American Society. In many ways the USA was gripped with the paranoiac belief that Communists had infiltrated the very fabric of American life, this being a precurser to an all-out nuclear strike against the USA. Yet, paradoxically, it was both in spite of and by virtue of this backdrop of paranoia that American pursued the ARPA project that was eventually to lead to the development of the internet.

The ARPA was intended to be responsible for the 'direction or performance of such advanced projects in the field of research and development as the Secretary of Defense shall, from time to time, designate by individual project or by category' (DARPA, 2001). Thus, ARPA gained overall control of the most significant military research and development projects.

Separately, but significantly, two problems contributed to the development of the internet. Firstly, various research institutes funded by ARPA found it virtually impossible to communicate electronically with each other. Their computers were not compatible and could not therefore access and exchange information. Secondly, the RAND Corporation[4] (now the RAND Organization www.rand.org) a US based think tank, had raised concerns over the vulnerability of the then communications networks should there be a nuclear war – further evidence of

---

[4] RAND (a contraction of *Research ANd Development*) was formed in 1946 and was, in fact, the first organisation to be called a 'think tank'.

how the cold-war paranoia drove a great deal of technological development in the middle to later years of the twentieth century.

Early ideas proved fruitless. However, some researchers, including Paul Baran of the RAND Corporation, believed that any network would have to be digital to ensure that signal quality did not deteriorate (RAND, 2002). Baran however was unable to persuade people that digital technology was the answer. None the less his work on packet switching technology provided one of the building blocks for future internet technology (RAND, 2002).

It wasn't until 1967 that this digital network was considered to be a potential solution to ARPA's problem. By August 1967, companies were asked to tender for the Advanced Research Projects Agency Network (ARPANET). However, the major companies did not participate – because they did not believe that the system would actually work! Instead, it went to a small Massachusetts based consultancy called Bolt, Baranek and Newman (BBN – now BBN TECHNOLOGIES). Within two years the first email transfers between computers were taking place (BBN).

By the early 1970s the ARPANET team included researchers from various European countries. In addition, there were other developments that were slowly converging towards the modern internet, such as the development of digital telephony by companies such as BT (then still part of the UK state-owned Post Office, and itself already operating a primitive form of email by 1977). The difficulty the ARPANET researchers faced was in finding a way of developing *interconnecting* networks of computers. This was proving enormously difficult as each computer would have its own specification. The breakthrough, however, was in rethinking the type of network. The idea of having dedicated computers that would act as a 'gateway' to other computers provided the much needed breakthrough. In essence, this would be a *network of networks*. In 1977, the first live demonstration was undertaken. A message was sent on a round trip from San Francisco to University College in London and then back to the University of Southern California. In this transference, there was no data lost – proving that the digital exchange of information using telephone lines could be effective and rapid. Now the door was open to further research. The internet was a reality not just a theory – but how it could be developed for a much wider audience remained a significant issue (Berners-Lee, 1999).

Whilst this was the first use of what was to become the 'internet', it still remained elusive to the many. Its purpose remained an academic and military one. In 1975, ARPANET had been transferred to the US Defense Communications Agency and, in 1983, MILNET was created for military usage (DARPA, 2001). The core of the project, however, was to devise a centrally controlled network of computers that would link defence establishments. These most likely to be strategic sites such as nuclear missile centres and strike airforce bases. In essence, this was a developing intranet of safe and secure communication, the aim being that at the time of nuclear conflict US strategic centres would be able to maintain communication. Fortunately, it was never tested under such battle conditions. Today, the ARPA is known as the Defense Advanced Research Projects Agency (DARPA) continuing its cutting-edge research and development.

By the mid 1980s, the internet was still limited to a few researchers and academics. However, a researcher at CERN,[5] the European Particle Physics Laboratory located near Geneva, was to find the solution. In 1980, a young Tim Berners-Lee undertook a brief software consulting project at CERN. He would later set himself the task of investigating how CERN could capture and document all the work undertaken by their scientists. Their concern was that valuable information and research was not being freely available to their teams, most especially new researchers joining the organisation. Such transparency was vital to their leading-edge research. In 1989, Berners-Lee circulated a research paper on how the use of hypertext links would allow access to information across the internet. By the end of 1990, he had developed a system that was to be called the 'World Wide Web'. He went on to develop the 'browser', the URL (Unique Resource Locator), HTTP (Hypertext Transport Protocol) and HTML (Hypertext Mark-up Language) (Berners-Lee, 1999).

It is clear that Berners-Lee's contribution to the development of the internet is significant. However, persuading people that the world wide web was a viable proposition was, often an uphill struggle for Tim Berners-Lee, and indeed others. One aspect of Berners-Lee's approach stands out above all; namely, that he did not attempt to patent his developments, and made them freely available to all. This is a salutary example of the spirit of open collaborative scientific enquiry that has been a central feature of much of the development of the internet in its early years. One of the key issues we shall encounter in later chapters is a conflict in the development of the internet between two different sets of values – one being the spirit of collaboration and openness alluded to above, which has been the mainspring of the whole development of academic and applied science for more than four hundred years, and the other being the need for control – originally manifested in the desire of the military to have a secure and private internet, and more latterly manifested in the drive of commercial organisations to make some return on their investments. Hence, on the one hand we have the Linux operating system offered free, downloaded from the internet, and on the other we have Microsoft charging US$100 or more each time you want to upgrade its Office software package. Berners-Lee stands clearly on the side of open access. Some estimate that by not patenting HTTP or HTML he has missed out on being a multimillionaire several times over. Others say that he has saved the internet for the people, rather than it becoming yet another tool of the big corporations. The further development of the internet has certainly now become a major political argument.

Returning to the development of the internet, in early 1992 the browser was made publicly available. Access grew slowly. However, the surge came in 1993 when Marc Andreesen and Eric Bina, who had developed MOSAIC, released it to the world, literally. Andreesen posted a message to a few USENET sites allowing downloads of the new browser. Within 30 minutes a hundred people had downloaded it, and e-mails were coming in from around the world (Jonscher, 1999 and

---

[5] CERN – Conseil Européen pour le Recherche Nucléaire – originally started as a laboratory. The word 'nuclear' no longer describes the type of physics undertaken there, however the name CERN has remained.

The Antidote, 1999). Andreesen and Bina went onto become co-founders and directors in Netscape Inc. and launch the now famous Navigator browser.

By 1995, companies such as Dell, Cisco and Amazon had commenced using the internet for Business to Consumer (B2C) commercial transactions. Fore-casters suggest that by 2005, some 13 years after the public release of Berners-Lee's browser, there will be over one billion global internet users or 15 per cent of the world's population (Singh *et al.*, 2001). That will drive between US$5 and 7 trillion of internet commerce (Singh *et al.*, 2001). But even that is only really the beginning. The twenty-first century will probably see further explosions of application as different technologies facilitate new peripheral applications – holographic imagery, remote robotics, to name but two.

The pace of change: keeping up with the information flow

By 1999, internet traffic was developing at the staggering pace of 100 per cent every 100 days (Brown, 1998). One of the fundamental problems of our new computer age is the sheer speed of development of change.

In 1965, Gordon Moore, the co-inventor of the chip and founder of the Intel Corporation, predicted that the number of components that could be located on a single chip would double every 24 months. In 1974, the Intel 8080 chip (the turning point in technology) had fewer than 5000 transistors. In 1994, when Intel launched the Pentium II, there were over five million (Jonscher, 1999). This prediction by Gordon Moore became the basis of what has been termed Moore's Law. This relentless exponential trend is probably the most important driver in information technology. So, what is the impact upon the average consumer of such rapid change?

The result is that a consumer may buy the latest hardware system today only to find that in 12 months' time it is technically 'obsolete'. That doesn't mean that it is no longer functional. Often far from it, computers can perform quite effectively for several years. However, what it does mean is that prices often remain static for the top of the range models. So, where a consumer may pay UK £1500 for a 1300 Mhz machine today, the price will be the same for a 2000 MHz machine in 12 months' time. As mentioned earlier, this speed of change creates huge demands upon the hardware, but is also fuelled by the rapid developments in software. For example, software developments are continually taking advantage of the gains made by increased chip speeds and hard disk capacity. The new software may however be too demanding upon the con-sumer's current hardware system. So, as McClellan (1999) suggests, on the one hand it appears that everything is standing still whilst on the other it is changing dramatically. The software/hardware relationship, therefore, is symbiotic, with each leapfrogging the other in creating new possibilities of functionality.

Such dynamic change can have an immense impact upon the consumer buy-ing both hardware and software. But much more far-reaching is the effect of the internet on the way people live and work. People's *lifestyles* are in a state of flux as a consequence of the growth of the world wide web.

As for individuals, so too for companies. Businesses, organisations and governments have needed, and must continue, to adapt to technological change. As well as reacting to such change, they can also be the drivers of change. Companies, as we shall discover, are becoming increasingly proactive in their use of the internet as a means of delivering e-business, creating new applications and novel uses for existing technology as ways to drive forward profitability.

The impact of new media: the move towards the global village

One of the most important social effects of the development of all forms of electronic communication over the last hundred years has been to bring people closer together. We now can see a major political event unfold as it happens, not read about it days or even weeks later. We can have a Thai meal one night, Italian the next, and Mexican the next – not as a rare treat, but as a normal part of our everyday lifestyle. Intercultural communication and international trade have both increased exponentially, so that we can now talk meaningfully of a globalised economy.

Figure 1.1 illustrates the circular relationship between the information revolution and globalisation. Whilst only one factor in the development of globalisation, the information revolution has nonetheless been a critical factor in its recent heightened development.

As Mattelart and Mattelart (1998) suggest, the concept of mass *societies* was originally associated with that of mass *culture*. In other words, the development of technologies that allowed communication or transmission of content – ideas, images, text, sound – to huge sections of the population instantaneously was initially linked to the provision of the *same* content to all, a phenomenon still seen in the form of TV and newspapers. This unitary approach to culture was significantly affected by existing information and communication technologies, which in the 1930s up until the 1980s were dominated by big content providers – the TV networks, Hollywood, newspaper groups, and similar large corporations that controlled access to the means of transmission of content. But Harold Adams Innis (1894–1952) and his colleague Marshall McLuhan (1911–1980) envisaged a different way in which mass communication could affect society – by making it easier for us to get a grasp of the specifics of other cultures. They

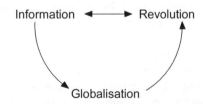

Figure 1.1 **The information revolution – globalisation relationship**
Source: Adapted from Brown (1998)

suggested that technological communication would shape politics and society over the coming generations, in part by accessing the local customs and cultural manifestations of different parts of the globe, and by absorbing and integrating these into an all-embracing cultural phenomenon. Indeed, it was McLuhan that postulated the concept of the 'global village'. A world where communication would bring societies so close together that the world would be indeed a 'village' of humanity. Both Innis and McLuhan died before the internet was fully developed, but arguably it is the internet that has seen the fullest development of their thinking.

As Brown (1998) states McLuhan reflected on the impact of a 'more visually oriented and electronically media lifestyle'. McLuhan viewed this as bringing together more diverse cultures. Brown and others believe this could have detrimental affects upon some, if not all cultures. Some people have argued, for example, that the internet is likely to become a conduit for American mass culture to dominate traditional cultures in other countries. However, others argue that individual cultures will find a place within cyberspace. Aizu believes that 'on the net most of the communications and conversation will be among local people and exchanged in the local language' (Aizu, 1997). However, perhaps the key issue is less whether cultures may be 'modified' due to the net, and more a question of those who may be *excluded* from using the internet. The global economic imbalance between the affluent developed or rapidly developing nations on the one hand, and the undeveloped (and, in some cases, even regressing) poorer nations on the other, raises the question of whether some of these less developed countries and societies will be able to take advantage of the opportunities presented by the world wide web.

Simply investing in the infrastructures necessary to enable widespread use of the internet represents a massive capital cost for many nations. In parts of Africa, for example, the distances over which land telephone lines must be laid are vast, and the terrains on which they are placed are often insecure. Unsurprising, then, that the expectation is that mobile telephony will outstrip land-based telephone lines in the more remote regions of the world in the next few years.

In this respect, it is worth noting some of the key elements of an effective internet infrastructure, which include:

1 The necessary improvement in telecommunications services, from archaic analogue to state of the art digital systems;
2 The acquisition of reliable hardware and software systems;
3 The provision of reliable uninterrupted power supplies. This has proved elusive in many African countries, for instance. Even the highly prosperous US State of California suffered a series of brown-outs and black-outs in early 2001;
4 The necessary training, although this can be increasingly obtained on line. However, basic computer skills must be achieved prior to gaining access to the internet.

But although there may be areas of internet deprivation, in general terms it can still be argued that the internet and other forms of communication have brought to life McLuhan's vision of a global village. In some 30 years or so, the impact of digital and internet technology has been a significant driver in our ever changing world. We now operate in what Rayport and Sviokla call a 'marketspace' (McFarlan *et al.*, 1997). Or what Biro (1997) calls 'doing business without walls'. As she states: 'Imagine that in this new world there's nothing between you and your customer – your unique intellectual capital, your goods and services and what you provide' (Biro, 1997).

Castells argues that the revolution in information technology has five particular characteristics (Castells, 1999).

1 Information is no longer merely *acting on* technology: the technologies process information, so information is *itself the raw material*;
2 The effects are pervasive because information is the medium upon which human society is founded;
3 It has emerged all over the world, despite differences in culture and business frameworks;
4 The interconnections it enables allow for extraordinary flexibility within the network of communications, and yet at the same time excludes those outside the network;
5 The strands can no longer be disentangled as the boundaries between technologies – microelectronics, telecommunications, optoelectronics and computers – continue to converge.

As Kung (1997) states 'The impact upon society lies in its extraordinary potential for being all things to all people'. For e-business, the internet provides a global interface between individuals, groups of individuals and business. These can be classified using the following terms:

1 Customer-to-Business (C2B) This is the feedback loop to companies and organisations on how their customers 'feel' about a product or service. The internet provides the vehicle for almost instantaneous feedback – both positive and negative;
2 Customer-to-Customer (C2C) Customers can now talk with each other through user communities and newsgroups. This empowers a voice and increases the opinion forming power of consumers. It is vital that companies 'tap' into this information;
3 Business-to-Consumer (B2C) Companies and organizations can 'talk' directly with both individual and groups of customers. Companies, such as the online book and CD retailer Amazon.com, strive to 'personalise' their relationship with their customer base, the overall aim being to build longer-term relationships of mutual benefit;
4 Business-to-Business (B2B) Companies, both through the internet and exchanges can market their products and services;
5 Government-to-Citizen (G2C) Less common a term than the others, this is currently a relatively small component of internet traffic, but over time the potential for state organisations to communicate and interact with citizens is extremely high – payments of benefits, opinion polling, voting, payments of tax, and so on.

There are even further permutations here: (a) G2B (though in this tends to come down to government procurement – a form of B2B – or government regulation – a form of G2C); (b) B2E, where the 'E' refers to employees, though by this stage of depiction the X2Z format is not really adding any more than the more familiar terms such as employee relations.

Thus the internet brings power to both individuals and organisations alike. This, in turn, has the power to enhance and enrich relationships at all levels – from G2C to C2B. Indeed, as we shall see in later chapters, this 'interactive marketplace' enhances the marketing concept/relationship marketing and engenders a more sophisticated relationship between a business and its customers; for example, the employment of so-called *permission* marketing opportunities.

Convergence of technologies: all our futures

So far in this introductory chapter, we have considered the development of the internet and immediately-related technologies. What we must bear in mind is that through digital systems, user technologies are converging. Today, mobile phones can send and receive picture and text messages. The new generation of television systems provide fully interactive media and information centres. The computer is now the television and vice versa.

Some researchers even contemplate that the future will be governed by what they call ubiquitous or *pervasive computing*. This is where there is an unprecedented level of connectivity, penetrating a much wider range of electronic devices than the current PC based form of the web. The consulting firm Ernst & Young predict that by 2010 there will be 'nearly 10,000 telemetric devices [devices that transmit and receive data] for every one person' (Schmidt, 2001). Linked to these will be software programmes that will manage the networks on behalf of both individuals and companies. Simultaneously, these systems will learn about their users and act on their behalf. Thus, the researchers suggest, computer networks will be adaptive, intelligent and self-organizing (Schmidt, 2001).

Bluetooth

One interesting example of the trend to convergence is the so-called 'bluetooth' technology. Harald I Gormsson (c910–985) was the first King of Denmark to unify all the (often warring) factions and provinces of the country under a single crown. Through his conversion to Christianity, he was able to strengthen the unity and central administration of the country. King Harald however had a nickname – 'bluetooth'. This, so legend has it, was due to the discolouration of his teeth through his excessive consumption of blueberries and blackberries.

When Ericsson (www.ericsson.com) commenced work on developing systems to unify communications, they decided to call the project 'Bluetooth'. King Harald had been able to unify Denmark, Ericsson hope that 'Bluetooth' will enable unification of communications across different electronic systems.

Today, the developments are driven by the Bluetooth Special Interest Group (www.bluetooth.com) which includes nine promoter companies – 3Com, Ericsson, IBM, Intel, Lucent, Microsoft, Motorola, Nokia and Toshiba. The objective is to create total *wireless* connectivity with all types of signal (voice and data) (Ruello and Renault, 2001). However, it is important to bear in mind that 'Bluetooth' is just *one* of many technologies that may be developed to create a truly ''wireless and connected' world.

The interconnected personal environment

During the 1950s and early 1960s there were numerous television programmes (mainly American) that described the house of the future; a home peopled by physical robots. Only in part have these predictions come true. However, such is the rapid pace of technologies today, that most of what was predicted is, in fact already here.

One version of this is the 'intelligent house', where microchip technology is located in a variety of points in a building and passes and processes data relating to key aspects of the domestic environment. This has led to the *intelligent refrigerator* concept. Already by early 2003, BT's Futurists (www.bt.com) had made significant contributions to the development of intelligent refrigerators that scan the barcodes on foods as they are placed in the refrigerator. An onboard computer can send to an individual's mobile phone a text message stating which products are near their use-by date, and thus need to be cooked and eaten soon. Technology is also being developed that informs the refrigerator's onboard computer which items need to be replenished. Additionally, the householder can inform the computer what other items need to be ordered. The computer then logs onto the approved store so that it can place the order online for delivery at a suitable time and date. The householder only has a 'minor' role to play. The computer undertakes the work load, and at an operational level, it also is perfectly able to make the decisions.

Mobile telephony

When reading through this text, it is vital to consider the ongoing developments in micro-electronic technology and how it impacts upon our lives. The most immediate current example of this is the expansion of functionality of mobile telephones. Mobile or (M) commerce is increasingly becoming a key feature of internet and intranet based systems. At the time of writing (2003) it is already possible to send both text and picture messages from mobile phones to a computer. Perhaps the real questions that people need to ask themselves are: (a) Where will this lead us in terms of future technologies – wristwatch video phones as a viable commercial entity, perhaps?; (b) How will people use these systems? Will they be purely for social interaction between friends and families, how far will business be involved as well? Will companies become involved in M-communicating offers and, in fact, transact M-deals?

The answer to these questions is most likely 'yes'. As already mentioned, technological development is growing (according to most research sources) at an exponential rate. Needless to say, not all new technological developments become commercial successes immediately, and many not at all. But technological proliferation continues to happen at such a rate that the key issue will not be whether initiatives will survive, but which ones will survive and which ones will dominate.

In Chapter 13, we will explore in more detail some ideas that may drive the future of e-business. The question is always whether the public will accept these developments and, crucially, use them. But one important feature of the development of computerised mobile telephony may be a signpost for the future. The sudden explosion of text messaging amongst the young was quite unanticipated by market analysts and strategists, whilst WAP, which was heralded as the great new thing, has – so far – flopped. Thus we see that the market is not entirely controlled by the providers – the customer still has an important role in determining the success of a product or service.

Defining e-business and e-commerce

Before we commence our examination of e-business, it is worthwhile considering some of the definitions that are in current usage.

- e-commerce: The online exchange of value, without geographical or time restrictions, between companies and their partners, employees, or customers (Singh *et al.*, 2001).
- e-business: In many ways e-business encompasses the above definition for e-commerce. However, wider implications must be considered. These, for example, would be the macro factors commonly known as the PESTLE factors. Here, we need to consider the influences of Politics, Economics, Society, Technology Legal and Environmental. How, for example, will these influence both businesses and customers in the future?
- e-procurement: The process of buying raw materials and supplies via the internet.

We should be aware that the terms 'internet' and 'world wide web' are not the same, even though people often use the terms interchangeably. The former is the general network of computers by which data can be transferred in a number of ways. The latter is the specific browser based service, where pages defined using HTML can present text, audio, or images.

These descriptors will be used throughout the text, and are important in understanding how the business aspects of the cyber world operate.

The size and scope of e-business

The purpose of this section is to illustrate the overall value of e-business currently and in the future. Whilst statistics are provided from reliable sources, students should remember that this is a dynamic and volatile marketplace. The

Table 1.3 World's online population

Region	2000	2001	2002
North America		180.1 (August)	181.2 (February)
South America	16.5 (November)	25.3 (August)	NA
Europe		154.3 (August)	171.4 (February)
Africa	3.1 (November)	4.2 (August)	NA
Middle East	2.4 (November)	4.7 (August)	NA
Asia Pacific		144.0 (August)	157.5 (February)
World Total		455.6 (February)	544.2 (February)

Notes: Figures are millions (estimated).
Source: Marketing News (2002).

statistics provided throughout the book should thus be taken as a *guide*: Moore's Law is equally applicable to the growth of the marketplace. Thus, we urge students to regularly check the websites of major market researchers to obtain a current status report on the market.

Table 1.3 illustrates the world's online population. As you can see from the comparative figures available, some regions of the world demonstrate significant growth rates. Even if the online population for a region remains small in comparison to others, it is the growth rate that is key to future development.

Research conducted by the Gartner Group suggests that the value of business to business e-commerce transactions will be significant by 2005 – Table 1.4 (Marketing News, 2001). According to the Gartner Group, a key component of this growth will be the development of electronic market makers. These are organisations that develop internet marketplaces for particular industries or geographic regions. These e-market makers provide an opportunity for other companies to buy inputs at lower cost and within a shorter time frame (Marketing News, 2001). The same researchers suggest that some 37 per cent of all B2B e-commerce transactions by 2004 will be by e-market makers.

As we can see from the above tables, the use of the internet is expected to grow rapidly. Of course, usage projections are only potential forecasts. Until the time comes, we will not really know whether these usage figures have been met or exceeded. Equally, *how* was the internet used? Was the emphasis towards

Table 1.4 The value of regional B2B e-commerce projections*, 1999–2005

Region	1999	2000	2001	2002	2003	2004	2005
North America	98.0	255.0	480.0	920.0	1 680.0	2 590.0	3 620.0
Europe	18.4	72.5	188.0	417.0	753.0	1 200.0	1 750.0
Asia	31.5	96.8	220.0	503.0	949.0	1 660.0	2 400.0
Rest of the World	2.15	9.0	31.0	89.0	250.0	500.0	760.0
World Total	150.15	433.3	919.0	1 929.0	3 632.0	5 950.0	8 530.0

Note: *In billions US$. Forecast now includes data from those companies that have released information on how much of their procurement has moved online, as well as actual e-commerce sales transaction data gathered through interviews.
Source: GartnerGroup/Marketing News (2001).

purchasing, information (for example, news) or a mixture? In March 2003, it was clear that the rapid rise in internet usage focused on society's thirst for up-to-date information of the War Against Iraq, and its various machinations. Clearly, it was complementary to the 24-hour news coverage presented by the major international television networks.

How does the e-environment work?

So far we have seen how the internet has developed and how technology has converged to work 'together' to enhance the overall internet experience. It is perhaps useful, at this stage, to consider how the internet and e-business currently works. To uncover the workings of the internet, we will review the various key words or 'jargon' associated with it. Much of this 'jargon' will be reflected throughout this text.

So where do you begin?

For those people who have a particular interest in the details of how one machine can send files or images to another far away, down a telephone line, an addendum to this chapter spells out the basic infrastructure of the internet.

For this section, we will assume that the computer is already up and running and logged onto an Internet Service Provider (ISP), such as AOL or BT. ISPs can be considered as the 'gateway' to the internet and the provision of email facilities.

Internet addresses

There are various components that comprise an internet address. It is useful to have some understanding of these components as it can save you time and energy when attempting to link to these sites.

- http:// This is the first element of the address and stands for Hyper Text Transfer Protocol. This is the protocol that allows the multimedia part of the world wide web to operate efficiently;
- www This is the world wide web. It is an indication of the part of the internet that we are attempting to communicate with. Not all websites are actually accessed through the world wide web – some may use a different route, bypassing the main network;
- Domain name this the name of the specific web site, for instance, www. palgrave.com is the website of the publishers of this book – Palgrave Macmillan. Domain names need to be registered with a name registration authority before they can become active.
- The fourth component of the address refers to the type of institution operating the site. Here are a few examples:
  www.amazon.co.uk The 'co.uk' refers to a UK company or commercial organization.
  www.brookes.ac.uk This is the website for Oxford Brookes University. The 'ac.uk' refers to an academic establishment in the UK. European countries, for

instance, will use the 'ac' but with their specific country identity. An example would be www.ucl.ac.be. This is the website for the Université Catholique de Louvain in Belgium; ucl.ac.uk is University College London.

www.wsu.edu   This is the web address of Washington State University in the USA. Whilst there is no country denoted for example 'usa' the 'edu' can be taken as a clear indication that it is an American university. A variation of this is used in Australia; for example, Monash University in Victoria is donated by www.monash.edu.au. Yet another variation is the use of 'u' to denote university. The following is the web address for Hong Kong University (note the hk at the end of the address to denote country) www.hku.hk.

www.mi5.gov.uk   This is the website for MI5, the historic name for the British Security Service whose task is to guard the UK and its interests against terrorist and espionage activities. As you can see, it uses 'gov' to designate that it is a government run site. Additionally, MI5 have an official recruitment site – www.mi5careers.info. Instead of using the 'gov' designator they use' info' for information site.

www.marketingpower.com   The use of 'com' rather than a country specific indentifer is generally used by companies and organisations to symbolize a 'global' business or presence. Marketing power is the website for the American Marketing Association, the world's largest association for individuals and companies involved in all forms of marketing, from university professors to marketing research practitioners.

www.dfas.mil   This is the web site for the US military department Defense Finance and Accounting Services, 'mil' being a designator for military sites most especially within the US Armed Services. The Defense Finance and Accounting Service is responsible for armed service pay as well as supplier invoicing (which can be processed online).

www.msf.org   This is the website for Médecins sans Frontières, an independent humanitarian medical and aid agency. As MSF is a non-governmental agency, as other non-profit organisations it uses the 'org' designator.

www.virgin.net   The use of the term 'net', short for internet, is generally used by Internet Service Providers (ISPs), in this case Virgin Net is part of the Virgin Group of Companies.

Whilst these are the current 'designators', we will probably see new ones entering e-vocabulary. Possibilities for ones could be .store, .dept, .biz (for business) and .sch (for school). The possibilities could be endless.

Designators, as most other features of the world wide web, are regulated by a number of international groups that deal with issues such as protocol rules. Perhaps the best known of these is the world wide web consortium (sometimes shortened to the W3 Consortium) which is responsible for the programming rules for HTML and its derivatives such as XML, as well as other programming conventions such as Cascading Style Sheets (CSS). Despite the existence of these regulators, or perhaps because of their proliferation, it is worth being aware that no one body – to date – has complete control of the internet or of the world wide web.

Table 1.5 B2C business models

B2C Model	Definition	Example
Consumer exchange	Online marketplaces that do not hold inventory.	e-bay
Internet service provider (ISP)	Suppliers of internet access services.	America Online (AOL)
Portal	Search and navigation sites. These are generally supported by advertising. They offer syndicated or user generated content.	Yahoo
Content service provider	These sites are supported by advertising revenue. They offer seller-affiliated content.	iVillage.com (see Chapter 7)
e-Tailer	A company that holds and sells products at retail margins.	The online bookstore Amazon and the online grocery store Tesco (see Chapter 5).

Source: Adapted from Bughin *et al.* (2001).

Table 1.5 illustrates the various B2C (business-to-consumer) business models. It demonstrates the different elements that create a B2C environment. If you regularly use the internet, you will have accessed some, or all, of these models.

Search capabilities

The way both individuals and companies use the internet are many and varied. An important tool is the search engine. This is a rapid growth area, and one of the most successful amongst internet based companies. Yahoo is probably the most recognised brand name, and thus the most used. Search engines allow the user to search vast databases or directories of links to various websites.

Search engines can be described as vast crawling beasts that roam around the e-world collecting snippets of information about different web pages. This information will normally consist of the page's URL (Uniform/Universal Resource Locator), the title of the page, key words (these are chosen by the creator of the page(s)).The following is a selection of popular search engines:

AltaVista	www.altavista.com
Jeeves	www.askjeeves.com
Infoseek	www.infoseek.go.com
Excite	www.excite.com
Lycos	www.lycos.com
Yahoo	www.yahoo.com
Google	www.google.com

These will deliver you to the main sites, usually based in North America. However, several, such as Yahoo, have regional search facilities; for example, www.yahoo.au (for Australia and New Zealand).

Not all search engines operate in the same way. This is why if you put the same term into different engines you may get quite different responses. Some will look solely at information provided in a specific part of the HTML web page source document, called the *head*. Others will look at the occurrence of the search term in the text of the page, ignoring the content of the head. Still others will attempt to translate the search term into closely related terms, and flag up those pages that show the greatest semantic similarity – it is likely that further development of textual analysis programmes will increase the prevalence of this kind of search mechanism. And yet others will display relevant pages in the order of the volume of external hot links that take those who access other pages to the page in question.

In Table 1.6 we illustrate some of the uses of search engines for both the individual and company alike.

In theory, at least, search engines are relatively easy to use. It is simply a matter of inputting the name of the company, organisation or subject you want to find. In terms of most organisations and companies this can be relatively

Table 1.6   B2C and B2B user areas

Areas	Description
Individuals	
Shopping	Online shopping now ranges from groceries to furniture. UK grocery retailer Tesco, through Tesco.com, is the largest online grocery store in the world, and currently operates in the UK and South Korea.
Study	Students from secondary school to university can extract a range of information from internet sites and specialist library and database sites. Additionally, various qualifications can be studied online. Oxford Brookes University through its partnership with the Association of Certified Chartered Accountants (ACCA) operates an online-supported MBA programme under the auspices of the Oxford Institute of International Finance – www.oxfordinstitute.org
News	All the major news channels – BBC, ITN, CNN – have launched online facilities. The benefit of many of these is the currency of the news. Where most broadcasters (except BBC News 24 and CNN) are confined to specific TV news slots, the internet is not. It can continuously update the news, as it happens. Equally, it can refer the reader to online links. During the 2003 Gulf Crisis, BBC News Online had links to the websites of the United Nations, Stop the War Coalition, The French Government, the UK Prime Minister's Office and the US Presidency.
Vacations	Hotels, resorts and transport details can be viewed and booked online. This applies equally to mass vacation reports; for example for Southern Spain as to luxury hotels such as the RF Group in Europe.

Areas	Description
Health and beauty	This ranges from websites that provide health and beauty advice to online purchasing of cosmetic products. Avon (www.avon.com), the world's largest direct marketing cosmetics company, has built a website that provides both advice and products to its global customer base.
Banking and finance	The internet has become the vehicle for two types of internet banking services. The first was created as an off-shoot of a bank or finance house. The aim here is to provide the 'off-shoot' with its own identity. An example is www.egg.com which is the internet and telesales arm of the insurance giant Prudential. The second is where a traditional 'bricks and mortar' bank has developed a website where customers can internet bank. An example of this is one of the fourth largest UK banks – Lloyds TSB (www.lloydstsb.com). Such services allow customers to monitor statements, transfer funds and organise payments 24 hours per day.
Job hunting and career advice	In addition to sites that offer advice on preparing CVs and interview techniques, there are sites advertising job opportunities. In the UK www.jobs.ac.uk advertises a range of college and university staff appointments. The job seeker can also arrange email alerts when new jobs are posted meeting their specific requirement.
Shared interests	The internet provides both individuals and groups the opportunity to share information and knowledge. This ranges from model trains to favourite composers and their work.
Companies	
e-Procurement	Several individuals and groups of companies are sourcing their supplies via closed intranet systems. This is developed further in Chapter 5.
Billing/invoicing	With e-procurement comes billing and invoicing via closed and secure intranets.
Online payments	In time, there will be an increase in electronic payments to suppliers. Such systems could eventually replace cheque payments and letters of credit for larger export/import consignments.
Online marketing	Provides a vehicle (often interactive) to market and sell products and services online. The online bookseller www.amazon.co.uk has developed a relatively sophisticated site that not only sells books and CDs to online customers, but also builds a relationship with them.

straightforward, most especially if they are an international business, such as the energy company BP. However, if they are a small enterprise or you are searching for a specific type of business, it may not be as easy as first thought. The search engine may actually state that there are several thousand pages available citing the input text. However, many of these will have little or no relevance to the search, save for a passing reference to one of the words.

Example:

The group of words 'marketing consultants' produces 1 710 000 website hits. However, the result shows every possible known combination of marketing consultant (from e-marketing through to marketing research). That in itself is a very broad span. Additionally, any websites that includes the words 'management consultants' or just 'consultants' (again a wide variety) have been selected.

The key to reducing this overload is to be more specific. There are various ways of achieving this aim.

1   Be clear as to what you are searching for. Have you been specific enough? In our example above, we may really want to find marketing consultants involved in internet marketing. Thus, the group of words 'Internet Marketing Consultants' is more specific.
2   However, to make sure that the internet is reading the exact group of words, they should be placed in quotation marks. Therefore 'Internet Marketing Consultants' should refine the search. However, do we want them worldwide or just in the UK? Thus, refining it further can help to reduce the information overload, although not remove it altogether. So, what does a search for 'Internet Marketing Consultants in the UK' actually reveal? Depending upon the search engine used, the result is in the region of 10. Some of these will also lead to other search engines. However, the process of significantly narrowing the field has begun.

Summary

This chapter has set the scene – the 'How did we get to this stage?' It is clear that if it had not been for a mixture of political pressures and individual ingenuity, the internet and the world wide web would not exist. Whilst we can trace developments back to pioneering work at Bletchley Park during World War II, it has been the 'rapid' developments since the early 1990s that have brought us to the point where we now stand and gaze into CyberSpace. But the effects of the internet go far beyond military communications – it has already changed our lives, and will do so to a far greater degree in the future.

Bill Gates, co-founder of Microsoft, wrote in 1995:

[the digital revolution] will give us more control over our lives and allow experiences and products to be custom tailored to our interests. Citizens of the information society will enjoy new opportunities for productivity, learning and entertainment. Countries that move boldly and in contact with each other will enjoy economic rewards. Whole new markets will emerge, and a myriad of new opportunities for employment will be created (Gates, 1995).

The chapters that follow consider the impact of the internet and e-business on our daily lives: how e-business has expanded and how its presence will change the way we think and undertake business now and in the future.

Further reading

John Naughton (1999) *A Brief History of the Future: The Origins of the Internet.* London: Weidenfeld & Nicolson.

Questions for review and reflection

1 Log on to the Bluetooth website and update progress on the convergence of Bluetooth technology. Consider how this will affect both the daily life of yourself and your family.
2 What initial factors do you believe led to the development of the internet? If these factors had not existed do you believe that the internet, as we know it, could still have been developed, or would there have been an alternative?
3 Speculate as to the future of the internet within the next five years. Look back at this when you come to the final chapter of this book.

Notes and references

Aizu, I. (1997) 'Cultural imperialism of the net'. *The Harvard Conference on The Internet and Society.* Cambridge: Harvard University Press.
The Antidote (1999) 'How did we get to a worldwide web?', *The Antidote*, no. 23, The Centre for Strategic Business Studies.
BBN. In 1997 BBN was acquired by GTE. In 2000, GTE merged with Bell Atlantic, forming a new corporation Verizon Communications.
Berners-Lee, T. (1999) *Weaving the Web: The Original Design and Ultimate Destiny of the World Wide Web by its Inventor.* San Francisco: Harper Books.
Biro, K. (1997) 'The new economics: how will value be created and selected?', in *The Harvard Conference on The Internet and Society.* Sebastopol, CA: O'Reilly & Associates, Inc.
Brown, D. (1998) *Cybertrends: Chaos, Power and Accountability in the Information Age.* London: Penguin.
Bughin, J.R., Hasker, S.J., Segel, H. and Zeisser, M.P. (2001) 'What went wrong for on-line media?' *The McKinsey Quarterly*, no. 4, web exclusive.
Castells, H. (1999) Toward a digitally networked world. *The Antidote.* 23. The Centre for Strategic Business Studies.
DARPA (2001) This is the US Defense Advanced Research Projects Agency. ARPA was the forerunner of DARPA. Their website provides background to the formation of the agency and the type of projects they undertake. www.darpa.mil
Dertouzous, M.L. (1997) *What Will Be: How the World of New Information Will Change Our Lives.* New York: HarperCollins.
Gates, B. (1995) *The Road Ahead.* London: Penguin.
Hodges, A. (1983) *Alan Turing: The Enigma.* London: Burnett Books.
Jonscher, C. (1999) *Wired Life: Who Are We in the Digital Age?* London: Bantam Press.

Kung, H.T. (1997) 'Introduction: Personal internet and common societal vision', *The Harvard Conference on The Internet and Society*. Cambridge: Harvard University Press.

Madden, R. (1999) *Colossus: The Forbin Project*, (review), www.spintechmag.com

Marketing News (2001) 2001 Marketing fact book, *Marketing News*, 2 July, American Marketing Association.

Marketing News (2002) 2002 Marketing fact book, *Marketing News*, 8 July, American Marketing Association.

Mattelart, A. and Mattelart, M. (1998) *Theories of Communication: A Short Introduction*. London: Sage.

McClellan, J. (1999) *The Guardian Guide to the Internet*. London: Fourth Estate.

McFarlan, F.W., Elmore, R., Jeffry, M. and Ottolenghi, L. (1997) Customer relationships: what happens to brands? in *The Harvard Conference on The Internet & Society*. Sebastopol, CA: O'Reilly & Associates Inc.

Neilsen//NetRatings (2002) Neilsen//NetRatings reports a record half billion people worldwide now have home internet access, News Release, ACNielsen eRatings.com

Ohmae, K. (1996) *The End of The Nation State: The Rise of Regional Economies*. London: HarperCollins.

RAND (2002) 50 years of service to the nation. *RAND's History* www.rand.org/history.

Ruello, A. and Renault, E. (2001) 'World without wires', *Connectis*, June, no. 12, pp. 22–4.

Schmidt, C. (2001) 'Beyond the internet', *Rand Report/ The Rand Organization*, May.

Singh, T., Jayashankar, J.V. and Singh, J. (2001) 'E-commerce in the US and Europe – Is Europe ready to compete?', *Business Horizons*, March/April, vol. 44. no 2, pp. 6–17.

Addendum: how the internet actually works

We start with the basic carrier media – sometimes called the *backbone* of the internet. These are the major telephone lines that carry internet as well as audio signals. The companies that own these – BT, AT&T, for example – are thus called *network service providers*. Increasingly, the demand is for *broadband* capacity, usually using dedicated internet carrying cables (such as Digital Subscriber Lines – DSL) and satellite signals. Broadband by-passes lines which until now have been shared with voice telephony, and thus facilitates much faster transmission of data.

Additional carrier capacity is available through mobile phones (using systems such as the *Wireless Application Protocol* – WAP) and through other forms of radio wave transmission. But, in general, these are – currently very much second string to the major land line systems. One of the major areas of development is in wireless communications – Bluetooth, mentioned earlier, uses a wireless sensing system (though constrained to devices within a few yards of the detector).

The backbone lines of the internet connect together large individual computers and computer networks – some of these will be networks in their own right, called *campus networks* (often a large and widely dispersed organisation may have its own campus network, and as the name suggests, many universities have such networks). Others will be *hubs* – large scale computing facilities that feed more local services.

Hubs, or as some call them 'global' Internet Service Providers (ISPs), then link to a network of more local ISPs, or smaller campus networks (these are sometimes called *local area networks* – LANs). The local ISP then provides Internet services (such as email or web access) to individual personal computers.

For all this to work, the final destination – the individual desktop computer, for example – needs to be relatively powerful in historical terms. It has been estimated that the typical office PC today is more powerful than all the computing power of 1950 put together. It needs to be able to handle text, images, audio, and soon it will need to link with other domestic appliances. This is based on a system often called the *client/server* system. 'Client' here refers to those desktop and laptop personal computers, whilst 'server' refers to the larger machines used by ISPs. Servers function as the basic link between a client machine and the outside world of the internet. As such, they run all the various programs and routines that are necessary for file and data to be transferred across the internet. One of the current areas where more work is being done on developing the ease of use of the internet is the balance between what is done on a client machine and what is done on a server. A currently fashionable notion is that of 'thin' clients that do little processing, leaving it all up to the server. This has some useful applications – such as the intelligent refrigerator concept discussed earlier, where all that is really needed is the facility to decode information and transmit relatively simple signals back to a server. But it has limitations where the computer user wants traditional office PC functionality such as good word processing or spreadsheet packages.

At the time of writing (March 2003), many websites make use of the client/server balance by installing 'cookies' on client machines, programs that run in the background but allow the machine to interact with the website in question whenever it is accessed. For example, a cookie may contain a company logo, so that this does not need to be downloaded every time the client machine accesses the website, but is taken from the memory on the client's own hard disc. The owner of the client machine may be unaware of the existence of the cookie for most of the time, though without it accessing a website may be much more protracted. There is clearly a potential ethical issue here, in that many less sophisticated users of the internet may not realise that as well as reading data in from a website, they may also be downloading a program – the potential for importing corrupt software, viruses and the like is there, though in practice many ISPs tend to have reasonably robust systems for managing this. All the same, there remains a degree of vulnerability in this respect.

So, the chain for sending an email goes something like this:

Client A – Server A – Hub A – Backbone – Hub B – Server B – Client B

The chain would be similar for a client accessing a website, with the exception that the site may be located on a server, and thus there is no instant access to the second client.

Clearly, all this may be faster or slower. Two clients may stand on the same server, though this is rare. More often, there has to be a process of searching or *routing*, as it is called, to get from one machine to another. Most of us think of our email addresses or websites in textual terms – with names such as jbloggs. clapham@freeserve.net, as discussed in the main body of this chapter. In fact, all computers linked to the internet have a numeric reference, which consists of four numbers (between 1 and 255) each separated by a full stop. This is called an *IP address*. So, in the fictitious example of j bloggs, the IP address might be something like 221.34.194.206, the first number referrring to the actual machine, and the others referring to the wider network addressing necessary to reach j bloggs's machine. The textual names we give computers and web sites are called *domain names*, and the domain names of web pages are usually called *uniform resource locators* (URL). Domain names are controlled by domain name registration authorities, who are themselves regulated by InterNIC, a group responsible for this aspect of the internet, who liaise with other regulatory bodies such as the W3 Consortium. Routing, however, will generally operate on the numeric version of the identification.

Routing is a key process of the internet. To get an email, for example, from downtown Clapham to uptown Beijing, it has to find an appropriate route through the telephone system, one that will optimise speed of delivery. To achieve this, each file that gets transferred is not delivered in one lump, but is broken up into many smaller parts. This is called *packet switching*. A file is chopped into many smaller parts, and then *each may be sent on its own route towards the recipient*, where it is reassembled. The process of chopping up and then reassembling is carried out by a program that conforms to a set of rules for disassembling and reassembling, called the *transmission control protocol* (TCP). This is usually seen on your computer combined with the *internet protocol* (IP), which represents the agreed rules and routines for sending data through the internet. So you may find reference at times to TCP/IP in your browser preferences, for example.

The beauty of packet switching is illustrated by an analogy. Suppose you wanted to send a large aero engine by road, from your factory in an urban region or city, to someone else's factory on the other side of the city. The lorry would be big, and would get caught up in heavy congestion in the city. So it would take ages. Imagine, however, instead that you had a fleet of motorcyclists (they would have to be cheap!). You take the engine apart, so that it is all in little pieces. Each motorcyclist takes just one part, and you tell them to get there by whatever was the quickest way. Assuming that none of them gets lost or hijacked or involved in an accident, the parts would get through much faster. Then, at the other end, the recipient has a manual that tells them how to put everything together again (they know that you used the same manual to take the thing apart in the first place). This works for the internet because the transmission times and the processing of data are, to human time scales, extremely fast.

So, the transmission of different packets or slices of a file, or of an image, may go along several different routes, depending on the methodology used by the routine program, and surprisingly it is unlikely to go the same way if you transmit the same thing twice to the same address. Routes depend on the volume of traffic at different points, which vary with the time of day, as well as on other local factors.

The simple act of sending an email or accessing a web page also requires a significant amount of processing to work effectively. As well as the transmission protocols (TCP/IP) there are also client side protocols, such as the HyperText Transfer Protocol (http) that enables your browser to recognise a web page and deal with it accordingly, or email protocols such as the Internet Mail Access Protocol (IMAP), Post Office Protocol (POP) or Simple Mail Transfer Protocol (SMTP) that enable your PC to get mail from the server or send mail to it. You may well have seen these in your browser or email package preferences and settings at some time.

We tend to think of email and the world wide web as 'the internet', but there are several other services and protocols that may be used. File Transfer Protocol (FTP) is one such, enabling people to move files between client and server machines – it may be used, for example, by people to load websites from their client machine, where they have done all the development work, onto a server. Another is Telnet, which is a program that allows a desktop computer to behave like a mainframe machine, and interact with a 'parent' mainframe remotely. This is particularly useful for a company with stored data that they want a remote employee to analyse, but that they do not want to send by email.

This is, in brief, the structure of the internet as of mid-2003. At the time of writing, there are many initiatives happening which may well change the internet within a few years to become a faster and more versatile facility. The Internet2 consortium, for example, is a group of nearly 200 companies, academic institutions and governmental organisations, which is developing and testing out new technologies in many areas of the internet, including new applications, new networking systems and transmission options.

One thing we can be sure of – the information in this addendum will be quite out of date by the year 2010, if not earlier!

◪ 2 The commercial impact of e-business

Introduction

The purpose of this chapter is to introduce you to some of the key management issues underlying e-business. So, you will see how e-business changes the standard approaches to business, though it still operates on the same basic principles. As stated in the preface, our key aim here is to create a sense of horizon, rather than spell out in close detail the specifics of current e-business models and approaches.

Learning objectives

On completion of this chapter you should be able to:

1 Evaluate the strategy of an e-business using standard management models such as industry analysis and market development ('Ansoff' model);
2 Identify the key features of some models that are specific to e-business.

A key theme of this book is that e-business is not a completely new and different approach, but rather the continuation of ordinary business by more dynamic means. It should therefore be seen as a *development of traditional business models*. To that end, in this chapter we shall, in the main, use standard tools of business analysis to obtain a clearer idea of what opportunities are presented by e-business.

The emphasis in this chapter is less on facts and figures of internet usage, but rather on the way in which existing strategic theory explains the overall range of opportunity presented by the existence of the internet. We shall look at e-business using the following three established models (readers interested in seeing these models explained in greater detail can consult one of the recommended titles given at the end of the chapter):

- *Product/market innovation matrix* which illustrates the opportunities to exploit new and existing markets.

- *Value chain analysis* which indicates how electronic technologies can transform every part of the operation of a business.
- *Industry analysis* which shows how the extensive use of electronic technologies changes the balance of power between different players in many markets.

How e-business can change the nature of products and services

We shall firstly look at potential impacts on products and services, using a model generally known as the *Ansoff Matrix*, after the person who devised it (Ansoff, 1985). This model presents four different approaches to innovation;

- *Market consolidation and penetration*: existing products are developed in their existing markets.
- *Market development (customer led strategy)*: new products are devised and introduced into existing markets.
- *Market expansion (product led strategy)*: existing products are introduced into new markets.
- *Diversification*: new products are devised and introduced into new markets.

These strategies depend upon the specific circumstances of the particular markets in that the organisation is operating. Market penetration is effective when the whole market is growing, but less so when it is static or in decline. Market development usually works well with an established brand that can be extended. Market expansion is effective where there is a highly profitable product with a good share of a specific segment of the market. The potential for a diversification strategy is less clear, though in a highly volatile market, involving high levels of innovation and rapid market growth, it can be appropriate.

In terms of the risks that a company runs, market consolidation draws on knowledge that the organisation already possesses and therefore is less risky than the other strategies. At the other extreme, there is the higher risk option of diversification. This occurs where an organisation is offering a product, for which they may have only limited know-how, to a market that they also may only understand to a limited extent.

The internet market is varied – people are buying some things they always did, such as machine parts, books, airline tickets. But they are also buying services they never had before – the well known *friends reunited* service would be possible but extraordinarily difficult to operate without the speed and ease of internet communications.

Hence one could argue that the *entire* internet market is relatively new in one way or another, and therefore the main task for every company is to understand the features of this market, and how it is changing. The biggest dangers in this situation are to go to one or other of the extremes – either regarding the world wide web as so novel that one can ignore standard approaches to marketing and strategic management, or presuming that this is just one market like others, and assuming that what works in a high street store will work on a website.

But having avoided these pitfalls, what are the opportunities for developing new products and markets? This naturally will depend on the market, but also on the organisation's position in the market.

There are some general features of the internet which are currently common to most markets – though not all of these will remain common for very many more years. These are:

Market growth: In 1999 it was estimated that about 1.5 homes in the UK had internet access; by the middle of 2001 this had grown to well over 5 million and is still on a steep upward curve;

New avenues of mass access: The internet provides huge opportunities for mass communication with potential and existing customers; large databases can be employed so that a vast number of people can receive a personalised email from a company, similar to personalised direct marketing by post, but with a much lower cost and a significantly lower irritation factor. Similarly, a banner advertisement on a popular website can achieve customer perception levels comparable to, say, radio or even television adverts but at a fraction of the cost;

Low entry barriers: If you are in the shoe selling business, then you have to have the physical logistical organisation to acquire, store and display shoes for the public; beyond that, however, the task of selling shoes on the internet is not much more difficult than selling them in a shop – in other words, the extra effort of trading on the world wide web is not very great;

Rapid innovation in trading platforms: In 1998 the internet was almost solely a desktop computer phenomenon – just a few years later we have TV, palmtop and mobile phone based internet access; whilst it is not likely that many other completely novel basic forms of internet access will come along in the next few years, the way that we use these will change dramatically; one application will be the steady increase in combining internet communications with other processing systems, so that the end user will find that the internet will do much more for them, without the chore of logging on, passwords, website addresses and so on (for example, diary style software will *automatically* place orders for weekly food shopping based on standard shopping lists, so that you will not even need to place the order – it will be done for you);

The public is still watching and waiting: Despite all this innovation, *far more people look at web pages than make purchases from them* – two misconceptions (amongst others) hold the public back:

1 transactions are generally, but falsely, believed to be less secure on the web; in fact, telephone ordering is much more easily accessed, and many e-traders use highly secured payments systems using encryption software that cannot be broken into (though people from the inside could still make public the encryption methodologies to others). See Chapter 4 for more details on security;
2 people are also reluctant to make purchases over the web because of not being able to see, feel or touch them; the common claim is that someone will not buy a pair of shoes unless they get the opportunity to try them on; in fact,

we do this all the time in another environment – mail order! In time, therefore, it is likely that this suspicion will die away.

The high tech trading platform raises expectations of high quality goods and services: The prime retail consumers who use the internet are more likely to come from higher income brackets, and have the characteristics of what has been dubbed the 'new consumer' (Lewis and Bridger, 2001) – prepared to pay a premium price for speed of delivery, for greater authenticity of product and for ease of purchase, and not tolerant of mistakes or poor quality.

These factors together provide a context for all e-business as it currently carries on. And this therefore significantly affects the product/market choices available to organisations.

It should be clear that there are great opportunities for companies to continue to offer their existing products, and/or deal with their existing customers, but adding an internet element to their operations. As we shall see in later chapters, however, not all companies have been completely successful in doing this. One interesting example where this has been done effectively is with retail supermarkets. Services such as 'Tesco Direct' or 'Sainsbury's to You' enable the existing customer to order their week's shopping and have it delivered direct to their door. A number of observations can be made about this:

- It is a service which will mainly appeal to the loyal customer – setting up these arrangements takes more time initially than going to the local supermarket.
- Once a web-based ordering arrangement is in place, it becomes much easier for the company to target specific promotions at specific customer groups (whilst it is possible to enter customer transactions on to a database via modern point-of-sale tills, it is still much less wieldy than the internet order).
- It is likely to change the way most people purchase; currently these stores operate list and table based shopping web pages, making impulse buying less likely; at the moment there are few if any virtual reality stores where you can feel what it is like to walk around a store (this will come within a couple of years, however); a service of the 'Tesco Direct' type has existed for some time, specifically for people with mobility restrictions (for example, the disabled, or the very infirm elderly person who remains in their own home) but was deliberately restricted in its offer and is therefore not generally known about.
- The change in the shopping platform may reduce the amount of physical store based activity, but increases the distribution activity of the supermarket – one of the classical economies of scale that supermarkets derived from having large stores was that there were fewer places to which to transport goods; the introduction of a 'direct to you' element means that Tesco and others have to move into the small transport field, leading to large numbers of vans driving around, creating greater road congestion in cities – potentially too great an expansion of this aspect of internet retail might lead to government restrictions on the extent of small vehicle transport in urban areas, thus indirectly constraining the growth of e-business.

The main basis of the original dot.com explosion, however, was centred not on existing business but was based on *new* types of service that the internet can offer, services that are not feasible using other forms of communication or data interchange. Unsurprisingly, then, much of the first wave of internet based e-business is, in effect, diversification.

To take one example, until the advent of the world wide web there were very few recruitment agencies that dealt with education posts for public colleges and universities – the money in it was very marginal compared with the revenues to be gained from recruitment for the financial services or computing industries. However, the much lower costs of operating a recruitment business over the internet, plus the relatively early entry of many academic staff to the internet world (one of the first internet applications was the Joint Academic Network – JANET for short – which was already creating a significant level of email traffic by the early 1990s), has meant that further and higher education – which have traditions of openly advertising all vacant posts – has become a key target for recruitment agencies, with some dedicated agencies as well as education divisions of more general agencies. The website www.jobs.ac.uk is a shop window of employment opportunities specifically targeted at people working in the University sector in Britain.

There are many other kinds of service that, in their present form, are sufficiently different from their pre-electronic versions that they are, in effect, new operations. For example, bulk purchasing of goods (discussed in more detail later in this chapter) used to be a relatively mundane affair – a purchasing manager scanned the industry periodicals, contacted people she or he had used before, compared a few prices and then made their order. In effect, the market for all but a small range of materials and products was local – depending on the goods or services, there might be a national element, but even then it tended to manifest itself in the form of local or regional sales representatives. Today, by contrast, if we want to buy goods we can look at international prices, using an online trading site. They will select the sellers with the best price and we can make the purchase online, secure in the knowledge that we could not have got a better price (we shall look at some aspects of this in the chapter on e-procurement). Whilst there may be some limits to this, it nevertheless illustrates the opportunities.

In summary, then, we can see that in all four of the Ansoff categories there are major opportunities for the existing business as well as for the start-up.

A value chain analysis of e-business

Having looked at the potential impact of e-business on an organisation's choices as to which services and products it will offer and to whom, now we can look at the broader implications for organisations. The model we shall use for this has been devised by Porter (1985) and depicts an organisation's key activities as being connected as *a chain of value* which is added by each link. This chain involves the activities which comprise the production or development of whatever the organisation provides for its customers – firstly, there is what the organisation needs to bring in (raw materials, information, and so on), then the key operations (such as manufacturing the product), then taking the product to the customers or point of sale, then the marketing and sales activity, and finally the service provided to the customer post-sales. In addition to this primary chain of value, there is a secondary cluster of support activities, such as HR, IT/systems, or purchasing. These enable the primary value chain to operate most effectively, though in themselves they are less directly connected to the details of the technical work.

Primary activities

Inbound and outbound logistics

Probably, the physical movement of materials and products is less dramatically affected by e-business than some other parts of the value chain. However, there are some effects – specialist distribution companies are able to use the internet not only to plot the fastest and most efficient routes (using data such as satellite navigation data) but also can combine same day collection and deliveries of even small quantities of goods (for example, using mobile telephony or radio devices for direct data entry – hand-held devices are now standard for many carriers such as UPS or Business Express).

Additionally, a large amount of the input of many organisations is information based in one way or another (market reports, stock prices, customer data, government regulations are just three examples) all of which can be (and often are) digitised and sent via the internet.

Operations

Here the main immediate beneficiaries of the internet revolution are service industries, which rely less on physical activities and more on the transfer and processing of information. So, for example, the travel industry has hardly been affected *physically* – trains and boats and planes still move about in exactly the same way – but, in striking contrast, ticket sales have been transformed, so that a growing proportion of travellers are booking through the internet, and those who go to high street travel agents are benefiting from the electronic databases that these agents access direct to identify or book seats.

One area where there is a direct impact is the computing industry itself; much software now can be easily obtained via the internet – with the added benefit that some of what physical stores sell is available over the internet for free.

Marketing and sales

Perhaps the biggest immediate usage of the internet has been for marketing purposes. Just about every major organisation has its own website these days. On these you may find any of the following (i) their annual report to the shareholders; (ii) brochure information about products and services; (iii) recruitment opportunities posted on a company site; and (iv) opportunities to purchase products or services over the web. In some cases there are additional promotional elements – a virtual walk around the business, for example. Sales in some areas have been transformed – easyJet, for example, has blazed the trail of low price airlines, partially supported by a heavy use of the internet (an interesting example of early diversification, as the airline has already developed a range of other services that can be purchased via their internet café style 'easy everything' high street outlets).

In addition to company marketing information, one of the largest applications of the web is the development of online broking or agency sales – companies that will find the best deals for you; for example, a Britney Spears' gig, or a Eurostar return ticket. This is a service that has existed in one form or another for many years, but the greatly widened range of sources of tickets has enhanced the quality of this service significantly.

Customer service

Surprisingly, few of the really big companies exploit this aspect to any great extent. Although it is common that a company will include their email contact details on a website, there is only rarely a direct contact to give feedback on products or make complaints (cynically, one might think that this would make complaints too easy, whereas the telephone still provides a significant barrier to some against making a complaint).

On the other hand, this aspect of customer (or in this case, citizen) communication is being exploited by local councils, who deliver a wide range of services, and often are having to juggle the areas where high quality is compromised by poor resources. Many local councils use their website as a major route for communication between citizens and their elected representatives, not necessarily as complaint but also as a natural part of the process of government.

Support activities

Firm infrastructure

Intranets – internet style systems, usually of a www type using HTML pages, but operating in a closed environment for employees of just one organisation – have become an essential component of larger or more dispersed organisations. Additionally, some global firms use products such as *Lotus Notes* to combine email and internet functions, so that information can be shared across continents – decisions can therefore be made involving key players even though they may be in offices thousands of miles apart.

Human resource management

Not very long ago, the most elaborate use that human resource (HR) departments made of computers was a staff database, but more recently a range of HR activities have sprung up, and it is clear that many more will follow. As mentioned above, for example, recruitment via the web is now a common phenomenon, whether on the company's own site or by means of a specialist recruitment website such as PeopleBank. In addition however, many HR departments use intranets to publish documents such as health and safety policies.

Perhaps most exciting of all, however, is the development of *e-learning* facilities such as on-line discussion forums, bulletin boards, programmed learning of technical knowledge or skills coaching, many of which are offered as distinct services by HR consultancies or are developed in-house. The university sector has also taken up the opportunities of online learning enthusiastically. The head of the UK eUniversities Worldwide organisation claimed that 'By 2005, it is forecast that online learning will be the most widely used web application' (Beaumont, 2003). Whilst this is an overstated piece of hyperbole, it is certainly the case that given the focus in general management theory currently on knowledge and learning, it is highly likely that this application of the internet will be a major growth area in the years to come.

Another relatively unexplored potential benefit is the use of *distributed human resources* – so that work can be allocated less on the basis of who is physically present at a certain place at a certain time, but more rationally on the basis of who has the skills and is accessible via the network. Because many elements of the value chain are data based or data driven, it is possible to make free use of individuals' skills on an international basis. In theory, a company that translates documents can receive the documents by email, send them out to a translator in just about whatever country is appropriate, get the translations returned electronically, and forward them on to the client without anything even being printed off in hard copy! Similarly, a computer company based in the USA may have analysts in Germany develop a system, then have it written up in computer code by Indian programmers, and put it all together in a package in the UK for a French client! Imagine that without email. A third illustration of this is the use of telephone switching technologies, so that a company such as Yellow Pages can have operators serving the UK, but based in India! Such individuals may be trained in UK local culture, including learning the names of current UK celebrities, being aware of current UK events, even the weather in London that morning! But the point is – although they are talking to UK residents, they are not there, they are somewhere completely different.

Technology development

As the last examples above indicated, even something as (relatively) straightforward as email can and has transformed the way in which an organisation does its business, where anything that can be digitised can, in theory, be done in any place in the world where the best resources can be obtained at the best price. In practice, it is never quite that simple – there are still very many parts of the world where telephony is simply not good enough yet to carry large amounts of data quickly and reliably, and there are often barriers to international trading based on tariffs or so-called 'non-tariff' barriers, such as requirements for professional qualifications. Nevertheless, rethinking an organisation's operations from an information perspective can often create surprising opportunities for doing much of the work at a distance, linked solely by electronic data communication.

Procurement (company purchasing)

By far the largest expansion of internet based services has been in the B2B market. Many of these are information related (such as the construction or onward sale of customer databases).

Additionally a number of internet sites are themselves shopfronts – sites where a whole range of services and products may be offered. There are several different models of this. One is the portal – where the customer can trawl sites but always within the environment of the original web site – so you never forget who has brought this service to you. www.AskJeeves.com is the most cited example of a portal. An alternative is where a site promises to trawl the rest of the internet and find the appropriate product at the best available price – one implication of this is that within distribution constraints, all producers of a certain product or service will be forced down to the lowest available price (in theory good for the customer, but in reality only so where a number of competitors can stay in the market. Once a couple of really major players manage to squeeze the rest out of that market altogether, then prices drift upwards again).

What this analysis of the value chain has indicated, then, is again the range of opportunities at each step in the chain. It is probably true to say that the customer end of the chain has received most overt attention, but it is worth bearing in mind that the B2B market is several times larger than the B2C one – so in terms of profitability there is probably as much, if not more, advantage to be gained at earlier stages of the value chain as at the 'sharp' end.

e-business and the five forces of industry dynamics

We have seen an illustration of some of the ways that e-business can affect services and products, and the impact on different parts of an organisation's operation.

In this section we shall look at how e-business can change the dynamics of an industry, using a well-established model, again popularised by Porter (1980), which depicts a industry in terms of *five key forces*:

- the power of the key competitive rivals
- the power of key suppliers to the industry
- the power of key customers
- the power of new entrants
- the power of organisations that offer an alternative or substitute for the main product/service provided by that industry.

Any particular industry is more or less defined in terms of the balance of power between these forces.

Competitive rivalry

The volatility created by the growth of the internet has disturbed the existing rivalry between key players in many markets. Most striking is the difference in approaches by high street banks and building societies in the UK. Some, such as the Prudential insurance company or the Co-Operative Bank, have gone for a separately branded internet bank. Others, such as HSBC, have utilised existing banking facilities and added on an internet arm – in HSBC's case they built their telephone division, FirstDirect. Others, such as Barclays and Lloyds TSB, have been slower to make a move in this area. Given this variety of different responses of the main players to internet trading, it is likely that the balance between them will change significantly. At the time of writing this, the reluctance of customers to make financial transactions over the web is a major restraint on the growth of internet banking. But in a few years, when people have grown more familiar with the idea of providing financial details over the internet, then those financial companies that have already established their internet brand will have a significant competitive advantage.

Suppliers

The power of suppliers is significantly affected by the internet, depending on the particular kind of market. Where there is a large range of suppliers and a relatively small range of different levels of quality, then internet purchasing services will tend to drive down prices as companies can shop around. Where there are fewer suppliers, or the product or service supplied admits of many significant variations, then there is greater room for suppliers to provide premium products for which the convenience of shopping around is less marked. The range of different procurement options we discuss in Chapter 9 illustrates an important general point, that the internet can generate a number of alternatives to a standard business model. The basic idea of one party wishing to purchase goods from another becomes vastly more complex when one looks at developments such as electronic auctions or collaborative commerce (both discussed in Chapter 9).

Customers

The power of customers also varies according to the kind of market. In general, the power of retail customers is low – they act individually, and are normally only able to influence the main players in an industry via specific events, such as high profile court cases. The vast majority of the time, retail customers do not act as a body and therefore do not exercise concentrated power. By contrast, business customers, or bulk purchasers (for example, airline charter companies) do have a significant level of power over their market – in some cases a determining influence.

Electronic delivery of services has different potential trends: (a) potential greater economies mean that smaller purchasers can anticipate the same degree of service that larger purchasers have always been able to demand; (b) aggressive large companies can make use of internet purchasing facilities to dominate the market even further; for example, by buying up as much of a certain product as possible and then reselling it to other competitors, or by setting up closed trading communities, even compelling small suppliers to either be engulfed or be excluded. As the B2B market dwarfs the B2C market in volume and value of trading, the role of the industrial customer is of dominating importance in the current internet environment. Whether it will remain so is unclear – as internet based applications grow, including the intelligent house concept mentioned in Chapter 1, so too the customer/supplier relationship will change, and intermediaries will grow in importance; for example, helping the retail customer manage the array of different internet based appliances and services they will enjoy domestically. Whilst the corporate purchaser will retain a majority of traded volumes, it is likely that the domestic purchase of appliances and services will gradually acquire an increasing role in the overall internet market. Indeed, it is arguable that the B2B/B2C distinction will eventually break down as the corporate purchasing function becomes ever more specific, and as the consumer opts for services that give them ever greater control over their product environment.

New entrants

As mentioned above, the barriers to internet commerce are in themselves relatively low – developing a website is a relatively low cost exercise compared with setting up retail stores that would cater for the same size market. But the key barriers in any industry remain the same whether or not the industry moves into e-commerce. Knowledge of the particular features of the market, understanding the potential variations on the production process, capital investment for that process and creating a market identity are critical elements, and are essentially not dependent on the level of e-commerce involved. So, those organisations whose internet presence is their first entry to a particular market are likely to underestimate the non-electronic barriers, simply because the electronic barriers are so low.

It is this which has dogged many of the dot.coms. Amazon was highly successful in their early years primarily because they were able to master the physical logistics – a wide range of books is available, and orders generally arrive within the time period stated (usually well before that, in our experience). Paradoxically, it is the less important price premium that has mainly contributed to their more recent financial difficulties – giving the company too small a return on each sale. Other companies that have not done so well have usually failed to deal with the physical element of their trade – most have reasonable websites, but that is nowhere near enough.

Substitutes

In any market there are many alternative ways of satisfying a need, which makes this a more amorphous category than the other forces. In industries where part of the value delivered to customers can be *digitised*, then the range of alternatives is potentially vast. For example, information services for financial markets can be provided in many different ways. One example is the Bloomberg information system, which originally was tied to the use of specific terminals and used its own private lines. As internet technology developed, the system was redeveloped so that it can now be accessed via the world wide web. Despite this, some information systems continue to offer their service via dedicated lines – often in financial trading where the sheer provision of data is enhanced by the promise of highly specialised and expert investment advice. Others are offered purely on standard websites that people can enter on payment of a membership fee. And there are some that maintain a degree of control by being restricted to CD-ROMs which are bought outright or sent on a regular basis – in practice, this is almost certainly not information relating to current share prices, as the speed of delivery of the data would be far too slow for that purpose (really only direct and immediate electronic access is appropriate for a financial trader). The slower forms of the service are more likely to be global analyses of trade patterns, company analyses, industry reports and so on.

What do we learn from the five forces analysis? Clearly, the impact of electronic trading is changing the balance between the existing main players in most industries. Similarly, the balance of power with suppliers is made more volatile whilst, with the power of customers, the retail customer remains fairly powerless and the business or bulk customer end of the industry is perhaps the least clear to predict, because of conflicting trends. Surprisingly, complete new entrants to the market are not necessarily made likely – because the existing barriers to entry remain the dominant issues to resolve. A much greater range of substitute or alternative services or means of distributing and selling products and services is possible, in proportion to the degree to which there is a digitisable element to the service.

Modelling e-business

The bulk of this chapter has been a demonstration of our theme that standard business analysis models are just as appropriate to e-business as to any other kind of business. Nevertheless, there are some key ideas that, although not completely specific to e-business, acquire a vastly different importance in this context.

One key idea is that of the *killer application*. This is the idea that an organisation that can develop a really strong and genuinely new addition to the value of a particular service can often gain a lion's share of the market that grows around it. In essence, this reflects the general marketing idea of whether it is best to be first or second into the market with your concept. In the UK, we all talk about 'biros' – though the functional name for these is 'ball point pens'. The name for transparent adhesives used on either side of the Atlantic betrays the different companies that managed to make this a killer application in their market – in the UK 'Sellotape', in the US 'Scotch Tape'.

What makes the idea of a 'killer app' (as they get referred to) so important in e-business is (a) the potentially large market; and (b) the speed of internet response, which means that a brand name that is immediately connected to an internet address gets accessed, whilst one that is well known but not so easy to find gets ignored. Add to these the innate conservatism of most consumers – people are more likely to stay with a provider – that offers acceptable service than take a risk on a new provider – and it is clear that an early and successful entry to a market is an important source of competitive advantage, though bear in mind – *successful* entry. A product that is faulty survives for a shorter time on the web than in the shops.

Many of the household names on the internet could be described as *killer apps*. However, it is important to distinguish between the service that gets into the market first and achieves an initial high level of response from that which achieves a lasting lead. The now ill-fated Napster is a case in point. Napster was the first structured attempt to harness the potential of the internet to deliver digital music – other approaches had been tried, but not in a customer oriented manner so much as for the benefit of the producer (that is, a record company or artist). Napster enabled people to swap digital music files for free, on something resembling a 'swapshop' basis. The industry, in the late 1990s, had converged on a file format called MP3 as the optimum way of storing and processing music files. In 1999, Shawn Fanning, an American student, produced a program that enabled people to access MP3 files very easily, and swap them with other inter-net users. In a matter of months it climbed to be the second – and, very briefly, the first – most accessed site on the whole of the world wide web. Unfortun-ately, it never managed to establish a sound legal footing, and eventually folded following unsuccessful litigation with the major record companies. Still, it established the idea of MP3 exchange, and other websites, such as Kazaa, flourish doing almost exactly the same thing.

Another key concept is that of *data mining*. Data mining is the idea of collec-ting mass information about the needs and choices of customers, and then extracting specific groups from these databases at which to target particular services or promotions. This is currently mostly a hybrid concept. Much of the data is collected through paper systems – market research questionnaires par-ticularly. Then it is entered on a database, and from that point it can be processed electronically like any database. So, if we have access to a sufficiently large database, we can pull out those groups most likely to be attracted to my product or service; families with under five children who holiday abroad, for example, or middle-aged women who are managers of large businesses, who drive top of the range saloon cars and use a health club. The opportunities for very precisely targeted market segmentation are enormous. In time, more data collection will be directly internet driven – some readers may already find that, inadvertently, they have provided information that has led companies to email them with various business offers.

This raises the current difficulties with 'spam' email. Spam is junk email – unsolicited and generally unfocused emails that are sent willy-nilly to hundreds of thousands of email addresses, offering goods or services. Some of these are legitimate, if rather sloppy, direct mail services. Others are ruses to get the consumer to respond – for example, pressing a 'delete this email' button may well send the recipients details back to the sender, who then has it on file for further junk mailing. Still others may be directly dishonest or dubious in other ways – planting cookies or viruses on a workstation. May 2003 saw a key land-mark, when, for the first time, spam email was for a few hours higher in number than legitimate email traffic. Although filters exist for spam, it is difficult to censor out every email, and there are many browsers and service providers that are ineffective at preventing spam. The general spirit of the world wide web as an unregulated environment has allowed spam to proliferate, but it is likely that, if the W3 consortium and related internet groups do not voluntarily deal with this problem, then governments will attempt to – whether they will succeed is a different matter.

A third key concept is that of an *internet community*. Where speed and ease of access are key features of the market, customers have less incentive to stay loyal to one particular service provider. Of course, good service is always one reason for someone to repeat their business with a company. But whereas for a high street store or a local plumbing company this can be sufficient, on the web there are too many competitors out there to rely on this. A key event in the securing of repeat business is the 'bookmark moment'. Once a website is on someone's list of bookmarks, it is much more likely to be visited regularly – it is easy to access, no fussing with complex addresses, just click on the bookmark. By comparison, even appearing very high on a search engine list is a lot less likely to secure a visit – a typical search engine result lists five hundred, maybe five thousand, results. Unless a site consistently appears near the top of several search engines' responses, it is nowhere near as likely to be visited repeatedly compared to the bookmarked site.

The key principle behind an internet community is to provide a reason for the visitor to want to come back to you – to create a bookmark moment. A sense of community is created by a range of different facilities – shopping that appears to focus on your specific needs (for example, reminding you that you bought an 'x' last month, did you know about the new version just out), special deals for registered visitors, feedback opportunities (especially where there may be a chat-room or an open bulletin board). Someone who is encouraged to make a contri-bution to a bulletin board is very likely to bookmark the site to see if anyone responds to their comment.

One example of how a sense of community can be a valuable way of developing and extending a market is provided by eBay – the online trading platform where individuals can offer their own goods for sale (generally, though not exclusively, second-hand). Individuals can rate the vendors they trade with (in text as well as grading), and some regular vendors use the space provided for them to describe what they are offering for sale as a vehicle for a chatty com-munication with their targeted audience (so much so that it appears in some cases that there may be a small elite of vendor/purchasers, especially where antiques are concerned). Chapter 12 will discuss the issue of user communities in more detail, but it is clear that this is a feature of the internet that can, at times, go beyond the *chosen* strategy of web designers, for example, and what can *emerge* is quite unanticipated – witness the text messaging boom referred to in Chapter 1. This underlines the point that the internet is an *extension* of 'normal' strategy – it is not a *replication* of it. The more functionality built into a website, the more versatile it is, and thus the wider the range of different ways it can be adapted. To take a mundane, non-electronic example of how versatility confers lasting potential, the adhesive used in 'Post-it' notes was originally developed for quite a different purpose, for which it ended up being not entirely suitable, but its potential to apply to many different everyday needs made it a 'killer app' of the stationery world.

In this chapter we have looked at some of the key features of the internet from a business perspective. The main theme has been that the most important e-business models are those of standard business, though there are some where the internet aspect significantly deepens and extends the concept, such as the killer app.

This chapter has been mainly concerned with e-*commerce* – the use of the internet for trading purposes. In the next chapter, we shall look at a different side of the web – its social impact and the use which not-for-profit organisations make of it.

Further reading

The strategic analysis models discussed may be found in any one of several textbooks on strategic management. Perhaps the most straightforward of these are:

Johnson, G. and Scholes, K. (1993) *Exploring Corporate Strategy*. Harlow: Prentice Hall.
Pettinger, R. (1996) *Introduction to Corporate Strategy*. Basingstoke: Palgrave.

A central article in the debate on how far e-business requires new or adapts existing models is Michael Porter's 'Strategy and the internet' (*Harvard Business Review*, March 2001).

Notes and references

Ansoff, I. (1985) *Corporate Strategy*. Harmondsworth: Penguin.
Beaumont, J. (2003) 'The ball's rolling but it needs a little push', article in *The Times Higher Education Supplement*, 16 May.
Lewis, D. and Bridger, D. (2001) *The Soul of the New Consumer*. London: Nicholas Brealey.
Porter, M.E. (1980) *Competitive Strategy*. New York: Free Press.
Porter, M.E. (1985) *Competitive Advantage*. New York: Free Press.

The following case study is intended as a stimulus to further research and investigation on the impact of the internet on business. It is provided as a resource to be used as appropriate by readers and tutors. There is no right or wrong answer – it is up to you as a reader to think through how you would deal with the issues raised here.

⊻ Case study   Action Leisure Centre

Action Leisure Centre is a sports/health club based in West London. It is based in a converted warehouse, and has a complex which comprises (a) an aerobics gym; (b) two squash courts; (c) four outdoor tennis courts; (d) a double swimming pool – one side for 'serious' swimmers, the other for leisure and toddlers; (e) a climbing/abseiling wall; (f) a shop selling sportswear and accessories; (g) a cafe/restaurant. In addition, there are changing/locker rooms and showering facilities.

The club has 1250 members, most of whom are relatively high income families living close to the complex. There are 45 staff, including shop staff, sports instructors, pool attendants, maintenance, and the cafe/restaurant team.

As well as providing the club facilities for members, the complex is occasionally hired by groups for a day – once this was for a wedding reception, several children's parties have used the pool and cafe, and on two occasions a local company has used the complex for an active management team event including use of the pool and climbing wall.

The management team is keen to expand, and there are plans to open another three clubs in West London over the next few years. This is not the only idea for expansion, however. The club has a healthy membership, but on average each family uses the facilities about 45 minutes a week. Early mornings see people swimming and using the gym; in the evening there are people relaxing after work, but during the day there are relatively few people in the club, which makes it look less attractive to those who do come.

You have been called in as an internet and management consultant. The chief executive wants to know how the internet could be used to improve the club's services. He is keen to leave as much open as possible – you have been told that it is a 'clean sheet' strategy. He and the board are committed to developing a website, and they have already appointed a web design company, though they need a report from you before giving the company a specific brief.

What advice will you give the board?

Questions for review and reflection

1   Think of an internet company you know about. Where would you place it on the Ansoff model? Why?
2   How does e-business affect the dynamics and balance of power in an industry? Apply this to a specific industry or sector, such as retail.
3   What are killer apps? Why are they important?
4   How can an e-business make use of an electronic community to enhance its operations?

Ideas for further study

1   As well as the strategic models we have used in this chapter, one exercise you could profitably conduct is a PESTLE analysis (political, economic, social, technological, legal, environmental affecting the context of an organisation) on a company you know that is involved in e-business.
2   Take a company you know something about that, so far as you know, is NOT doing any business via the internet. What are the key issues they would have to address in order to trade on the internet?

⊻ 3 The social impact of e-business

Introduction

In the first two chapters, we have looked at the development of the internet and the range of implications of this for business; note, incidentally, the *range* of implications, not an exhaustive list. As our intention is to develop a sense of *horizon* and opportunity, rather than compile a manual of facilities, we are seeking to give an indication of the opportunities in this fast growing field, rather than make an audit of specifics.

At first sight, you may wonder why we are dealing with issues such as *social aspects* in a book about *e-business*. Our view is that all elements of contemporary life have a business aspect to them. People spend a third of their life at work. But then, what happens with the other two thirds? They mainly spend that time benefiting from the results of business activity (treated in the widest sense to include not just commercial profit-related activities, but also not-for-profit business activity such as is provided by government and the voluntary sector). We watch TV (produced by electronics companies, maybe marketed via the internet). We shop for goods which may have been sourced via the web. We go on holidays using aircraft manufactured by companies that have purchased raw materials over the web, and which are regulated by governments that publish their requirements over the internet. We may use personal computers to surf the web directly. All of these are making direct and indirect use of the internet.

So, the impact of the internet is as much about how we will live our lives in the future as how commercial business will be conducted. This book is not solely about e-commerce, but about e-business in this broader sense. But business only exists because it has social value – people buy (or the State provides) goods and services because they meet social needs. It is therefore important to have some sense of the impact of the internet in social as well as commercial terms ones. This is important for the crucial issues of marketing which will be considered at length in Part Two of the book, but it will also be important for issues of the ethics of internet operations, for the management of different kinds of risk on the internet (the subject matter of the next chapter) as well as for the future development of internet based activities.

We will use for this purpose the PESTLE model of environmental analysis referred to at the end of Chapter 2. Crudely, this is really an acronym that sets up a series of categories – one could as easily call them bins – into which one can assign the various different external features of the working environment.

It helps the analyst create some sense of order out of chaos. For those who are unfamiliar with this concept, the acronym is made up of the initial letters of the following features of the external environment – Political, Economic, Social, Technological, Legal, and Environmental. This is not the only way to split up the external environment – Cartwright (2001) uses a broader acronym, 'SPECTACLES', that includes our concepts plus others (for example, he separates out customers, whilst we will here include this in the social category). But for our purposes, PESTLE is sufficient.

Learning objectives

On completion of this chapter you should be able to:

1 Identify some of the key social, political legal and ethical aspects of the development of the internet;
2 Identify some of the long-term themes that affect the internet as it is now and as it is likely to change over the next few years.

Political implications

There is a potentially wide range of political consequences of the growth of the internet, including:

- decision making and voting
- provision of government services and information
- communication and consultation relating to policy options
- the development of post-national senses of community and identity
- the web as an arena for direct political action
- exclusion of individuals or communities.

Many of these are in their infancy at the time of writing, though we can see already the shape of the future. Some governments, most notably Hong Kong, have opted for an integrated wide ranging e-government strategy. More often, however, in this relatively early stage of the internet, governments have allowed individual departments to develop their own websites, but there is relatively little direct data transfer between them. In the UK, for example, whilst there are cross-departmental facilities such as access to documents on policy or legislation, there is little evidence of government departments automatically sharing information. For instance, little has been done to develop the option of linking health, social security, taxation and housing databases (the latter is relevant in this discussion, because, in the UK, a large amount of State financial aid to poorer families consists in housing benefit – a payment to assist people to pay their rents or other housing costs). There is a significant political issue here – many fear the coming of the 'Big Brother' state, where all our personal affairs are overseen and controlled by an impersonal state apparatus. This has therefore created a resistance to the use of the internet simply for developing quicker and more reliable citizen communication.

But in each of these categories, there is a clear series of opportunities, at least in part driven by what aspect of the government activity is information based (and hence can be made digital) and by what underlying political issues pertain – such as security with voting, or accuracy with health records.

Decisions and voting

It is only a matter of time before the more technological nations make voting a net-based activity. The fiasco of the November 2000 US presidential election, where the controversial and highly disputed question of physical holes punched in ballot papers in one county of the State of Florida determined the final result, has underlined the need for voting to become as sophisticated as the people that cast the votes.

Voting for political representation, or in referendums, is precisely the kind of activity that can be very easily put on to a computer system. Whether it can be made sufficiently secure is a bigger issue. There is a general confidence in most western democracies that by and large (with the possible exception of the 2000 US election referred to above) the election systems are acceptably fair. In part, this is due to the physical evidence of voting and the fact that if there were a serious dispute over votes, then the actual ballot papers could be retrieved and visually re-checked (as indeed did happen in the USA in Florida in November 2000). It is likely that on-line voting will only occur on a wide scale when there is public confidence that the system could not be hijacked and unrepresentative results engineered. As it stands, some countries have made some moves towards this, though none of the major developed countries have gone as far as making their major presidential or parliamentary elections online. There seems no reason, though, why this is not merely a matter of time.

Government service delivery

After major businesses, it is governments that have taken advantage of the growth of the internet most effectively. A wide range of government services can and have been made web-amenable, with the result that the internet has penetrated deep into the workings of many western governments.

It is not hard to see why. Any service which can be made digital has the potential to be delivered via the web. Movements of government funds (such as grants) are an obvious example. Appointments to meet government workers (hospital appointments, for example) and related rostering/scheduling activities relating to government or State activity is already partially conducted via electronic databases, and from this it is but a short step to full web based provision.

Payment of taxes is already well advanced in some countries. Again, Hong Kong has taken a lead with this, where tax returns as well as payments can be made online. The UK made a false start with online tax returns in 2002, though the major flaws in the system have, allegedly, been corrected now. Many minor aspects of the tax service, such as online delivery of appropriate forms and guidance booklets, are well advanced in most developed countries.

Local authority registration of land transactions is another example, where all the relevant service is information, and therefore reducible to digital information. The provision of education – mainly a government service – is already well advanced in the penetration of e-business methods, as well as having its own booming area of e-learning. Provision of some social services and social housing is already on the threshold of becoming more web-amenable. So it is possible, for example, that someone seeking housing provided by a local council may make their application online, have the council's response online, and may ultimately be able initially to view the property offered them online as well. Whether all potential recipients of such social provision have access to the appropriate computing facilities is another issue – which we shall address later in this chapter.

Clearly some services, such as the council collecting waste, are physical and therefore not in themselves changed much by e-government. But there are features of even these services that can be made more effective by means of the internet. What if, by mistake, your rubbish is not collected? What if there are problems with the street lighting in your area? The reporting of these to the relevant authorities can, and in time will, be a standard internet activity – whereas at the time of writing they remain a protracted and inefficient affair in most countries, with telephone calls being rerouted between different departments and no one being sure who is responsible.

If the reader refers to government or local council websites, they will get an indication of the degree of internet penetration that has already occurred – by the time you read these words, it will doubtless have increased significantly.

Communication and consultation

The internet has already become a major source of government information. Most UK government consultation papers are available on the web, and in some cases there are opportunities for online feedback from the public. The website set up for members of the British public to express condolences over the death of Princess Diana in 1997 was a graphic and striking example of how the web has become an essential component of the way we interact with governments and those associated with the machinery of the state.

Postnationalism

This is as much a social issue as a political one. There is a growing feeling that the great spur to globalisation which the internet provided has led to the really big global businesses (for example, Microsoft, McDonalds, Sony) acquiring greater influence than national governments.

The web is based partially on communities and establishing regular navigation tracks – there is too much out there for individuals to make complete use of it unaided. Therefore, any organisation that can create its own user community can thereby communicate directly with people about its services and products, no matter where they live. We shall return to this issue in Chapter 12.

In the past, governments were able to regulate trade by several techniques, only one of which was customs restrictions at the port or border. One important mechanism one was simply not allowing or not licensing the sale of certain items within its borders. For example, you cannot walk into a shop and buy a gun in the UK – you need permits, and any shop that did sell you a gun is obliged to inform the police. But you can buy a gun over the internet, no questions asked – If someone can get the item across national borders, though this is illegal in itself, they have effectively avoided government regulation.

This is an extreme example. However it is an indirect illustration of the point that, whereas in the past, people who lived in a certain region tended to have a wide range of common interests that made it sensible to work collaboratively in nation states, today you may find that many of your key concerns are not shared by someone in your location. Instead you share a lot more with a community comprising of people drawn from widely separated geographical regions. This morning one of us played chess on the internet – we played someone from Finland, whilst we live in the UK. Last week, we played people from the USA, India and several east-European countries. We have become part of an international community, whereas not so very long ago we would have played chess at our local chess club down the road. What tends to facilitate this being described as a user community rather than simply a number of people using the same facilities, is the domination of English in international contexts. This is a general feature of international business, but it is reflected at least as much on the internet as in physical trade.

So, if someone is a member of a number of communities, only some of which are based in their own country, a number of major questions for nation states has to be addressed, such as:

1   to whom do people owe *allegiance* today, if they spend a large amount of their activities communicating and collaborating with people from other countries?
2   who *should be* regulating and governing people, when much of what they do is no longer purely nationally based?
3   who really *does* regulate the operations of internet based facilities at the moment, and do they act in the best interests of the people who use the web?

Direct political action

It has become clear in the last few years how powerful a tool the world wide web can be for political groups. Especially those which represent a fringe, or which for other reasons may be excluded from the traditional sources of public communication such as TV, radio or the press, the web is an opportunity to present ideas free of many of the constraints of the standard political media.

This has both an up and a down side. The positive aspect is that groups that may be excluded from standard debate on political developments may find a voice via the web. So, many of the street protesters demonstrating against the growing dominance of global capitalism have been able to coordinate their activities as well as publicise their views via the web.

The downside is that some groups that are excluded from standard popular debate because their views are unacceptable to the vast majority may be able to express their anti-social views via the web. Racists, for example, have found a new and dangerous opportunity to communicate with each other to organise demonstrations and avoid police detection. Whilst racism is clearly immoral, the issue of terrorism is more complex. Some 'terrorists' end up being pillars of their societies – witness Nelson Mandela or a number of the leaders of Israel – and the public accept, at such later times, their justification of methods of political violence, on the basis that they were fighting an immoral or evil regime. Arguably, this is not necessarily a case where the majority at any one time is simply in the right in rejecting terrorism. Whatever the pros and cons here, it remains true that terrorist organisations, using methods of extreme violence to further their political aims, have also found that it is really very difficult for police and military authorities to track websites that may only be used for a short time to organise some act of violence and then be shut down. The growth in mobile internet technology may only accentuate this dangerous position.

Exclusion

An argument that is gaining ground in the west is that the idea that a nation can govern itself more or less as it chooses is giving way to a recognition that the major global companies are now, partially (though not entirely) due to the growth of the internet, able to dictate to governments. Rather as the barons and earls of the Middle Ages could exercise much more influence over the activities of the king than ordinary subjects, we seem to have entered an era where some are more equal than others. This raises the issue of internet inclusion and exclusion. The company that has a strong web presence, pays for lots of banner advertising, pops up near the top of most search engines, and is linked inwards by many other web sites, has a major presence on the web. It thus exercises, simply by its visibility, some influence on the content and on the style of the web in general, if only by the growth of imitators.

Now, it is true that individuals trying to advance unpopular or controversial views on the world wide web certainly find places to express themselves – as, for example, in the thousands of discussion groups on just about any subject you care to imagine, from Abba's hit singles to the role of the USA in supressing data on crop circles. But, arguably, the style and manner of exposition is vastly different. The amenity of the world wide web is that you can find so much there. The *impact* of it, though, is related to what is most easily accessed. In this respect, it is not essentially different from the proliferation of cable and satellite TV channels – on any evening in most counties, you can watch documentaries about global warming, political events, history, geography, education, and so on. But the major content of TV shows in the UK in recent years has been the fates of leading entertainment celebrities, who are written up in the tabloid press, invited on to talk shows, and so on. It is not a matter of what is available to us, so much as what is easily available and promoted to us.

One aspect of exclusion is that political disagreement is easy to load on to the world wide web, but very hard to press on to the consciousness of the majority of the population.

Another aspect of exclusion is the potential barriers of access to the less well off parts of society. It takes a computer, or at the least a decent mobile phone, to get access to the internet plus, to make much headway with it, some assistance with learning is usually required. Over time, the costs of computers should slowly diminish, though market factors affecting pricing come into play here. Standard PCs tend to be priced in the UK at £800–£1 200, and this tendency has persisted now for almost a decade. (Interestingly, the same models usually can be found in the USA at the same number of *dollars*) – that is, a third cheaper). So, a really poor individual will have significant difficulties funding this.

One way in which some countries have tried to overcome exclusion is by using state facilities, such as local colleges, as centres for individuals to use computing facilities and, in the commercial world, the phenomenon of the internet café is now well established. But these have had only limited success – the poorest families in a society may often feel that education is not for them, and avoid colleges even when the college is making provision designed for them specifically. Similarly, the largest single category of user of internet cafés is the young middle-class traveller, sending emails back home via an MSN or Hotmail account.

Political and social exclusion is a growing phenomenon in the western world. It has been estimated that less than half the US population ever intends to vote in presidential elections. Additionally, in many European countries, there has been a large increase in a migrant population, many of whom are political or economic refugees from undeveloped countries in political turmoil, who are disenfranchised politically as well as usually at the very bottom of the social and economic ladder. The argument given above suggests that despite the potential for the internet to provide a levelling opportunity, in practice its dominance by e-commercial interests has resulted in inclusion of the 'standard' citizen/consumer at the expense of the less politically or socially established individual. A generic political issue to be sure, but one that retains its character despite the existence of the internet.

Overall, the political impact of the internet is potentially vast. It is clear that it offers great opportunities for governments to change the way they deal with the communities they serve. But it also is creating fresh opportunities for those on the fringes of society to further their own ends. Also, although the potential for extending state provision to communities is greatly enhanced, the global nature of the internet undermines the idea that the population of a country can be defined as a nation in terms of their shared interests – if, indeed, this is generally true anyway.

Economic implications

We have already explored many of the key economic implications of the growth of e-business in Chapter 2, where we identified some of the commercial opportunities and how these are likely to affect industries. This exploration will continue in some ways in the Chapter 5, on marketing, and in Chapter 11, on the finances of e-business.

There are other potential implications, however. Internet-driven sourcing of goods and services means that orders can be placed at great speed, taking into account a wide range of price information around the globe. Prices can be globally influenced, therefore. A knock-on effect of this is that unemployment patterns can be affected more rapidly by global trends, and in a wider range of industries. For example, until the advent of internet bookshops, employment in the book trade was entirely a national affair – even local, in many respects. National chains of bookshops competed with independent individual book-shops and each found a niche. Now a local bookshop in, for example, North London has to compete not solely with national chains (in itself quite a tall order these days) but also with the discount pricing of the internet bookstores, and even with the internet sales of publishing houses themselves.

So, there are not merely commercial mico-economic trading implications, there is also a macro-economic impact on countries via the pressure of global pricing and in terms of international fluctuations in sales and employment in industries which have formerly been nationally based.

Social implications

Perhaps the least easy area in which to identify trends is the social sphere. Some trends have already become clear – for example, the rapid rise in usage of email has revived the art of letter writing. The explosion, amongst the young, of the related practice of text messaging via mobile telephones is another mani-festation (of a completely different style) of the convenience of instant written communication, and its sometime advantages over spoken communications.

Texting provides an interesting confirmation of the predictions of McLuhan, that electronic media will create their own forms of communication, rather than simply be alternative vehicles of existing forms. So, texting has developed its own language, based on the need to be quick and economical with characters. Because this is essentially a youth phenomenon, it has also evolved in a manner consistent with modern youth cultures.

Box 3.1 Text language example

One example of text language is as follows:

d u w 2 g on a d8 w m = Do you want to go on a date with me?

In some cases, common words have been truncated to their initials. In others, there have been phonographic substitutions – '8' for the sound 'ate'. In other cases (not represented here), there may be specific codes – 'lol' meaning 'laugh out loud', and used as an appreciative response if someone says something funny.

The range of social implications, potential as well as actual, is so vast that it would be impossible to list even a small number of them. We shall therefore confine our discussion to a few examples.

The death of confinement

One major potential social effect of the internet is the liberation of immobile members of society. People with severe physical difficulties often find it very difficult to travel or even to visit local facilities, despite the fact that many countries these days have legislation requiring public facilities to be adapted to be convenient for the disabled. Few forms of public transport are convenient for someone who is confined to a wheelchair, for example. Few amenities, such as restaurants or cinemas, are well adapted to accommodate those who are differently abled from the walking majority. In the past, such individuals were marginalised and excluded from the vast proportion of social activity, because it involved travelling around – even a walk down to a local pub or a church hall could have proved an insurmountable obstacle for someone who needed to be taken in a wheelchair. Of course, there still is a great deal of that kind of exclusion, but as well as a growing sense that this has not been a positive feature for society in general – as well as being terribly isolating for the people concerned – the internet has proved a boon for the disabled. Where once meeting and communicating with people who shared the same interests required movement, now it can be effected electronically. This has been particularly important for the elderly, amongst whom there is a larger proportion of those with mobility difficulties. Indeed, the over-65s have been the fastest growing group of internet users as the twenty-first century starts. Internet shopping, online communities and interest groups, and chat rooms are all facilitators of a growing inclusion of those whom previously society had excluded.

A society that never sleeps

With the development of international user communities, there has been a significant spur to the so called '24/7' society – operating 24 hours a day 7 days a week. This is an example of a trend which is already in evidence and, in some ways, has required a physical presence (so that in major urban areas, such as western capital cities, some shops stay open '24/7' and others have continually lengthened their hours of opening so that there is a much smaller window of non-trading time than in previous decades). But as well as the physical element, the internet has accelerated this process. It is possible to trade shares, to carry out bank transactions, to buy goods, to interact in chat rooms or connect to people via other communications platforms – all at *any* time of the day. A not uncommon pattern of work that has started to emerge – especially with the self-employed or those who do a certain amount of their work at home – is to start doing some work very early in the morning, maybe stop for a more extended breakfast, work during 'normal' office hours and then later in the evening, maybe after having had an evening meal and relaxed with family or friends, do a last thing check on email. It is not necessarily healthy, of course, but it is happening, and more and more so.

The other side to the '24/7' society is that the people who *service* this have also to live 24/7. So, low paid supermarket employees may end up having to work all-night shifts, without the financial rewards received by their customers, the 24/7 professionals. The impact of night work on a family is significant, and can create great tensions in a marriage. The growth of the 'never sleeping' city is likely to bring greater stresses and strains upon the social fabric of urban populations.

One last example of social impact is that as well as bringing people together, the internet can have a negative personal side. Already we read of 'internet widows' – partnerships and marriages where one person gets so engrossed in surfing or chatting that they use up all their spare time and neglect their part-ner – and of young people becoming obsessed with chatting to their friends via the web (though for anyone who has lived in a household with adolescents, or remembers their own adolescence, this seems simply to have replaced the phone with the web rather than present any radically new phenomenon).

One aspect of this increased personal element to the internet is the phe-nomenon of web dating – where people have close relationships with people conducted solely via the internet. In the 'privacy' of a closed chat room, such relationships can involve as much intimacy in terms of verbal disclosure as a physical relationship – though, of course, the physical element is what makes it very different! Some may write these off as the sad activities of lonely people – that may often be true, though probably less so than one might at first expect. Be that as it may, the judgement as to whether it is sad, or fun, or fantasy, or flirtatious or just plain desperate, is not really the main point here – which is simply that it happens. In some cases, people have made the very unfortunate mistake of thinking that a 'virtual lover' will be just as good in the flesh. People have made marriage vows over the web, only to find that the person they married is not the kind of person they expected – wrong personality, wrong colour hair, wrong age, sometimes wrong gender!

The main conclusion to draw from this discussion is that the web is not just a commercial enterprise. It is a communications network, and its social uses are as many and as varied as human ingenuity.

Technological implications

In many ways this category is here for completeness – because it is a major category in most PESTLE analyses. Much of what is said throughout this book is an expansion on the technological implications of e-business. Nevertheless, there are some specific technological aspects which merit attention.

One of these is that internet computing, just like all electronics since World War II, is subject to the speed/power/size trends of the whole industry, symbol-ised by the now-famous Moore's Law referred to in Chapter 1. In fact, this is an average, and at certain times over the last decade it has been doubling at an even faster rate, only to slow down whilst other parts of the industry catch up. Originally, a decade or more ago, the global network was based around a few major providers run off large scale super-computers – space research labs, university computing networks, government computing installations (the US Pentagon being the most important of these). It has however, in the last few years, become possible to access the web via progressively smaller devices; from mainframes to mini-computers to PCs (via servers) to handheld palm devices; to WAP phones and beyond. Similarly, the email based academic network of some ten years ago with which the authors were familiar has given way to the HTML visually oriented web page of today. Already a wide range of additional features are being built upon this, using further software devices created via Java or Javascript languages. The features include ever higher quality graphics, text that moves, blinks, changes colour as you watch it or even disappears. The website of the Icelandic singer Bjork loaded in late 2000 is a striking example of this; individual words appear on a white screen as if emerging from the fog and then disappear as mysteriously, and music and video clips as standard. It is clear that whilst the delivery mechanisms for extensive multimedia web activities are limited by current telecommunications power and the available bandwidths, the potential is there for yet further extension – holographic representations coming down your modem is clearly a technical possibility, though maybe a few years away at the moment.

Legal implications

Some broader legal issues have been considered in the political discussion. For example, the facilitation of international trade and communication means that it is difficult for an individual nation state to maintain its own jurisdiction. To take an extreme, and perhaps controversial, kind of example, in Afghanistan at present it is illegal for someone to try to convert Afghanis from Islam to Christianity. If someone in, say, Italy, puts up a website aimed at persuading Afghanis to convert to Christianity – whose laws are being broken here? Not Italian laws. Maybe not the current legal framework of the rules of Afghanistan (because they apply within the country, not beyond it), though one could understand that they might feel that an attempt was being made to subvert that framework. In some countries, legislation is intended to apply across the globe: Belgium's war crime laws, or the US anti-bribery laws. In practice, these are only as good as the apparatus behind the enforcement.

Certain specific elements of commercial and civil law are adversely affected by the internet. One example is intellectual property. It is remarkably difficult to completely protect your interests if the key information relating to a commercial product or innovation is made available on the web. The existence of copyright symbols for example, or the demonstration of trademark or patent registration in one country is unlikely to deter those in distant jurisdictions wishing to copy or pass off an innovation as their own. There is the option of not putting the innovation on the web, but this is not likely to be a successful long-term strategy. For one thing, if you hold off with your innovation, another party may come along with an idea that does the same kind of thing, put it up, and then get the so-called 'first mover advantage' of being identified with the product, often itself generating 'killer app' status (as we saw earlier – electric carpet sweepers are called Hoovers, and adhesive tape is called 'Sellotape' in Britain).

Napster, discussed in Chapter 2, provides a classic example as well as a salutary lesson. Recorded music is perfect for digitisation (though it often leads to large file sizes, though that is a minor issue here). Once Shaun Fanning had distributed Napster free, within months millions of people were swapping MP3 files. The effect of this was to side-step the record companies. So, if one person paid for an MP3 version of a song, within a very short period of time this could be passed on to hundreds or thousands of other Napster users. In this case, the US legal system rode to the rescue of the record companies. Napster was operated in the USA by US citizens, so when the courts ruled that it had to pay record companies or cease to carry their music, it was not difficult for this to be enforced. Imagine if the software had been developed in, say, Bulgaria, where the power of the US Government to control people's actions is negligible.

The Afghanistan example also indicates another legal aspect of the internet. Uploading a website is, in effect, a form of publication. Therefore, laws relating to free speech (or restrictions thereof), libel, treason, all apply to websites. (It is not well known that in the apparently liberal UK, it is treasonable to call for the abolition of the Monarchy in print. Hence, a website that did just that – which, on the face of it, would seem a legitimate if controversial political position in the UK – could find itself in violation of British legislation.) A further complication here is where a site has a form of streamed user communication – a chat room. There have already been some cases where the host and developers of a website have been sued for libel due to material which was put on their chat rooms by a third party. It is generally taken that 100 per cent control is not possible, but that some measures should be taken to inhibit or prevent abuse, libel or whatever constitutes illegal expression. For example, a web page setting out principles of good behaviour on a site is accepted in the UK as part of a reasonable approach to chat room management, and elimination of any illegal or offensive material as soon as it is detected.

The other side to the legal issues relating to the internet is who governs the net itself? As mentioned in Chapters 1 and 2, there is a cluster of organisations that work loosely together, each having a responsibility for some aspect of the web, among these being programming languages and conventions, or registration of domain names.

In addition, governments have adopted laws that are intended to regulate internet activity to some extent: the USA produced a Framework for Global Electronic Commerce in 1997 and, in the European Union, there has been the Electronic Commerce Directive of 2002. Whilst the overall effect of legislations such as these is to make the internet more of an open and orderly environment, not dominated by any one set of interests, it would be a mistake to think that the total impact of legislation has or will be likely to extend this feature. Many other pieces of legislation can apply to the internet, covering laws relating to libel, discrimination, terrorism or other criminal activities, and so on. Whilst these laws are passed and enforced for the good running of society as a whole – in theory, at least – it is certainly the case that the overall effect is to constrain activity.

The tension between those who see the internet as a free resource for the population without any hindrance, and those who wish to harness it to drive economic and social development more efficiently, is a central theme which affects the whole ethical, social, political and legal development of the web. This tension goes back to the origins of the internet.

One strand of internet development came from the international academic community, especially university researchers into physics and other natural science subjects. For academics, open dissemination of results and theories has always been a key feature of the research process. Scientists and other researchers are keen to present their views to the public scrutiny of their peers, both so that it may be tested and confirmed, but also so that further work may be build upon their results. For such a community, the internet was a perfect way to share results quickly, especially where the process of approval of research papers can take many months. Out of this group came a strong feeling that the academic traditions of freedom of expression should drive the development of the internet. Many of the most active contributors to the development of the world wide web have shared their results freely without any attempt to control or 'own' them – the behaviour of Tim Berners-Lee referred to in Chapter 1 being perhaps the most altruistic manifestation of this attitude. So far, this group has had its way – apart from the relatively low level of regulation referred to earlier, the web has been allowed to progress without a heavy hand of control.

On the other side of this argument are the big guns of the huge corporations and the western governments. The larger primary source of the original internet was the Pentagon, which needed to share and disseminate information around the world quickly. Inevitably, such an organisation developed secure systems to enable information to be moved around the network without being accessed by foreign powers.

In contrast, the corporate players have so far been surprisingly free about the internet. By and large, this has been because the development of computing power and software is still proceeding at so fast a rate that any attempt to copy-right or in some other way control or own the network would be doomed to be obsolete within weeks rather than months.

Nevertheless, there have been some hints that the web may not last in so liberalised an environment. The issue of security is one reason – criminal and politically subversive activity is greatly facilitated by the internet (which is not surprising, given that most forms of organised human activity have been made more efficient). Another is the impact of web activity on non-web commerce – as we have seen in the case of Napster and downloading music files. Yet another is the continuing tendency of the largest companies in the computing industry to find their own 'killer apps'. Arguably, Microsoft's bundling together of its internet software with its operating system could be seen as an attempt to ensure that the brand has a hand in the bulk of internet activities, not by presence inside the network itself, but through user systems of accessing it. This issue was only partially resolved by the US courts. However, the opportunity for an organisation to exercise 'long range' control over large parts of the web will probably remain, even though more direct attempts to take control of the network itself are unlikely to be successful. Overall, then, the balance of this argument seems to be that the freedom of content and wide dispersal of access will remain, but that progressively, major computing and other firms will place specific constraints on the web.

Environmental implications

It would seem, at first sight, as if the environmental implications of the world wide web are restricted to the construction of computers, the expansion of tele-communications and the use of electricity. Not that these are to be ignored – although any individual desktop computer terminal consumes a small amount of electricity compared with, say, an electric heater, the sheer volume of activity means that a lot of electric power is involved (not only are there millions of users online at any one time, there are servers, telecommunications links and corporate mainframes, as well as the internet backbone networks through which so much traffic passes in one way or another, such as the CERN or MIT networks). But over and above the environmental impact of internet platforms and activities, there are also wider implications, many of which stem from some of the economic consequences alluded to before.

For example, global-scale price pressure (as one may encounter with internet-based purchasing platforms) means that companies need to find ways to cut costs. In more developed economies, these are likely to come through techno-logical innovation. In less developed ones, whilst the will to innovate may be present, it may be easier to cut costs by eroding standards of operation. A classic example of this is ignoring environmental regulations. Indeed, some western companies themselves have chosen to locate production facilities in developing countries where environmental or employment regulation is a lower priority than sheer commercial survival.

The growth of the internet has been a significant contributing factor to the greater globalisation of business. A key consequence of globalisation is the effect of 'social dumping' – in other words, where an organisation operates in very many countries, they always have opportunities to shift production from one country to another. This is often concealed behind apparently sound economic principles, such as locating factories 'where there are lower labour costs.' The effect of this is not only that labour rates can be squeezed by multinationals, reducing operations in the countries with high wages, but also that government regulation of employment comes under pressure to be relaxed, with often severe consequences for the well-being, job security or even the health and safety of employees. Similarly, the example of the previous paragraph indicates that envi-ronmental protection can be squeezed in the same way.

There are other implications which are partially the result of the growth of the web. The greater ease of global sourcing means that goods may be transported greater distances – with the obvious increase in pollution. Surprisingly, labour and other production costs can vary so much around the world that it can be more profitable in some cases for a company to ship raw materials from country A to country B, employ local labour in country B to produce the goods, and then ship the finished products back to country A for retail sale, than to do it all in country A. Continued technological innovations in propulsion engineering mean that the costs of transport are at an all time low in real terms; to be fair, many of these innovations do tend to reduce the negative environmental impact of transport, but often these are more than offset by the consequent increases in use of shipping or air freight.

Ethical implications

As with other aspects, the ethical issues are not so much specific to e-business, but the internet environment puts existing ethical concepts into a different perspective.

Clearly, one over-riding ethical issue is the scale of potential access on the internet. The famous website loaded in 1999 by a Turkish man entitled 'A (chaste) kiss for my friends', which was apparently put up for no purpose other than to express friendship, went round the world, receiving literally thousands of hits, and being written up in national newspapers around the planet. This is a rare example of well publicised positive ethical uses of the web. Far more common, regrettably, are the less ethically acceptable ones. Typical of these is the case of an employee of a British bank, who was dismissed after he produced a web page detailing the sexual history of a female colleague – it ended up being seen by over half a million people.

One of the biggest issues with the scale of potential access is the behaviour of hackers and those who develop viruses. This is sufficiently large an issue that we shall defer it to the next chapter. There is an image in the popular press that all hackers are destructive – as we shall see later, it is not always as simple as that (though there are lots of cases where it *is* as simple as that as well).

Many of the unethical or dubious practices of physical marketing can be observed on the web. Advertisements that promise fantastic deals, but when you visit the site you find that the promise is rather greater than the reality. One twist with an internet advertisement is that once you visit a site, it can have software which will place a 'cookie' in your system – a small piece of coding, usually there make it easier to upload that site in the future (but clearly open to abuses, such as making that site a default location, or much more dangerously sending details of your hard drive back to a third party).

'Spam' email is another, and growing, menace on the internet. Spam is the computer-based version of junk mail – someone has gained your email address, possibly through your visiting a site, possibly via a database generated via a commercial transaction (in many cases buried in the small print is a request for your assent to a company releasing your details to other organisations, usually assent is presumed to be given *unless* you state otherwise). Then you receive unsolicited emails advertising goods, sometimes with an annoying frequency. The volume of this category of email is threatening to create internet gridlock in the coming years unless an effective means of controlling it is developed – this is likely to be as much technical as legislative.

It is inappropriate to summarise the key points of this chapter, as there is too much detail. But there are certain key themes:

- The web is still in its infancy, and there are many areas where technological or other innovations may change the face of the web substantially
- The tension between liberality and control will continue to be the determining factor in the development of the web, with potentially a gradual but not overwhelming increase in control by governments and corporations
- In social and political terms, the growth of the web is both extending and placing major strains on the lifestyle that western fostered nations developed in the second half of the twentieth century
- The potential of the web to revolutionise social relationships and develop a new sense of community is vast.

Further reading

As with Chapter 2, the main model used here is a standard strategic analysis tool. Hence, readers are directed to the same references as Chapter 2 for further study of strategic models.

With regard to the content of this chapter, the reader is directed to look frequently at regular publications, specifically a quality newspaper – the UK's *Financial Times* is particularly good on e-business. In addition, there are many internet magazines, and the best strategy is to read one good one regularly, and occasionally to buy a different one. The content of this chapter is changing at so fast a rate that there are few sources that remain current for very long.

Notes and reference

Cartwright, R. (2001) *Mastering the Business Environment.* Basingstoke: Palgrave Macmillan.

Questions for review and reflection

1 What effects might the growth of the internet have on economic factors such as employment?
2 How has the growth of the internet created opportunities for governments?
3 What are the main arguments for and against increasing the amount of control over the world wide web?
4 If you were asked to set up a web site for a political group, what legal issues would you need to take account of?

Ideas for further study

1 Identify a social group that in some way is disadvantaged in current society. In what ways could the internet be used to reduce or offset this disadvantage?

2   Try to make contact with people who are working directly on the internet – either developing or maintaining websites, or as regular and frequent users of services such as online auction sites. What trends do they foresee for the web? What aspects of its development do they see as positive and which do they have concerns about?

☑ 4 e-risk: security and vulnerability on the internet

Introduction

There is a range of different sources of risk associated with conducting business on the internet. Some of these are direct consequences of having a website at all. Some derive from the particular nature of your business, some from the technicalities of your presence on the web. Still other risks derive from the activities of your staff. It is important in this respect to recognise that *not all e-business related risk is electronically based, even when it has an electronic manifestation.*

Learning objectives

On completion of this chapter you should be able to:

1 Identify the prime areas of risk associated with e-business;
2 Analyse the respective roles of system and human factors involved in such risks;
3 Evaluate the effectiveness of different overall approaches to the management of electronic risk.

The scale of exposure

The often cited Forrester Research study on the difficulties involved in (global) e-commerce (Percival-Straunik, 2001) identified eight prime sources of difficulty:

1 internal politics;
2 the global/local balance;
3 regional coordination;
4 cultural differences;
5 inadequate service provision;
6 the transition from a global to a web strategy;
7 global logistics;
8 product complexity.

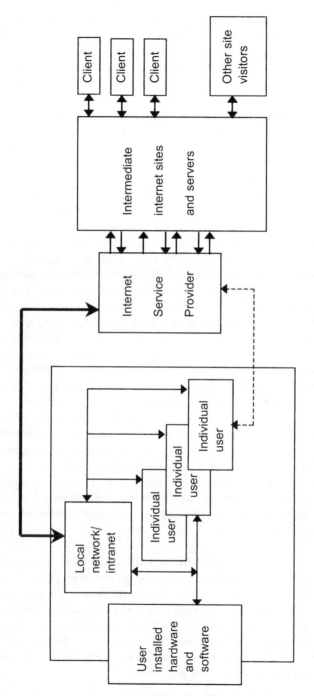

Figure 4.1 **The network of potential vulnerability**

But interestingly, the issue of *security* did not figure on this list. Issues relating to strategy were, on this survey, seen as more important factors. It is unlikely that a similar result would be derived, if such research were conducted again in the early 2000s. The growth of 'spam', mentioned earlier, the evidence of large-scale financial fraud perpetrated on the internet,[1] the use of email by criminal gangs – all these and more have brought the issues of security to the centre stage in the further development of the internet. All require some measure of control, which in turn affects speed and cost of internet operations.

Figure 4.1 illustrates the range of potential sources of risks and vulnerability for an organisation conducting some of its business via the world wide web.

In this diagram, we see a simplified model of some of the key elements of an organisation and its e-business operation. The reader can see that even though simplified, this is not a simple matter – there are very many possible sources of risks and of vulnerability to some kind of hazard. At each point of interface (indicated by arrows in the diagram), there is potential for some kind of damaging event or process. For example, an organisation may have specifications and security procedures for software that its specialist computer staff install, but have no system-based protection against the installation of unauthorised software, or even connection of hardware, at local PCs or workstations located in different parts of the company. The fact that some piece of software is not authorised does not mean that it will necessarily lead to damage or loss of any kind, but it increases the risk. For instance, most organisations will have quite elaborate procedures for checking for viruses and related packages – so-called *malware* – and cleaning any disks or other sources used for storing software. However, in many organisations the culture may well be compatible with individuals bringing in discs containing unauthorised material, such as that which is downloaded from an open website, copied from a friend, or even from a free CD given away with a computer magazine. Quite apart from the obvious potential of malware contamination, there is the additional possibility that the installation of a piece of unauthorised software may well involve the turning on or off some feature of the operating system that then renders existing software ineffective.

The model of exposure in Figure 4.1 indicates the sources or potential points of vulnerability. This can give rise to a wide range of different types of security weakness. Laudon and Traver (2001) identify six major forms of security risk related to e-commerce:

- *Integrity*: Is the information obtained via the internet what it purports to be, or has it been in some way altered by an unknown party?
- *Non-repudiation*: A company may send something out that was ordered on the internet, and find that the recipient refuses to pay because they claim it never arrived; potentially this can combine with an integrity failure, allowing someone other than the real customer to have taken delivery of the goods.
- *Authenticity*: Is the person or organisation with whom you are communicating over the web who they purport to be?

---

[1] In just one area – the theft of proprietary information – one estimate puts the loss at $45 *billion* in 2000 (IDG 2002).

- *Confidentiality*: If I send important personal information to an other party, can I be sure that no one else will be able to access it whilst in transit?
- *Privacy*: If I send important personal information to another party, can I be sure they will use it responsibly and only use it for the purpose for which I provided it?
- *Availability*: Is the internet service I seek from a company there as and when I want it, or is it sometimes offline?

In what follows, we shall call the potential for damage *exposure*; the degree of likelihood of damage, the *level* of exposure, and the potential severity of the damage, the *extent* of the exposure. We can distinguish in Figure 4.1 above two overarching categories of sources of risk:

- Internal to the organisation.
- Externally, either via a website, email or other party computer system, or via the internet interface, the internet transmission link, or the internet service provider.

We shall go through both of these main sources of exposure, and identify both the general level and extent, as well as identify some of the methods by which exposure can be minimised.

Internal exposure

Thematically, in all areas of exposure there are human and technical factors. By and large, the human factors are the most problematic, and require the more careful attention. Technical factors may create weaknesses, but these can be identified and plugged in one way or another. The human aspect, however, is that each of us has a unique and highly complex blend of interests and intentions and, as a result of this, there are very many different reasons why someone might inadvertently or deliberately exploit any e-business related vulnerability of an organisation or network.

Malware

We commonly hear about viruses, worms, Trojan horses and similar forms of software contamination. These are all forms of software package devised deliberately in order to create some kind of effect or problem for a recipient computer system – usually this is called malicious code, or *malware* for short. Malware contamination is one of the biggest single sources of exposure for smaller organisations (though, as we shall see later, other threats can be more serious for the really large firms). It has both an internal and an external aspect to it. The comments below will focus initially on the internal weaknesses that can lead to contamination, and then look at the external aspect.

What is 'malware'?

There are three main kinds of malicious programs:

Virus: This is the best known term, often used misleadingly for all such programs; a virus is a program that will generally lodge inside a file (usually, though not always, an executable file or program) copy itself and spread those copies to other files, along the way it may do something else such as display a picture, or rewrite part of someone's operating system, or erase data saved on a hard drive.

Worm: This can do similar things to a virus, but whilst the virus spreads from file to file within a single computer, a worm will travel around a network; for this reason viruses can just as frequently be spread via the exchanging of disks, whilst worms will more often be transferred via the internet; usually the method of transmission is by the worm accessing someone's address book in an email program and then sending itself to all addresses contained therein.

Trojan horse: This is where the software package does not actively transfer itself directly, but lies concealed within some file that looks harmless and maybe of utility to the user (a game is a common vehicle for this purpose), inducing them to open the infected file (hence the name).

A fourth form of malicious code is beginning to be seen. Many web pages use applets (small programs that add various forms of functionality to them, such as pop up menus, or mouse related events; these are often written in Java or Javascript languages). *Bad applets* are such routines that are written with malicious intent, and are transmitted to anyone who accesses a particular web page or interacts with a certain element (such as clicking on a radio button on a page).

Dealing with malware

Almost all major organisations have more or less elaborate methods of protection against malware contamination This level of coverage shrinks rapidly once one moves down to the level of small businesses and individuals. Some surveys have suggested that less than a third of all SMEs are protected against wholesale loss of data due to malware exposure. The general lower level of smaller user protection, compared with major corporations, is primarily down to cost: the larger organisation can sustain the sizeable overhead that is necessary if one is to protect against all the major risk elements. This may require not only malware protection software – which carries a cost in its own right – but also maintenance, updating, computing support, and so on. All of these are factors that may make a small business or sole trader feel that the cost is more important than the risk that is being run.

But when one adds to this the fact that the vast majority of companies in almost every country in the world are small businesses, running on tight margins, then the potential scale of worldwide exposure becomes enormous.

It is important to recall in this context the analogy with human infection: the more people there are out there with flu, the more chance you have of catching it.

Apart from a very virulent infection, slight contact with just one person carries a far lower level of exposure than prolonged contact or contact with many infected people. Similarly, if one PC somewhere has a malware based infection, then it is likely that this will be transmitted to a few others. If these all have some form of protection then the onward transmission rate is reduced significantly. If they are all small businesses with out of date or no protection, then the transmission rate will increase dramatically, in some cases to a rate of millions per hour.

In this respect, then, the relatively low levels of individual or SME protection against so called malware are a serious compromising factor in internet and e-business security. A trading company, for example, may be well protected, but the key question is how well are their clients or their customers protected.

Many of the major difficulties with malware infection are not so much down to the technical features of the protection as to do with the comprehensiveness and completeness of the protective methodology, or with the way the technology is managed. The most common protection methods are (a) commercial anti-malware software such as McAfee or Norton (b) *firewalling*, where filtration software is installed at the entry points of internet-connected systems. Both approaches have drawbacks, however.

One drawback with commercial anti-malware software is that it is usually out of date by the time it reaches the customer. That is to say, the risks against which it is designed to protect the customer have already been identified by major users and steps have already been taken by those major users to combat them. For example, Microsoft has whole departments concerned with the identification and disarming of viruses and worms. Many malware entities are dealt with without end users even being aware that this has happened, sometimes because they are directed towards larger systems or against the framework of the internet itself – the major servers. But sophisticated and determined malware writers have continued to develop their own 'products' to avoid such protections. For example, the famous 'concept' virus now has literally dozens of variants.

But commercial anti-malware software being out of date is not a reason to go without. Long after a package has been identified and a solution or defence found for it, there will be clusters of nodes of the world wide web that have not benefited from the solution, and there will be individual personal computers that have the infection standing on their hard disks and feeding it out – sometimes unknown to the PC owner – for months or even years to come. Again, this reflects the role of human vectors in the spread and combat of disease – long after a cure may have been found and the majority of the population protected against a disease, there will remain individual carriers in less closely surveyed regions.

A related drawback is that these kinds of protections are only of limited forward value. In general, they will prevent an existing package entering a system, and often too will protect against a new form of malware based on an existing strategy. If a particular kind of infection has been identified (say that a worm, when activated, emails a copy of every one of the user's emails to an undisclosed location), then steps can be taken to deal with this and with other similar programs that might gain entry to the system via the same kind of process, and do similar things with the address book. So, once a protection system has identified against one program that sends an image to the whole of your address book, then it will generally also deal with any that sends a text file, or an email message as well.

But, as mentioned above, the ingenuity of the malware-writers (see later in this chapter) is at least as high as that of the malware-protectors, so there is a continual catching up process in motion, leaving most users exposed for a certain period of time until up to date protection is installed.

This last point underlines another, non-technical, weakness about software protection. It is only as good as the people who activate and update it. Most commercial providers of anti-virus software provide regular online updates, but these still need to be specifically enacted by the user. Even in larger corporations, where there is generally a much higher awareness of this kind of exposure, it can be the case that individual users of workstations or PCs fail to take advantage of updating services that may be provided centrally. If there is insufficient corporate commitment to electronic protection, then it may be that staff are unaware of the extent or level of exposure that casual security activity may create.

A parallel weakness is that unless the staff have a relatively acute sense of exposure in general, they are likely to be casual or sloppy in their use of un-authorised software. Some organisations are very strict about this and ban all software that has not been rigorously vetted. In some banks, for example, it is a serious disciplinary offence to introduce software that has not been checked carefully by an internal computer security department.

Again, though, strict rules are one thing, and a genuine sense of commitment from the staff is another. If people know that the organisation could be seriously damaged, just by them 'harmlessly' slipping this disk they got from a friend into their disk drive, then they are likely to be just that step more vigilant than if there is no such confidence. If, on the other hand, they are unconvinced of the hazard, then sooner or later they will think 'Just this once won't matter', and thus the integrity of the system will be violated. With all of these risks and their pre-vention, it is often less a case of being able to eliminate the risk completely so much as significantly reducing the likelihood that the exposure will turn into actual damage.

Firewalling is generally a much tougher defence. But this too has some draw-backs. Again, there is the historical element – you can only protect yourself against something that you think someone 'out there' has devised or is con-sidering using. So, by definition, potential attacks that have not been thought of yet are not yet protected against.

More important is that firewalling tends to be of a blanket nature. Typically, a firewall may filter every email or accessed web page and screen these for content or attachments, preventing the user from accessing something that the firewall designers have deemed to create unacceptable exposure. Some of the results of firewalling activities can be absurd in themselves – for example, a firewall that is intended to protect not just against infected file attachments but also to screen out inappropriate content (such as obscenities, potential terrorist communica-tions, or pornography) may prevent the transmission of legitimate messages. One anecdotal example is of someone who ordered a book online for them-selves, but using their work PC, only to have the confirmation message stopped at the firewall – the book's title was *Does my bum look big in this?*, a popular novel in the UK in 2000; the explanation given was that 'bum' was on the list of words that suggested potential pornographic content.

Another mechanism that fulfils a similar role to a firewall is a *proxy server*. This is a server that stands at the point of interface or gateway between an organisation's system and the public network. It can therefore operate similar filtering processes as firewall methodologies, but it will tend to operate in the opposite direction. The firewall tries to prevent undesirable material getting in, whilst the proxy server tries to keep internal users from bringing in undesirable material.

Firewalls and proxy servers will generally slow down transmission rates. Some firewalls – for example, a number of those sitting on government email servers – simply avoid this problem by banning the transmission, one way or another, of any attached file of a certain type at all. This gains security at the expense of forfeiting one of the key benefits of email.

As with the potential exposure of commercial anti-malware software not being comprehensively adopted throughout an organisation, a firewall has the potential for 'holes' – that is, parts of the overall local network that operate without the firewall protection but still interact with the rest of the network. This can happen for many reasons. One may be that a system has been upgraded piecemeal to a point where it is believed (in error) that all workstations are on a particular system or have a given set of settings, and then the firewall that is introduced works on machines in virtue of those settings or systems. But an individual workstation may have been overlooked, an individual user may have chosen not to do whatever was necessary to trigger the upgrading, or there might simply be a technical error where the central electronic record for workstations is corrupted or deficient in some other way, leaving some machines 'off the list' so to speak.

A further complication with all methods of internal protection is that the 'internal network' is not entirely self-contained. The steady growth of people working at home, or away from the office, means that people are using laptops and PCs that may connect to the local network intermediately (for example, via an email connection through a third party internet service provider such as MSN or AOL) or indirectly (via work stored on a disk or handheld device and then loaded into the workplace machine at a later date). It is often the case that well firewalled networks end up importing major items of malicious software because staff laptops are not so well protected. Yet a further problem here is that even when working in the office, someone may be using a telephone line that stands outside the general network. It is common for very senior managers to have a line that is separate from the main switchboard that is used for highly confidential calls. The growth of 'airport' and other remote modem devices means that the manager might then be able to use this line to access the internet completely independently of the organisation's firewalling technologies, creating an exposure that may at a later date facilitate the introduction of malware packages into the main system.

In short, then, malware infection can be protected by software designed to 'disinfect' once they have been 'caught,' or by firewall or similar technologies designed to prevent initial introduction to a system or network. In practice, however, there are significant drawbacks with both of these.

Above all, though, the principal weak link is when there is a lack of recognition by users of the importance of protection against this type of exposure, a theme we shall come back to in later areas.

Personal data protection

Many corporate systems will contain a great deal of personal information, about clients and about staff. In many countries, there is significant legislation requiring that the data held is only used in very specifically defined ways, and that it is not on open inspection. Quite apart from the legislative requirement, it is clearly good practice not to allow all and sundry look at the disciplinary records of members of staff, for example, or to have the private addresses of customers open to public inspection.

A standard way of protecting this information is by password protection of files or servers. Most corporate local networks will also use password protection for individual email accounts, for access to a particular user account, for use of the network, or even for any level of access to a workstation. One result of this is that people may hold some items of confidential information independently of any corporate database. This in itself may create exposure that an organisation may not even realise it has.

There are three permanent problems with passwords in general (these comments apply also to the use of passwords as an external protection method):

- People find it difficult to remember passwords, so given the choice they often pick something memorable for them, such as the name of their pet hamster, or their date of birth. Someone who knows just a little bit about an individual might then have a fair chance of guessing their password.
- When passwords are set centrally, or the system sets parameters on password choice (such as the prohibition of recognisable words, or the requirement to include numeric as well as alphabetic characters into a password), then it becomes difficult for the average user to remember. The majority of individuals using computer systems are likely to have multiple passwords to remember (such as e-store or internet discussion groups, banking security pin codes, ISP recognition data sets). The volume of security information that a consumer may have to remember creates a great temptation to write some of it down. For a company employee to do this is to create a fresh form of exposure, based on the risk that the written password is seen by the wrong person.
- Passwords need to be regularly reviewed to remain secure. Hackers use programs that will not only generate huge numbers of random character strings that might act as passwords, but then will attempt to use these to gain entry to a secure network. The longer the period of time that a particular string is extant, the greater the likelihood that it will be captured by one of these programs and used, to gain entry. Also, the longer a password is used, the greater the chance that someone else may discover it. Unfortunately, the

more frequently passwords are changed, the more likely it is that people will want to write them down to remember them.

As well, there are short-term issues with password-protected entry to data sets. Individuals may have data on a screen and be called away suddenly to a meeting, leaving the 'secure' information visible to who ever happens to pass by their desk. Even when someone is at their desk, open plan offices make it easy for one person to catch a glimpse when walking past someone working at their desk. The risk that that someone is intent on acting inappropriately with the information, or that they can actually see something sensitive may be small, but it is present and therefore creates an additional exposure for the organisation.

Of course, each new development in technology increases the potential protections – the use of webcams, for instance, can be harnessed to iris recognition software, so that a screen saver could only be turned off by the person responsible for the desktop appliance. Voice recognition software has a similar potential. both of these are used extensively in other applications of personal identification – such as airport security.

Human factors in internal exposure

The preceding forms of exposure represent mixtures of human and technical weakness. The following are primarily human and user related matters, rather than ones involving system design.

Commercial confidentiality

Needless to say, any company using computers even to a minimal degree will hold information therein that they would like to keep to themselves. Commercial confidentiality is perceived to be a central feature of the competitive advantage for most organisations. It is not always quite as true as some of them believe. Most really new developments have been leaked to the press, or the technology has been communicated via research papers, or 'beta' versions have already been tried out by members of staff, or simply competitors have guessed what is happening (because they too may be working on similar lines). But all the same, the timing and the nature of a new development can be crucial to its success. In addition, information relating to the weaknesses or problems of an organisation is likely to be highly sensitive, in some cases open knowledge could lead to clients cancelling orders, suppliers demanding immediate payment of invoices (with all the attendant problems this creates for cash flow), for example.

Commercial information is thus extremely precious, and its dissemination can be a major blow to an organisation. Many of the protections outlined in this chapter (firewalling, encryption, passwords) will help to maintain commercial confidentiality. There remain the same kinds of technical and human problems with these remedies. In addition, however, there are other potential problems with confidential information and internet or email usage.

The simplest problem is sheer failure by individuals to perceive the commercial importance of an item of information. Many years ago, one of the authors of this book worked in a major communications organisation, and used to produce a regular newsletter for computer users. On one occasion, he chose to run an article about what seemed to him to be a harmless but interesting aspect of internal computer usage. His divisional manager (two levels up) just happened to see the edition before it was disseminated, and realised that a major project involving several millions of pounds sterling might be prejudiced if this information were made public. The author simply was not in a position to recognise the sensitivity of the article.

Other potential weaknesses involve the way in which information may be disseminated. Usually a web page takes a little bit of time to produce, several people within an organisation get to see it before it is uploaded, and therefore the oversight of one person is counterbalanced by the perceptions of others, and sheer accidental release of information is thereby reduced. Emails, however, which form an important subsidiary to much web-based trading (for example, confirming sales or delivery addresses, sending passwords, and so on) as well as other aspects of e-business, can all too easily involve slips of disclosure. For example, 'reply' buttons are often right next to 'reply to all' buttons, so that a slip of a finger or mouse can mean that many people see what was intended for only one. Or sometimes a reader does not scroll all the way down a message and forwards on information that is not intended (this is especially prevalent when emails include a long list of the replies bouncing back and forth between individuals, so that eventually a user forgets what exactly they said four emails ago – but it is there nonetheless for any fresh eye to see).

Contractual commitment

In common with any other form of communication, web page or email statements can form part of a legally binding contract. Again, whilst this is less likely to be overlooked in the more lengthy process of putting together a web page, it can be easily overlooked with an email. It is also important to recognise that different statements can have different import, culturally or legally, in different countries. By definition, the internet is global, which means that an organisation should at the very least bear in mind the different kinds of interpretation that may be made about statements about goods or services offered. This has led to somewhat farcical situations where companies fearful of potential litigation based on staff sending ill thought out or unauthorised emails now insert long disclaimer notices, usually far larger than the text of the message itself.

There is also a degree of ambiguity about the *legal* jurisdiction concerning a statement made on the internet. Generally it may be assumed that the country in which the company is based or in which the web page originated will be the legal system under which any claim might be heard, but this is not quite as simple as it looks. A multinational organisation, with an intranet that stretches across many countries, for example, may have a website where the contributions were made in different places, which relate to different countries, may specify services or goods specific to different countries, and where the source files themselves are held at different places on servers in different countries.

Publicity

The risks of bad publicity are less pronounced with websites than they are with sloppy use of email. Emails in which people use obscene language, for example, or which include jokes or unflattering comments about a colleagues, may well get into the wrong hands or, by accident or even design, are spread around the internet. Such cases immediately create a liability not just on the direct perpetrators, but also on the employer. For example, under English law the employer would be expected to take reasonable steps to protect all staff against sexual or racial abuse, and this would certainly extend to cover sexual discussion of a colleague over the internet. For instance, in a recent case of this kind, a leading financial trader was required to leave their job immediately after disseminating an email not even written by him describing a sexual act carried out by a colleague.

But publicity is also created through the efficiency and effectiveness of the website itself. A customer will form a poor view of a company whose website is difficult to load, or has technical errors (such as links to non-existent pages, or pages that have not been properly checked and lines overwrite each other, or there are images that cannot be displayed). As will be discussed later, one major mistake here is that many organisations overestimate the capacities of the browsers and systems of their clients and customers, so that a page that seems to work well when tested out on their own machines performs far less well with lower grade hardware or software. In some cases, a page may simply fail to load properly, or leave out significant areas of content. The exhortation of website developers in the early days was to test out pages on as wide a range of browsers as possible, and still to leave a text version of the page accessible just in case.

Some website designers have taken a leaf from the kinds of quality test used by popular music companies – the so-called 'car radio' style test. This is where a deliberate choice is made to test out the product on the least suitable apparatus (in this context, such a test might be to see how the site performed on an old PC running on an obsolete operating system, with an early version of a browser, and using a slow telephone line). The assumption is that if the product works well then, it should work well in any context.

In general, the style and appropriateness of the content of a web page is a major marketing factor, as discussed in a later chapter. The more wide the testing of a site against different browsers, different operating systems, different hardware, different speed telecommunications lines, the more likely the site is to be appropriately received by the target audience.

A further level of exposure to publicity risk is the possibility of theft of a website or website name. An acquaintance of one of the authors of this book had a website that was 'stolen' briefly. The name of the site needed to be renewed, and the individual, rather inefficiently, did this on the last date before it ran out. This resulted in the site coming off public view for a day or two whilst the payment was processed (in itself an undesirable feature). But when it came back, the site had been swapped for another that was running pornography! It appears that the pornographer was trawling sites that were down or seemed to be dormant and then switching their server's details, so that a visitor would be routed to the porno site rather than the real one. A little rewriting of server details on the web registration was all that was needed to restore the status quo, but it did result in some embarrassment with a couple of clients! Another source of publicity problems here comes when a website address suggests one body although it is really used by another. Individuals have, for example, registered names of celebrities or famous brand names, and then run legal but damaging content on those sites, so that the celebrity or corporation is almost forced to purchase the site in order to suppress it. (This has been outlawed in several countries, but if it is legal somewhere, then it can be done by registration in that country.) This underlines the potential vulnerability of websites to publicity damage.

We can see from these examples, that there is a degree of ambiguity about the internal/external division when it comes to internet related exposure. This will remain a thematic issue with the rest of this discussion. As stated at the start of this chapter, much of the exposure is due less to system design than the way that people use or abuse systems. This underlines a theme of this chapter, that human resource management is at least as important in the management of an e-business as computing technicalities.

External exposure

The prime forms of external exposure stem from malware infection and the breaking into people's computers or to their telecommunication links remotely (*hacking*, as it has come to be known). Again, the main source of such exposure is at least as much down to human factors as it is to system design or technical flaws.

The varieties of hacking and the mind of the hacker

The common perception of hackers is that their prime motives are either greed or malevolence – that is, that either the hacking is going on to facilitate criminal gain such as theft or embezzlement, or it is intended wilfully to damage the organisation or, indeed, the global market (or capitalist) economy itself. This is a great oversimplification of the situation, however, and unless one gets some idea of the motives of the different groups of hackers around, one will not be able to deal with them appropriately.

It is important, though, before embarking on this discussion, to emphasise that hacking is almost always a criminal act in itself, just as breaking and entering. As we shall see below, not every hacker has criminal or even malicious intent – just as not everyone who breaks into a property has malicious intent. But the very act, nevertheless, is criminal (apart from *white hat* hacking – see Box 4.1 on p. 80.)

Having said that, we should bear in mind the different reasons why someone might choose to hack into a system (which of course will say something about what they are likely to do once they have got in). These include:

- *Play*: Some computer enthusiasts (many of them adolescent boys – sometimes described rather condescendingly as 'script kiddies') enjoy simply the challenge of trying to get in to a closed system; there have been several cases where a 'script kiddie' has managed to gain entry to top secret computer systems (including the Pentagon's) only to have no use for the information to which they then had access.

- *Computer enthusiasts and purists*: There are many computer enthusiasts who use hacking as a means to develop their own skills and understanding, and also in some cases as a means of identifying systemic weaknesses; there are many discussion groups and loose collections of individuals who share ideas and experiences about hacking publicly; one group that called itself 'the cult of the dead cow' in the late 1990s had many contributions from individuals claiming that hacking was the only way they could get major software companies (Microsoft was the prime candidate in most cases) to pay attention to the weaknesses they had uncovered – possibly some of these might have been a cover-up for people with more malign intent, but on the face of it at least there was evidence that some hackers were motivated by interest and a desire to see systems made more effective[2].

- *Commercial competition*: As indicated in the discussion of email, it is rare in the modern era that any new commercial development is entirely secret. However, there are other aspects of commercial operations that may have a significant degree of confidentiality about them – records of complaints, legal proceedings settled out of court, personnel files and financial records perhaps above all. All of these and more can be valuable ammunition for an aggressive competitor or litigator, and thus hacking can be a useful but unethical vehicle for industrial espionage.

- *International warfare*: During the armed conflicts in south-east Europe in the 1990s, there were at least two cases of major malicious programs that appeared to have been launched from within combatant countries, believed to have been intended to cause some kind of damage, or at least difficulty, to the main countries providing military assistance to the UN. In addition, any entry into a country's military computer systems (such as the hacking into the Pentagon mentioned above) is clearly a major national security breach with potentially catastrophic implications.

- *Anti-corporation*: Some people (they even have a name for this – *hacktivism*) hack into the systems of a particular corporation as a means of getting back at them, perhaps an employee who was fired, perhaps a customer who received poor service, perhaps a member of the public who suffered a severe loss (for example, having an accident as a result of using a certain firm's kitchen equipment) and has a grudge against the firm. Of these, the resentful employee is potentially the most dangerous, as they may know not simply their own route into a system, but the basic architecture of a system, and where they could cause most damage.

- *Anti-capitalism*: The concept of the market, or capitalist, economy has been criticised since even before the time of Karl Marx; nevertheless, there remain some whose critical views of this approach lead them to undertake

---

[2] There are even publications that – perhaps naively – attempt to support and meet the needs of hackers. One such is the French language 'Hackerz Voix' newspaper.

direct action in opposition to capitalism. Many of these are intent mainly on undermining the self-confidence of the contemporary market economy, but there are some who believe (wisely or not) that they can destroy – or perhaps punish – those who profit from capitalism as an ideology. For these (another type of hacktivist) hacking provides a particularly ironic source of activity, seeing as it is a central part of modern capitalism.

- *Criminality*: Last, but by no means least, are those with a simple criminal intent to defraud and steal for whom entry to a computer system may provide the crucial information they need to carry out the crime – bank account details are an obvious example.

The most important aspect of the list given above is that the criminology of all these groups is quite different (remember, by the way, that even in the harmless cases it is still criminal). For different kinds of motive different kinds of protection are appropriate, some of which may lie in long term re-education rather than in simple 'prevent, detect and punish' style approaches. Box 4.1 illustrates this.

We can see in Box 4.1 a broad categorisation of hacking, though the bulleted list given earlier identifies a range of more specific motives that can be operating when people hack into systems. The key issue, though, is that different motives imply different kinds of hacking behaviour, which themselves require different kinds of reaction. For example, many (though maybe not all) anti-capitalist

---

Box 4.1 The colour of your hat

It has become customary in computing circles to distinguish three levels of hacking:

'white hat' hackers sometimes working in groups called 'tiger teams', are actually working for computing companies, trying to test their systems to the limit, to see where the weaknesses are; they are the only people who can legally hack into a system.

'black hat' hackers whose main intent is to bring about results that the organisation sees as damaging (though in some cases the black hat hacker may see themselves as liberating information that should be freely available on the web for all); a subclass of the black hat hacker is the so-called *cracker* – the hacker with criminal intent; not all black hats are crackers – some have political motives (that is, the 'hactivists').

'grey hat' hackers are those who claim to be working for similar rasons to the white hats – that is, to identify weaknesses in systems – but they are unauthorised independent operators, and thus there is a suspicion that some may be crackers in disguise; in addition many of the big computing firms fear that grey hats may inadvertently, out of naiveté, alert crackers to system flaws.

---

protesters are most concerned to have a place where they can voice their views and express their difference of opinion. Not all will want to 'smash' the ruling class – some may merely want to reform the current approaches to business that large corporations demonstrate. A heavy handed legal and policing style reaction to their activity can be counterproductive, as it may turn people who are mildly against your corporation into those who positively detest you.

The appropriate reaction here may, then, not be a simple systems response of tightening up loopholes (though that always should be done anyway) or of evoking due processes of law, so much as an educative one of trying to provide opportunities for the protested to engage in a more positive dialogue. For example, setting up a discussion zone where protesters can make their points and managers can make responses to them. This is not possible for every organisation – it takes a great deal of time and considerable diplomacy, and can distract from the business of business. But for the large multinational (who are the usual targets of anti-capitalist protesters), it might be that this kind of approach may yield longer-term benefits than a heavy handed legal response. It certainly would be good PR, if nothing else. Of course, it only works if the organisation thinks that it can genuinely defend its position. If managers know that their organisation is acting unethically, for example, then they will be unlikely to go down this route. But then, they should not be in business at all if they cannot defend what they do. On the other hand, the harder core black hat hackers, such as those involved in criminal activity, or acting as part of a military conflict, will not be deterred by such an approach. In these cases, it is a matter of prevention, detection and sanction.

Types of hacking

There are many different forms that hacking can take, including:

- *Access to and theft of data from databases*:   much of the concern in this area has been with potential loss of financial data, such as bank and credit card account data.
- *Covert monitoring of information*:   sometimes called 'sniffing', this is where a program may be introduced as a virus or Trojan; one common form of this is the *email wiretap*, where a program simply reads and forwards on internal or external email messages (some of which might contain confidential corporate information, or compromising information about the private lives of senior managers, which then can be used for blackmail purposes, and so on).
- *Identity misrepresentation*:   sometimes called 'spoofing', a hacker may masquerade as a legitimate organisation, for example, to induce a supplier to send goods to a new address.
- *Denial of service (often called DoS attacks)*:   perhaps the most dramatic kind of hacking occurs when an organisation is flooded with traffic, so much so that its internal systems crash and the organisation's e-business operations are offline for a period of time; more and more extensive versions of these are continuing to be developed: distributed DoS attacks use a large number of

computers to launch the traffic; a *smurf* goes one further and induces large numbers of potential users and customers to send verification messages to an organisation; much of all this is likely to be used by hactivists rather than the professional fraudster.

An additional issue which does not actually represent a security risk, though it can sometimes stem from one, is spamming, as discussed earlier. It is important to recognise that spam is *unsolicited* email, not unlike 'junk' direct postal mail. One needs to distinguish here between direct mail (or electronic or paper form) that is sent to an individual who has freely and knowingly chosen to disclose their name and address to an organisation, and spam proper, which uses people's names and addresses without their knowledge or consent. Not all disclosures are knowing – many organisations either on the internet or in call centre scripts, require the disclosure of personal details before any further activity can be progressed, and in some cases these may be passed on without the individual realising this.

Spam is a growing phenomenon – some estimates put it as high as 40 per cent of the entire email traffic on the internet. Whilst it is not a security weakness, in itself it may relate to one – as people have become more wise to spam mail, the spammers have taken to disguising their addresses; for example, spoofing by using information taken illicitly from third parties or by using a routine to distort the recipient's own email address (so that jsmith@isp.com becomes aljsmith@isp.com, for example). There are filter programs that will deal with spam, as well as firewalls and similar designs. For any organisation, the receipt of spam can represent a major waste of time, but the sending of it can be equally difficult; for example, by diminishing the credibility of the organisation.

Remedies for external exposure

It is important to remember the points made earlier, that the sources and reasons for security risks existing are various, and hence the remedies also need to be diversified, not only to address the different motives that people may have for exploiting security weaknesses, but also to spread the degree of general protection. In the case of criminal activity, for example, it is generally presumed that they will go where the pickings are easiest. A well defended organisational network, for example, though not foolproof, may offer a less promising location than one that seems to have a less general focus on security. It is an analogy with burglary – the house with no evidence of security consciousness at all is more vulnerable than one where someone just puts up an empty box that resembles an alarm.

There are three key themes that need to be taken careful note of when developing protection systems for an e-business operation:

- The specific vulnerability of the organisation and all its stakeholders.
- The extent to which security systems curtail performance of the system.
- The general social benefits of having an open, accessible yet safe world wide resource.

These three tend not to work together. The safer the security system, usually the slower. The greater the benefits of public accessibility, the more likely this will conflict with the specific interests and needs of a particular e-business. For the organisational manager, this therefore means that a balance needs to be struck between these three considerations.

Legal protection

There are various laws in different countries that deal with some of the above issues. For example, many countries have data protection and privacy legislation, protecting the individual from the unauthorised use of their details. Similarly, the USA has legislation regulating the use of spam, and the UK and other EU countries are also in the process of developing similar regulations. Financial fraud is covered in detail in the legislation of most countries in the world. Basic employment law in many countries involves (in addition to workers rights) certain responsibilities for employees not to act recklessly or without due care and attention to the interests of their employer. And there is legislation covering areas such as child protection, which arguably would extend to internet based child pornography and similar activities.

The main difficulty for governments is not the issuing of laws but their ability to detect and prevent or punish prohibited activities. By and large, the countries with the most extensive usage of the internet tend to have extensive detection apparatus for such areas as financial fraud, but many fraud detection professionals anecdotally report that their ability to stop fraud occurring is diminishing constantly, as criminals find ever more effective ways of exploiting the vast opportunities of the internet.

Staff related

As has been the theme of this chapter overall, many of the key remedies lie in addressing human factors. These will not eliminate the risks associated with e-business – every activity under the sun carries some kind of risk. But they can address some of the main sources of vulnerability, and thereby reduce the level and degree of exposure.

Some of the exposure identified earlier in this chapter stems from loose organisational practice. It is easy for a systems expert to identify ways in which such looseness can be tightened up. This has to be balanced, though, against the general culture of the organisation. A university, for example, is one of the most risky environments when it comes to electronic security – many students gaining access, swapping files between their university email and their personal email, staff sending files with research material all over the world to colleagues and fellow researchers, and so on. But it is also one of the loosest kinds of organisational culture. A high degree of autonomy is the norm in any university. Academics will shout loudest of all when it comes to the restriction of their right to go about their chosen business (that is, teaching and research). Hence, simply setting policies and processes to regulate behaviours would win a battle but lose a war – the academics might well simply ignore it. This is the reality of organisational change relating to the internet; it has to fit around other features of a business if it is to work.

Nevertheless, certain policies and practices, when implemented in a manner that takes account of the organisational culture and norms, can have a significant effect in reducing the degree and level of exposure, though rarely in eliminating it. These include:

- A set of education and development options that will keep all users of a system aware of the kinds of risk they may run not only to a mythical organisation (from which even well educated employees such as university lecturers can sometimes feel alienated and therefore unwilling to support) but also to their own work and security.
- An open dialogue on security and the preservation of the huge utility of the internet, possibly conducted through organisation wide forums or via working parties.
- A set of clear rules and sanctions, so that when people do feel tempted to slacken off their vigilance, their mind can be concentrated by the prospect of some direct sanction to which their slackness might render them liable.
- Regular audits and random checks to establish how far organisational rules are being complied with or violated – it is important that this process is introduced in a manner consistent with good employee relations practice, otherwise it may be counterproductive, if people resent it (and thus will try to subvert it).
- A clear information management strategy in the broadest sense will also help to clarify what information goes where, who can have access to what, what kind of authentication is required, and so on – many criminals gain access to systems simply by asking a question of someone who is not sure who they should or should not tell.

Such activity achieves so much, but not more – the well meaning individual who leaves their username or password lying about may well change their behaviour as a result of a combination of education, encouragement and sanction. But the ill-meaning individual, who is intent on damaging the business or, worse, on criminal activity, will remain untouched by all of this. Nevertheless, the more awareness there is of security issues in general, the harder it is for an individual to take advantage of the system. As simple a matter as the policy on out of hours working is also important here – if someone is to commit industrial espionage, of an electronic or physical form, they are far more likely to do it when there are few people around than when there are many. A policy of notification of out of hours working, and of recording who accesses what data, can significantly reduce the degree of exposure, sufficiently so that a criminal decides to go elsewhere to get what they want.

Controlling data access

The prime feature of any violation of security for an e-business is where some unauthorised party reads, and maybe changes, data. One natural way of preventing this happening is to make the transmission medium as secure as possible – we shall deal with that to some extent in the following section.

Another way is to make the data useless, because it makes no sense to the reader. This is the concept behind *encryption*, the transformation of data via a code or key so that only authorised people can read it. It is as old as the Elizabethans (if not older), though recent developments in mathematics have made it a much more powerful tool.

Box 4.2   Internet data encryption

There are two prime methods of data encryption used with the internet:

Private key (or symmetrical):   This is where each party has access to the same key, so that the sender uses this key to codify data before transmission, and the receiver uses the same key to reverse the codification; it is relatively quick but amongst its drawbacks are (a) the potential for one or other party to lose their copy of the key or allow it to be accessed by unauthorised individuals, and (b) the need for e-businesses with large numbers of users and clients to hold vast numbers of such keys.

Public key (or asymmetrical):   More popular nowadays (though generally a slower process) involves two different keys; one is a public key that can be used to encrypt the data of a wide range of users, the other is a private key, held only by the e-business, which enables the data to be decrypted. This approach is only possible because certain mathematical functions are non-reversible, but can be further transformed by other functions to yield the original data again; in principle, a hacker with an enormous amount of computing power might be able to retrieve the private key, but as these system often use keys that are 256 or even 512 bits in length, we are talking years at current computing rates, which clearly makes such an exercise redundant for the purposes of getting quick access to the underbelly of an organisation's data sets.

Public key encryption has been welcomed by the computing industry, but as yet has not had a major impact, primarily because of the loss of performance involved. Some approaches try to make the most of the relative speed of symmetric keys and the relative security of asymmetric, using technologies such as *digital envelopes*, where the bulk of the data is transmitted using the faster symmetric method, but the symmetric key is itself transmitted using an asymmetric key.

User identification

Spoofing, website theft, and similar moves underline the need for a business to establish clearly who they are dealing with. We have seen that passwords, though extremely easy to use, have a plethora of potential limitations – loss of password, inadvertent disclosure, sloppy password security, naive password choice, amongst others. Despite these, password driven entry remains an important, if limited, component of the overall security system of an organisation.

There are, however, further and more sophisticated forms of authentication of users. Public key encryption can be used to develop additional protections, such as:

- *Digital signatures*: Each document is processed initially by a special function (called a hash function) to produce material that functions as the signature; this along with the original data is then encrypted in the normal asymmetric way; the recipient then decrypts in the usual way, and also reverses the hashed material; if the de-hashed material mirrors the original message, then there has been no tampering with it since initiation from source; in this way each document has a unique identification.
- *Digital certificates*: There are now a number of central authorities, called certificate authorities, that issue certificates that verify the identity of an e-business, including digital signature and other relevant information; these authorities include private organisations such as Verisign, and state bodies such as Post Offices.

One advantage of these methods is that it is harder for an individual to repudiate a message – hence its value for legal purposes. Though it cannot do much about repudiation of receipt of physical goods, it can establish that a certain individual really was the person who ordered certain goods or services.

Transmission security

Potentially, there can be many different kinds of signature, many different kinds of certificate structure. Two protocols have been developed that standardise this aspect of security:

- *Secure sockets layer*: SSL – also known as TLS or Transport Layer Security – is a standard relating to authentification and certification.
- *Secure Electronic Transaction*: SET is a more comprehensive approach to authentication developed to facilitate online credit card transactions; not only does it verify who someone is, it also carries out the other electronic messaging necessary to complete a transaction, such as contacting the credit card company.

All of these initiatives are being continually developed and strengthened via a range of government initiatives. The USA, in particular, has set up several bodies to improve the management of security for the internet, partially as a means of improving their detection of criminal, and more latterly terrorist, internet activity.

Summary

- Much of the risk with e-business is due to human factors.
- Virus like programs – malware – are continually developed.

- There is a wide range of different kinds of hacker, not all of whom are malicious in intent.
- Encryption – especially asymmetric – is the prime method of protecting data.
- Public key encryption can be extended to provide further forms of security suich as digital certification.

References

IDG (2001) *Securing the Internet Economy*. Holliston, MA: IDG/Infoworks.

Laudon, K. and Traver, C. (2001) *E-commerce: Business, Technology, Society*. Boston, MA: Addison Wesley.

Percival-Straunik, L.L. (2001) *E-Commerce*. London: Economist Books.

Questions for review and reflection

1 Consider one particular aspect of the internet with which you have a good personal familiarity. Identify the prime sources of risk here. How far are they based on systemic weaknesses, and how far is it a matter of developing the appropriate attitudes and skills with people?

2 What considerations would a manager in an e-business need to take account of when deciding the level of security they will adopt for their internet operations?

Part II

✓ Marketing and the internet

In Part I, we looked at the general context of the internet, its development, the business and social implications, and finally the levels of risk that e-business activities may run. The main lesson to draw from these discussions is the broad point that internet activity is not a radically new and different kind of business, but rather a novel way of doing the same business, one that creates new opportunities – but still within the basic framework.

We shall see this argument extended and developed in the next four chapters, all of which deal with marketing in one way or another. The devotion of so large a proportion of this book to marketing is justified by the fact that the role of the website is, above all, a relational one, showing customers what goods or services they can acquire, creating an environment for a customer dialogue on products or services, conducting transactions, and so on.

What we will see in these chapters is a confirmation that the 'web' aspect of website activity is only the half of it – if that. The underpinning marketing infrastructure is at least as crucial as the physical appearance of a series of web pages.

■ ☑ 5 e-marketing: the same people, same needs, different services?

The Internet represents an extremely efficient medium for accessing, organizing and communicating information. As such, the Internet subsumes communication technologies ranging from the written and spoken word to visual images. Internet marketing is one of the newest distribution channels marketers use to reach the customer. It is different from traditional channels in that it is also a communication network. Like all communication networks, the Internet is all about establishing and reinforcing connections between people.

(Yelkur and DaCosta, 2001)

The above quote by Yelkur and DaCosta provides a focal point for the understanding of e-marketing. The internet is the perfect medium for both conducting business and building/managing relationships. It is global, immediate, dynamic and relatively inexpensive. The internet remains open 24-hours a day, 7 days a week, 365 days per year. Customers can usually do business on their own terms, when it is most convenient or urgent for them. Unlike printed material that can become outdated relatively quickly, information can be revised and posted within a much shorter time frame. The internet is a key element of what is now a 24-hour society. The term '24/7' has become an everyday part of our vocabulary.

The key purpose of this chapter is to set e-marketing within the context of e-business. In part, it is a scene setter for several chapters to follow. In this chapter, we will consider the development and analysis of e-marketing. These include such issues as how e-marketing relates to contemporary 'bricks and mortar' marketing; how e-marketing relates to the standard marketing principles and practices as described within so many textbooks and university courses.

As we will see as the chapters progress, it is not a question of just the front-end elements of marketing that are important within the e-world. It is one thing building a website, it is a totally different experience 'delivering off that web site'. We need to think how marketing, logistics and distribution together can inhabit the e-world. Later in this chapter, we will consider how the low-cost UK-based company easyJet has accomplished it, at least so far.

The role of marketing in the e-business world

Over this and the following two chapters, we will investigate the role of marketing within the e-business world. We will consider the views of several writers who have different thoughts on e-marketing, and their impact upon the subject area. Additionally, we will guide you through the key marketing concepts and their relevance to the e-world that we now inhabit. Firstly, though, we must return to basics.

How do we define marketing?

Depending upon the sources that you read marketing can have several different interpretations. For example, the American Marketing Association defines marketing as:

> the process of planning and executing the conception, pricing, promotion and distribution of ideas, goods and services to create exchanges that satisfy individual and organisational objectives (AMA, 2002).

The UK's Chartered Institute of Marketing defines it thus:

> Marketing is the management process responsible for identifying, anticipating and satisfying customer requirements profitably (CIM, 1996).

Chee and Harris (1993) believe that there are certain points that are key to suggested definitions. Market variables, such as price, promotion, distribution and product, are used to provide customer satisfaction. (We would also add here the importance of people, physical evidence and process of customer satisfaction. These are issues that we will return to later in this chapter.) They assume that the customer segments to be satisfied through the organisation's production and marketing activities have been selected and analysed prior to production. So, the customer, client or public actually determine the marketing programme. Chee and Harris (1993) recognise that marketing concepts and techniques pertain to non-profit organisations, as well as profit-oriented organisations.

Much of this filters down into what a company creates for their customer. This is far from a new concept. In the 1950s, management thinker and visionary Peter Drucker wrote:

> There is only one valid definition of business purpose: *to create a customer* [emphasis in original].
>
> Because of its purpose to create a customer, any business enterprise has two – and only these two – basic functions: marketing and innovation. They are the entrepreneurial functions.
>
> Marketing is the distinguishing, the unique function of the business ... Marketing is not only much broader than selling, it is not a specialised activity at all. It encompasses the entire business. It is the whole business seen from the point of view of its final result, that is from the customer's point of view. Concern and responsibility must therefore permeate all areas of the marketplace (Drucker, 1994).

Guptara (1990) identifies six activities that come under the umbrella title of marketing. They are:

1 Identifying the needs of existing and potential customers (an emphasis on satisfying customer requirements is central to any definition of marketing);
2 Determining the best product strategy.
3 Ensuring the effective distribution of products. (This is a topic that we will refer to again within this text.).
4 Informing customers of the existence of products and persuading them to buy those products.
5 Determining the prices at which products should be sold.
6 Ensuring that after sales service is of the right quality.

It is the view of Varianini and Vaturia (2000) that 'many of the basic elements of the traditional marketing process still hold good'. What is clear, reading the general literature on e-business, is that many writers feels that e-marketing is something totally different from conventional marketing. Whilst some of the rules of the game may have changed, that does not mean that the overall fundamentals have resultantly changed. What we shall see in the following chapters is that many marketers share concern that companies do not take into consideration the need for these basic fundamentals. The end result has often been the collapse of dot.com companies. It is not that the basic premise of the company is flawed, it is often that the basic marketing of the business has not been taken seriously.

What is very different is the development of e-marketplaces. This may become a radical area for development within the B2B arena.

The internet is transforming not only the way companies do business, but the way customers and suppliers want to do business. They are becoming e-customers and e-suppliers. Consumer expectations are being redefined, and it is the technology that is enabling new marketing opportunities and capabilities. Thus, companies must adopt new mindsets and build new skill sets within their organisations.

- New competitors will emerge with innovative value propositions.
- Companies must stay connected to their customers, whether directly over the web and/or through links to the e-supply chain.
- e-Marketing does not negate marketing fundamentals such as segmentation, targeting, positioning, the marketing mix, customer satisfaction and value. However, it does create radically new challenges for the marketer.

Erin Kinkin CRM Analyst at Giga Group states:

> True marketing automation starts with discovery and ends with near real-time measurement. But the biggest difference between traditional and e-marking is that e-marketing cuts the cycle time from months to hours. That real-time feedback is critical, because if you don't like the response to an ad or a campaign, you can change it while it's active, which was not possible when it took months to get feedback (Longworth, 2000).

While the technology is certainly available to profile customers and market to them in real time, the impact upon marketing departments is not only misunderstood, but, in many cases, ignored totally.

Ryan (2000) suggests that companies that engage in e-commerce/e-marketing can receive four e-benefits.

Table 5.1 e-Benefits

e-Benefits	Descriptors
Efficiency	Sales and distribution cycle times as well as transaction times can be significantly reduced, thus allowing for improved revenue streams.
Enhancement	The addition of e-commerce can make the customer experience much better, provided that the company uses technology in a way that does not create a barrier between the company and the customer. Effective and efficient customer relationship will be crucial, especially in highly competitive environments. (This will be discussed in Chapter 8).
Expansion	A means of expanding product line and/or geographical market coverage. The internet will allow many companies to expand internationally with minimal cost implications.
Eyeball share	It is not just revenue that counts, it's exposure. A well-designed, integrated site is one that provides a reason for customers to return.

Source: Adapted from Ryan (2000).

What is e-marketing?

Before we consider what is e-marketing, let us briefly list what e-marketing is not. It is not:

- simply a static company brochure online.
- doing exactly what the company has always done before – life is now very different.
- sending masses of unsolicited emails (spamming) to 'possible' potential buyers.
- using out of date information, such as the features and benefits of the previous product version.
- Monday–Friday 9am–5pm delivery service. Companies that lock themselves into such a rigid delivery time frame, will discover that more flexible companies will gain advantages. Indeed, overtime the flexible companies may take significant market share away from companies that either can not be or do not want to be flexible. In the Information Age, flexibility is a critical word.

Essentially, e-marketing is about connectivity. In this environment, customers will gain enormous power. They will be able to compare product attributes and define their own needs through 'communities of interest'. For example, Amazon.com supply their customers with recommended reading based on their purchases, and the opportunity to review the book they have purchased. This is a sharing of thought within a community.

Additionally, companies will have to consider establishing new types of relationships with the customer: the delivery of added value through 'tailoring' offers to identifiable groups. For example, consider Dell who have placed the internet at the heart of the company. Equally, the San Francisco-based company Planet U used the net to help packaged goods companies and supermarket chains target their clip coupons to individual shoppers. Using loyalty cards to track purchases, supermarkets send the information over the net to a printer, and a unique package of coupons is mailed out to each customer. Even the amount of discount on each product can be varied according to how much customers usually buy – thus rewarding their loyalty. Although the coupons cost two to four times as much to print, customers try the products as many as ten times or more (Hof, 1999).

The world wide web, in particular, is a haven of opportunities to enhance customer connectivity. Companies can capture customer preference information through store loyalty systems – whether in the retail outlet or via the web. Therefore, information about individual customers will become increasingly valuable. However, one of the great threats to many companies is whether they have the knowledge and expertise to manage vast levels of information. How many companies currently data mine their own data warehouses efficiently and effectively?

A further dynamic difference with internet marketing is the transformation of the customer's experience of buying. Screen and mouse now replace shopping trolley and store aisles. This is likely to affect consumers in very different ways, depending on the goods involved. Short-term consumables seem as easy to shift on websites as they are in physical supermarkets. On the other hand, designer clothes are likely to have significant resistances for some time to come.

Real-time capabilities

There is the opportunity for instant measurable results, low-cost delivery of information, and the ability to adjust promotions (at speed) is much easier to implement and monitor.

We now talk in terms of *e-pricing*. Companies can update prices in real time to match or better their competitors. They can even price according to the customer. An automated system can handle this. However, it is still beyond the abilities (indeed, the imagination) of most companies.

The marketing mix and the e-environment

One of the mainstays of marketing has been the marketing mix. McCarthy in the 1950s developed the now famous mnemonic 'the 4Ps' (Product, Price, Promotion and Placement) – perhaps the most widely recognized concept in marketing. Since then, there has been much debate regarding extending the mix, or indeed replacing it. Booms and Bitner (1981) suggested that 3Ps were needed to cover service marketing. Subsequently, a 7P generic marketing mix framework has received general acceptability, although debate continues. For the purpose of this book, we have adopted the 7P framework. However, we encourage readers who are interested in the debates on the marketing mix to explore further.

Dutta and Segev (1999) have classified the internet's marketing functions based upon the original 4Ps. We have extended this further to include the additional 3Ps of Process, People (Participants) and Physical Evidence. Table 5.2 illustrates the relationship between the 7Ps of the marketing mix and the internet.

As you can see from the table, the marketing mix framework is applicable to the e-environment. When you read through the following marketing chapters, consider how the issues discussed relate to the marketing mix.

Who are e-marketers' customers?

As stated in Chapter 1, by the end of 2001 some 498 million people had internet access from home (Nielson//NetRatings, 2002). At the time of writing (2003), most sources suggest that the majority of net users are young people, with people over 35 not using it as much. As the younger generation develops, it will become the middle-aged surfers of the net (or whatever they may be called then).

According to AC Nielson, female web surfers have overtaken men in the USA and are a potential customer base in the Asia-Pacific Region (Nielsen//NetRatings, 2001). Coinciding with this overall growth is a trend that suggests that women are increasingly willing to purchase online.

Table 5.2 The 7Ps of the marketing mix and the internet

Marketing mix function	Relationship to internet
Product	Online product information Value added information on products Online advice on choosing the product Mass customisation of products Customer participation in product design.
Price	Online, real-time price information Metered pricing Customisation of pricing; this may link to product customisation – for example, Dell Computers or easyJet airlines Online only pricing. May be cheaper to buy online rather than from the company's retail outlet.
Placement (Place)	Online ordering of products Online distribution of products – for example, airline tickets (vouchers).
Promotion	Online-only promotions Links to other partner companies (opportunity for joint promotions) Customer participation – for example, competitions or viral (contagion marketing).
People (Participants)	e-mail contact to answer queries and provide general assistance. This, at times, may be labour intensive; however, it can help build strong relationships between the customer and the company. Can be used as an integrated or blended solution along with traditional postal services and telemarketing Feedback from customers Development of customer communities Customer identification – can be used to track valuable customers and build customer relationships over the longer term (see Chapter 8).
Process	Secure online ordering and payment systems Rapid confirmation of order/payment Online tracking of delivery With the development of 'intelligent' refrigerators, for instance, the process of ordering groceries will be done automatically via the refrigerator's onboard computer directly with the internet site of the grocery store. This type of 'processing' reduces the customer's involvement time. All they will have to do is place the groceries in the refrigerator itself!
Physical evidence	In 'bricks and mortar' scenarios, physical evidence tends to be associated with the physical construction and layout of the building. In an e-environment, the physical evidence could be (1) the website itself – its look and layout; (2) the confirmation email that the transaction (for example, the purchase of concert tickets) has been successful.

Source: Adapted from Dutta and Segev (1999).

Also, the surfing times appear to be different. For example, in the Asia-Pacific region women spread their surfing over a longer period, with over 50 per cent of women surfers within that region active between the afternoon and evening prime time hours of 4pm–10pm. By comparison, men's surfing times peak later at night, with more than 70 per cent of male surfers active in each hour between 8pm and 10pm (Neilsen//NetRatings, 2001).

According to Nielsen//NetRatings (2001):

Women were late adopters of the Internet but are making up for that lag now, and the speed with which they are coming online means, as a demographic, women must become a priority for most e-tailers.

Globally we have found that women are a fussier breed of surfer than their male counterparts. Women are much more efficient in their web usage – they spend less time online as they generally know what they're looking for and leave once they achieve their goal. E-markets should take this tendency into account by ensuring their sites focus on ease and convenience.

In terms of online purchasing, while women have historically been more concerned about security and privacy than men, US data shows that women are just as willing to make purchases at major shopping sites with trusted brand names. In Australia, big brand retailers such as www.myerdirect.com.au and www.davidjones.co.au have succeeded in seducing the female demographic online. (Neilsen//NetRatings, 2001)

Table 5.3 illustrates the increasing number of women using the internet. What is clear is that e-tailers will have to develop well-targeted marketing to establish

Table 5.3   Female composition of the internet universe (at home, May 2001)

Country	Female %
USA	52
Canada	51
Australia	48
New Zealand	46
Finland	46
South Korea	45
Sweden	45
Denmark	45
Ireland	45
Hong Kong	44
Singapore	42
Brazil	42
Taiwan	41
UK	41
Netherlands	41
Spain	40
France	39
Germany	37
Italy	37

Source: Nielsen//Net Ratings, 2002.

brand loyalty within this influential group. This is an area that we will return to in Chapter 8 (Relationship Marketing).

Understanding e-customers

One of the keys to success within any contemporary business environment is through an understanding of customers. Companies, whether they are 'bricks and mortar', 'clicks and mortar' or both, must have a detailed understanding of their customer basis. Those companies that do not will eventually fail within the marketplace – a victim of increased local, regional and global competition. Within our increasingly global environment, it is vital that companies become customer-focused or customer-oriented, for competition within the e-world can emanate from any location.

In Chapter 8, we will consider how companies build longer-term relationships with their customers.

Marketing research

As Varianini and Vaturi (2000) suggest, there are various marketing research techniques that can be used to develop an understanding of a company's customer base. These techniques are not new in themselves, although their application is. There are two key components to marketing research – primary and secondary research. We will consider these key areas in turn and with their subsets.

Primary research

This is original research gathered by the company on its current and potential customers directly. The concepts detailed below apply for any organisation, we have added an 'e' before each word to define the environment in which they operate.

e-questionnaires

It is standard within primary research to ask people questions. Questionnaires often take the form of one-to-one interviews. These can take place in the home, the office or indeed in the street. Shopping centres or malls and major railway stations are a key location to undertake such questionnaires. Within the e-environment there are also opportunities to gauge the views of current and potential customers. Increasingly, companies, online, need to determine reactions to their products and services. The questionnaire is an ideal way of gathering such qualitative and quantitative information.

e-focus groups

Focus groups can be described as a small group of people, with similar attributes, brought together to discuss a relevant topic. These groups typically comprise between six and twelve people and provide companies with direct feedback on a particular issue. That issue can be a new product in development, modifications to a current product or standards of service. Focus groups are usually under the guidance of a moderator whose role it is to make sure that the group remains focused on the topic.

Again, within the e-environment, companies can form such groups to gather relevant information. One additional vehicle for feedback is, of course, the chat room. However, in most cases chat rooms are not moderated in the same way as focus groups. Thus, chat rooms can become a wider talking shop that often debates points 'off topic'. The key to e-focus groups is that they retain the moderation element. This is an advantage to both the participants and the company alike.

e-observations

Customer observations are nothing new. For several decades, supermarkets, for instance, have been observing their shoppers, and indeed their staff, on a regular basis. This type of observation occured within both a human and a mechanical form. Specially trained observers have watched people to see how they shop. For instance, at the fresh fruit and vegetable stalls, do shoppers examine the produce prior to buying? Many people do – squeezing tomatoes to see if they are fresh and avocados to see if they are ripe are the often quoted examples within the marketing research literature. With the advent of sophisticated video technology, these observations can be recorded without the customer's knowledge and examined later. Of course, this does raise the issue of the ethics of such surveillance, a point we will return to later.

Equally, retail staff can be observed. The most used procedure is the secret shopper whose role it is to see how staff react to and with customers. This covers such areas as customer services and support.

People have watched others shop in order to determine or understand how they shop. The supermarket that could cater closest to shoppers' demands would win advantage within a highly competitive marketplace; e-observations are similar, except in terms of their environment.

Within the e-environment, such observation focuses on how the 'target' (the surfer, potential or current customer) reacts within the web space.

Secondary research

This can be subdivided into internal and external secondary research.

Internal secondary research: This is data that companies already hold themselves. This can be in the form of sales invoices, customers' purchasing and financial histories and previous marketing research reports. Companies tend to make three key errors where internal secondary data is concerned:

1. They do not realise the value of such data. They are considered 'old files' when, in fact they may inform the company or organisation about their

customers, their habits, needs, wants and desires. You could argue that this is a basic tenet of marketing – understanding and appreciating the customer. Sadly, still not all companies take this perspective.

2 There is no cross-referencing or relationship of the data stored internally. This does not need to be a manual function. Computer technology can assist in the storing and sorting of complex information. This is a point we refer to again below when we discuss data warehousing and data mining.

3 Too much emphasis is placed upon the information, without considering the implications. You may think here that we have just contradicted ourselves, especially in the light of the points above. In some ways – yes. However, the point to be made here is this. Internal information is valuable to a company or organisation. Indeed, many companies fail to appreciate fully the information they already hold. However, data needs to be continually updated and analysed. A company cannot just 'pigeon-hole' customers with the view that customer behaviour never changes. For some, the behaviour may not change, however, for the vast majority it probably will. Thus, internal data must be continually updated. This is where there is a strong and relevant relationship between primary research and internal secondary research – a point often overlooked by companies and organisations.

External secondary research: This is research that is gathered from a range of external (to the company/organisation) sources. Before we proceed to discuss these sources, there needs to be a word of caution. Marketing and marketing research textbooks are good at stating the range of materials that are available. However, such research must be considered within a geographic perspective. For instance, in the UK there is a plethora of information available. However, in other countries, such a wealth of information may not be available. This may be for political reasons, lack of technology, problems of collecting and organizing such data.

In general secondary research, the following sources are normally available:

- *Government sources*:   This can be a range of general government information; for example, export statistics, the census.
- *Indexes*:   These can be directories of companies and organisations; for example, Dun and Bradstreet (www.dnb.com) company directories.
- *Industry sources*:   These can be trade publications, professional organisations (including trade associations) and reports supplied by individual companies. These reports will have an industry focus, perhaps promoting strategic alliances to maintain viability within the industry.
- *Commercial sources*:   These are research reports written by such companies as A.C. Nielsen, Mintel and others. They focus on specific topic areas such as the retail sectors.
- *Institute reports*:   It is often overlooked that institutes and universities are a major contributor to research. These vary over the full spectrum of subject areas from business issues through to engineering and manufacturing techniques.

As you can see from the above snapshot, there is wealth of secondary data potentially available. The e-environment provides the opportunity to wider access to such information. In some cases, this information is free (for example, from government sources), in other cases, it is available on subscription or by one-off payments. Students at major universities are, through the web, gaining increasing access to an enormous wealth of information.

Data warehousing and data mining

As intimated earlier (and in Chapter 2), companies can hold a vast array of internal data. As we suggested, this information can cover purchasing and payment history. If you consider the amount and type of information that a credit card company, or indeed a supermarket, holds on customers, you will probably come to the conclusion that they can track a customer's movements and purchasing habits. That is an accurate assessment.

Computer technology, as we witnessed in Chapter 1, has developed rapidly over the past 20 years or so. Today, vast amounts of data can be stored within 'warehouses' or databanks. By using sophisticated software, companies can analyse that data to provide profiles on customers. They can also attach values to these customers, indicating which are the most and least profitable.

This data mining software allows companies to 'drill down and across' seams of data to extract the most relevant information. It is then down to how that company uses that 'extracted' data to their best advantage. It may be to offer the customer – on a one-to-one basis – a series of special offers, thus encouraging further purchasing activity. Alternatively, it may be used to discover what the customer likes and dislikes about the service provided. Linked into this is the ability to uncover the customer's potential needs, wants and desires. You may want to reflect here upon: (1) the potential links to both primary and secondary research; (2) the potential ethical implications of obtaining, storing and mining information on individuals.

We will return to data warehousing and data mining in Chapter 8 when we consider relationship marketing in further depth.

The development of e-procurement and e-marketplaces

E-marketplaces can be described as trading exchanges and are becoming an important aspect of both B2C and B2B marketing within the e-environment. We will deal with these from an operational aspect in Part III. For the moment, they are considered from a marketing perspective.

These marketplaces can be described as online portals that function as an information broker and gateway to services. The e-marketplace offers the expertise of a particular vertical sector, the purpose being to ensure that information and services offered are of a high value to the participants within that e-marketplace. MacIver (2001) suggests that 'procurement through e-marketplaces is just the start of what many believe is the single biggest change in business opportunity for over a century'.

E-marketplaces can be divided into three types: public, consortium-based and private exchanges.

Public exchanges: Also known as Independent Trading Exchanges (ITEs), these are independently-operated B2B trading platforms that any relevant business or group of businesses can join. The objective being to establish online interaction and transactions with a community of trading partners. As Masood (2001) indicates 'they capture the most obvious advantage of the web – the ability to contact and share transactions with a wide network of business partners across the globe'; for example, CheMatch (www.chematch.com), the chemical industry exchange.

Consortium exchanges: These are owned and operated by a group of competitors, bringing them into contact with suppliers, the aim of which is to lower the buying costs of the companies by consolidating their overall buying power. The key issue for such consortia, though, is the transference of information. There will be occasions where commercially sensitive information may be revealed. Thus, rival companies could, unethically, gain an unfair advantage. In order for such consortia to survive and prosper in the future, there may need to be a radical restructuring and rethinking on how industry operates within such forum.

Private exchanges: These are exchanges that are owned and operated by a single company or organisation. These sites are specifically tailored so that the company can link their trading systems directly to their suppliers. Thus, this becomes a potential strategic advantage for the company. However, it is not without cost. Forrester Research estimate that a fully-functioning site could cost in the region of €11 million (Masood, 2001). An example would be the car manufacturers Volkswagen and BMW in the B2B sector and iVillage.com in the B2C environment.

In theory, the efficiencies and greater transparency through the demand and supply chain leads to significant benefits. These potential benefits, for companies who engage in these exchanges, include:

- increased speed of transactions
- access to more information
- enhanced customer relationships
- optimisation of the supply chain (This can be achieved though the use of sophisticated planning and forecasting tools. These assist in the automation of business processes.)
- improvement in the overall branding of products and services
- a reduction in processing costs.
- increased speed in terms of settling payments.

☑ Case study   Bayer AG (www.bayer.com)

Bayer AG is a global business that operates in four key business segments: health care, agriculture, polymers and chemicals. The company actively participates within several e-marketplaces; for example, Omnexus™ (www.omnexus.com), a global trading marketplace for plastics.

Now, online B2B transactions form the cornerstone of Bayer's e-business activities. They participate in and have co-founded several e-marketplaces, where raw materials, products, scientific expertise and services, and even complete pre-assembled systems for production facilities are traded.

One of the key e-marketplaces for Bayer is cc-Chemplorer (www.cc-chemplorer.com). This is an independent platform formed by the merger of two e-marketplaces. Chemplorer was originally developed specially for the chemical industry by Bayer, Infraserve Höchst and Deutshe Telekom; whilst cc-markets was founded by BASF, Degussa, Henkel and SAPMarkets. They merged in July 2001 to form cc-Chemplorer.

cc-Chemplorer pools information regarding products and suppliers and compiles it for onscreen delivery. Facts such as size, technical specification, colour, delivery date and price are thereby easily displayed. The combined platforms provide a selection of 18 assortments and 1.6 million products.

There are several potential advantages for purchasing companies:

- By using its online catalogues, purchasing processes can be automated, optimised with processing costs reduced.
- The market becomes more transparent. The buyer can compare products/price without additional costs incurred.

Potential advantages for suppliers include:

- New growth markets – achieving potential international presence.
- Use of new processes which optimise marketing channels – often at reduced costs.

This e-procurement allows Bayer to order from more than 100 traders and distributors representing over 2 000 manufacturers. For Bayer, internal procedures have been revised so that each organisational unit can order directly from the website. This has simplified business processes and has provided cost savings of over 60 per cent compared to traditional purchasing methods.

Source: Bayer Annual Report 2000/cc-Chemplorer.

However, whilst e-marketplaces can contribute significant values to B2B environments, they are not a given success. In the late twentieth and early twenty-first centuries, there were several high-profile failures. Difficult economic trading conditions lead to several e-marketplaces failing to achieve necessary liquidity, with resultant collapse. As Masood (2001) suggests, many industry observers indicated that, during 2000, as many as three quarters of Europe's initial e-marketplaces collapsed. However, it can be argued that there will always be failures within new business operations. This is the very nature of business itself. It is clear, however, that e-marketplaces will continue to be developed – some will fail others will be a great success. Forrester Research suggest that that the value of online B2B trading will reach €2 trillion by 2005 (Masood, 2001).

As Twentyman (2001) suggests: 'in order to achieve faster liquidity e-market-places are rapidly evolving their business models in order to better fit the needs of customers; many are now offering increasingly sophisticated "value-added services" in order to increase their appeal'.

Masood (2001) further contends that 'the most significant development is arguably yet to come. Many analysts argue that increasingly marketplaces will connect to each other, filling gaps in functions and creating ever-wider networks of business partners ... But the creation of complex networks offering sophisti-cated functionality will require a massive effort by both marketplace operators and marketplace users.

However, there is a further issue that needs to be considered. In Chapter 2, we considered the PESTLE factors. Within those, we witnessed both political and legal influences. E-Marketplaces have come under increased scrutiny, especially in Europe and North America. Both politicians and the judiciary are concerned that e-marketplaces, especially consortia, can become 'cartels'. The concern is that if e-marketplaces begin to operate as cartels, then they create an unfair advantage over rivals not within the e-marketplace. For Europe and North American governments, this would constitute anti-competitive behaviour on the part of the companies trading within the e-marketplace.

Currently, there is much debate regarding the use of regulatory procedures to prevent e-marketplaces become cartels, whether by accident or design.

The relationship between e-marketing and direct marketing

If we take as a basic premise that e-marketing is about building relationships, then it is not a new concept. The delivery mechanism may be different, but the concept is not. Here, we can look to direct marketing and how it operates for some guidance. The fundamental premise of direct marketing focuses on build-ing relationships – indeed, long-term relationships.

Direct marketing, as a subset of marketing, can be traced back to the eight-eenth century. In both the UK and the USA, entrepreneurs such as Josiah Wedgwood, through mail order catalogues, were using direct marketing tech-niques to build customer relationships. The term 'direct marketing' was not introduced until the 1960s, when Lester Wunderman (founder of the advertising agency Wunderman Worldwide) coined the phrase.

We can debate whether e-marketing is a standalone marketing tactic or, indeed, a subset of direct marketing. The point is that e-marketing is about build-ing relationships, maintaining activity and delivering that activity over distance and at speed. This is reflective of the e-marketplaces described earlier within this chapter.

In Chapter 8, we will bring the relationship between e-marketing and direct marketing into focus when we introduce *permission marketing*. This is aimed at building mutual relationships between the provider and the customer.

e-marketing, e-logistics and e-distribution

In the introduction to this chapter, we stated that we would consider the relationship between e-marketing and traditional 'bricks and mortar' marketing. We can make comparisons with retailers. For example, you enter a grocery store, such as the UK's Tesco or the American company Wal-Mart. Displayed before you is a combination of instore marketing and a range of produce (fresh and packaged). The instore marketing, for instance point-of-sale (POS), may entice you to purchase an item on special offer. As you walk around the store, you collect in your basket both the produce you set out to buy – the essentials – and along the way you may also decide to purchase a selection of other products or indeed services. Supermarkets now sell additional services such as insurance and credit cards.

On completing your shopping, you enter the checkout zone, pay for the goods (cash, cheque or more likely through a debit or credit card) then leave. Your car is loaded with the purchases and the weekly or monthly grocery 'adventure' is complete.

What the above demonstrates is an action that society, virtually worldwide, has been used to for decades. We have been able to see the produce, test it (refer back to observations earlier) and then make a decision to purchase. With the grocery example, we have chosen the produce off the shelves and transported it to the checkout zone and then to our cars or public transport.

There is still a need for 'bricks and mortar' environments. It is unlikely, at least for some time, that they will be replaced, But the big question is how e-marketing can link into the supply chain activities that we have all become familiar with? Whilst this will be explored in more depth in Chapter 9, it is worthwhile setting the scene here.

As stated earlier, the key question is the relationship between the e-environment and the physical one. This is a 'relationship' that has caused significant problems for would-be 'dot.com' operations. It is 'relatively' straightforward to set up the 'front-end' part of the operation. However, customers expect that the product to be delivered, almost in the same way as if they went to the 'bricks and mortar' stores themselves. Companies 'delivering' via the e-environment have to meet those expectations. Otherwise, why should a customer shop online? This is what so many dot.com operations failed to factor into their business plans. As a result, there was little in the way of revenue generation, they used their capital resources. Slowly they haemorrhaged their financial reserves and withered.

The two case studies below illustrate how companies can market themselves on the web and deliver their promises. Once you have read Chapter 9, you should reflect back upon these cases.

Case studies

Finally in this chapter, we will consider two case studies: Tesco and easyJet.

▼ Case study Tesco plc (www.tesco.com)

As at April 2003, Tesco was the UK's largest supermarket chain. The company generated revenues of UK£25.6 Billion in 2002. They have 979 stores employing some 260 000 people accessing a population of 280 million across 10 markets (UK, Europe and Asia). Whilst they remained primarily a 'bricks and mortar' retailer, it has added value to its business through e-tailing. It has become an excellent example, to date, of 'clicks and mortar'.

Tesco.com has become the largest internet grocery retailer in the world. Tesco allows their customers to purchase produce via the internet and arrange a suitable time for home delivery. As inferred earlier, e-marketing, within certain business areas, is another form of catalogue or mail order marketing. This time, though, the transaction and delivery times are significantly shorter.

Tesco introduced a virtual store which allowed them to make further increases in product offers, especially within non-food items. Thus, they are able to stock a wider range of items than they would be able to house within their super-markets; for example, books and CDs. Online, they have created separate sites for electrical goods, clothing, gifts, wine and Tesco Personal Finance. They have undertaken a joint venture with iVillage.com which provides a UK-based version of the successful US-based women's internet portal (see Chapter 7, Marketing Communications).

In 2001, Tesco launched Tesco.com in South Korea, also providing their staff with the first online training facility.

Tesco's UK Statistics (April 2002)

Sales:	85 000 orders per week.
Area covered:	692 stores, 94 per cent of the population.
Products on offer:	Over 10 000.
Delivery charge:	UK£5.00
Registered users:	Approximately 1 million.
Turnover:	UK£356 million
Average sales per customer:	UK£85.00

Sources: Tesco.com/MediaGuardian.co.uk Wednesday April 10, 2002; Annual Report and Accounts 2002.

▼ Case study easyJet (www.easyjet.com)

A few statistics highlight the phenomenal growth of this airline, making it now Europe's largest low-cost airline.

- Launched in November 1995 with two aircraft flying to Glasgow and Edinburgh.

- By November 2002, it was offering 89 routes from 36 different European locations.
- In the 12 months ending February 2003, the airline had carried over 18 million passengers.
- During the financial year to 30 September 2002, the company reported pre-tax profits of UK£7.1 million on a turnover of UK£552 million.

The internet has been a key element in the development of easyJet, and is critical to its ongoing success. The company started selling seats via the internet in April 1998. By October 1999, over 1 million seats had been sold via the internet. However, this was dramatically superseded five months later when, in March 2000, 2 million seats had been reached, only to reach 3 million a mere three months later.

By February 2003, approximately 90 per cent of all seats are sold over the internet, making easyjet one of Europe's largest internet retailers.

easyJet operate a ticketless travel system. Passengers receive an email containing their travel details and confirmation number when they book online. For the airline, this reduces significantly the cost of issuing, distributing, processing and reconciling millions of tickets per year. This helps to reduce costs to the individual traveller. Additionally, it reduces the amount of paperwork for the passenger. All they need is their passport and confirmation number.

easyJet also operates a system whereby they sell one-way fares rather than return tickets. This allows the passenger to return when they wish, rather than being tied to specific return fares or minimum stays at a location. Again, a customer may consider this a benefit to their ease of purchase, a convenience. For others this may not be; they may prefer an inclusive return ticket package.

Source: www.easyjet.com

Summary

In this chapter, we have introduced marketing to the e-world. Our original premise was that marketing is marketing, whether it is within the structure of either the old or new economies. We contend that successful e-marketing is determined by how the company integrates marketing into its e-environment. It is how companies use the medium of the internet to market their products or services that is vital. For an example, we reflect upon e-marketplaces within the B2B environment. Companies would sell their products within 'markets' and companies would procure products and services from these markets. e-Marketplaces provide the benefits of transparency, massive information stores and transaction speed.

We have also considered how several companies have used the internet medium to market and sell their products and services via the web. In the following chapters, we will refine the marketing role further by considering branding, communication and relationship building.

Further reading

Burns, A.C. and Bush, R.F. (2000) *Marketing Research* (3rd edn). Harlow: Prentice Hall.

Questions for review and reflection

Take a website that you know well and have used for purchasing something (or have seriously considered for making a purchase).

1 How far does it address your specific needs?
2 How different is it from the physical experience of buying that product or service?
3 Finally, how far did the structure of the website and its user-style help or hinder you in making a purchase. Would you have been better off going into a physical store or making a telephone call, for example?

Notes and references

AMA (2002) There have been several definitions of marketing since the formation of the American Marketing Association in the early 1930s. The AMA's current definition first appeared in their publication *Marketing News* in 1985.

Booms, B.H. and Bitner, M.J. (1981) 'Marketing strategies and organisation structures for service firms', in *Marketing of Services*, J. Donnelly and W.R. George (eds), American Marketing Association.

CIM (1996) *CIM Marketing Dictionary*. CIM.

Chee, H. and Harris, R. (1993) *Marketing – A Global Perspective*. London: Pitman.

Drucker, P.F (1994) *The Practice of Management* (revised edn) London: Butterworth-Heinemann.

Dutta, S. and Segev, A. (1999) 'Business transformation on the Internet', *European Management Journal*, vol 17, no 5, pp. 466–76.

Guptara, P. (1990) *The Basic Arts of Marketing*. London: Hutchinson.

Hof, R.D. (1999) 'A new era of bright hopes and terrible fears', *Business Week Online*, 4 October.

Longworth, D. (2000) 'Rule of thumb marketing theory', *Customer Strategy*, issue 9 May, pp. 19–22.

Maclver, K. (2001) 'Efficiency drive', *Information Age Business Briefing*, no. 16, pp. B17–B19.

Masood, S. (2001) 'Model options', *Information Age Business Briefing*, no. 16, pp. B10–B12.

Neilsen//NetRatings (2001) 'Women a formidable force on the web', News Release, AC Neilsen eRatings.com

Neilsen//NetRatings (2002) 'Neilsen//NetRatings reports a record half billion people worldwide now have internet access', News Release, AC Nielsen eRatings.com

Ryan, C. (2000) 'How disintermediation is changing the rules of marketing, sales and distribution', *Interactive Marketing*, vol. 1, no 4, April/June.

Twentyman, J. (2001) 'Market dynamics', *Information Age Business Briefing*, no. 16, pp. B6–B7.

Varianini, V. and Vaturi, D. (2000) 'Marketing lessons from e-failures', *McKinsey Quarterly*, issue 4, pp. 86–98.

Yelkur, R. and DaCosta, M. (2001) 'Differential pricing and segmentation on the Internet: the case of hotels', *Management Decision*, vol. 39, no 4, pp. 252–61.

⅀ 6 Segmentation, targeting and positioning

Introduction

In this chapter, we consider how and why companies need to segment their markets and position their services to reach the right target market. The fundamentals of segmentation, targeting and positioning remain the same as in any other type or range of marketing operation. What is, of course, different is the medium in which it operates and the fact that it is not a 'one-way' means of communication but two-way. Equally, it could be argued that that the quality and range of information available to companies operating within an e-environment could be greatly enhanced.

Lerer (2002) states that the internet 'forces us to think about the individual customer and, while it is impossible to deal with every individual there is considerable virtue in thinking about smaller groups of customers'.

In an earlier chapter, we discussed the role of *permission marketing* and how it provides the opportunity for a greater flow of information between the e-business and their current and potential customer base. Indeed, it can greatly assist in the building of strong and longer-term relationships. To achieve this position, the e-business needs to gain some understanding of the market in which it intends to operate. This is precisely where segmentation, targeting and positioning are key drivers to success within the marketplace.

Learning objectives

On the completion of this chapter you should be able to:

1 Explain the purpose of segmentation, targeting and positioning;
2 Debate the relevance of these tools within an e-business environment.

What business is the organisation in?

In order *effectively* to understand the role of segmentation, targeting and positioning, the company needs to know what business it is in. Now this may sound like an 'odd' statement; however, it is an important strategic question. For some companies, such as a restaurant, it may 'seem' relatively clear that they are in the restaurant or catering business. Not so. There are many different types of restaurants catering for a diverse range of customers. Thus, the owners of that restaurant need carefully to match their offering (products and services) to the right audience, in the right location, at the right price and so on. This is especially so in a highly competitive market where the customer has significant choice and only limited disposable income. Therefore, the restaurant needs to understand its customer base. The same is true for any business, whether it has a physical location, such as a retail outlet, or is located on the internet.

What are segmentation, targeting and positioning?

Before considering their specific roles within an e-business environment, it is important to understand the principles behind each element.

Segmentation

Generally speaking, many people assume that a market is purely 'a large collection of people'. This could not be further from the truth. Not everyone buys the same product or service. As Yelkur and DaCosta (2001) state 'the more specific the segment, the easier it is to estimate demand'.

For example, not everyone who buys books, for instance, will buy this book. This text will interest specific groups of people; for instance, undergraduate business students who want gain knowledge of e-business as part of their studies. Another group may be young entrepreneurs who want to gain some background to e-business before setting up their own business.

Louvier and Driver (2001) suggest that segmentation is 'key to the marketing strategy process because it influences strategic decisions concerning competitive positioning, organizational structure and resource allocation'. They further contend that it is 'how a company perceives market structures and its ability to determine target market segments appropriate to its competencies and resources [that] will govern its competitive advantage' (Louvier and Driver, 2001). Therefore, an organization needs to identify carefully those individuals or groups who are specifically interested in its product or service. However, this must not be viewed as 'static'. Segments and markets change and thus companies must react to such changes.

Kotler (2000) suggests that market segmentation is: 'the subdividing of a market into homogeneous subsets of customers, where any subset may conceivably be selected as a target market to be reached with a distinct marketing mix'.

Dibb *et al.* (1997) enhance Kotler's (2000) view by linking the possible outcome to the action of segmentation. They state that 'segmentation can deliver an enhanced understanding of a customer's needs and wants, thus providing a greater responsiveness in terms of the product or service being presented to the customer'.

It is this mixture of appropriately dividing the population and understanding their needs and wants that is a key component to business success. Whilst many of the traditional elements of market segmentation apply to the internet, companies are operating within vastly different media. Therefore, companies need to be able to combine methods or tools to exploit segmentation opportunities successfully. Below, we consider the different types of segmentation processes attempting to link the more 'traditional' with current and future methodologies.

How are markets segmented?

Generally, markets are segmented on five key criteria: geographical/cultural, demographic, behaviour, geodemographic and psychographic.

Geographical/Cultural: In terms of geographical location, this has normally been associated with, for example, the physical entity of a shop or restaurant. To a greater extent, geographical location does not have the same limitations within an e-environment. Within this environment, an individual or company can purchase via a website from virtually any company within the world. There are limitations, most especially if there are political or legal constraints associated with the purchase. For instance, a person in England can legitimately purchase computer software CDs from the USA. However, depending upon the total value of these CDs, they may be subject to additional customs duties upon arrival in the UK.

Demographics: This focuses on the customer's age, sex and cultural/ethnic background. These can be used as a basis for determining a specific market. For instance, a website can focus on a specific age range within the female market. Here, several groups could be considered:

- Pre-teenage
- Teenage
- Young adults
- Mature adults
- Elderly.

There could even be subsets of each of these groups. This would be determined upon the particular products or services on offer.

Behaviour: This is a very complex area especially as: (1) individuals buy for numerous reasons, many of which are interrelated; and (2) how and when they buy can be governed by many factors, some of which are emotionally driven.

e-Businesses, as any other business operation, need to go some way to understanding why their customers buy a certain range of products or service at certain times. Yet, as Louvier and Driver (2001) point out, there is another factor at work here – the technology itself. Companies have to consider the 'socio-technical' nature of buyer behaviour, where the technology as represented by the purchasing system is an integral component of the behaviour process (Louvier and Driver, 2001). Understanding such behaviour, or at least trying to, allows the company to focus on a segment of the market that is most likely to buy their product or service.

For instance, take online banking as a possible example. An individual may use the services of an online bank because they want to be able to access their accounts at any time, day or night. This provides them with an element of 'control' over their circumstances. This is something that is clearly impossible with a normal 'bricks and mortar' banking service. Therefore, an online banking service can lock into this individual's personal needs and wants. If an online banking service could discover who fitted into such a category, then they would have a segment to whom they could target relevant information, and possibly convert from using a standard high-street banking service to an online service. Equally, once signed up to the online service, the bank could reinforce the link with the customer by discovering needs and wants. Thus, developing a relationship with the customer enhances the opportunity for increased loyalty with the online bank.

Geodemographics: This is a mixture of geographic and demographic information that can be used to help build profiles of individuals or groups of people. This has, since the 1970s when this was actively developed, been of immense benefit to companies, especially those utilising direct marketing strategies and techniques.

Although e-business is not limited to zip or post codes, it is still useful in understanding, for instance, the composition of socio-economic groups that may use the companies' internet services. Let us not forget that whilst the internet has a worldwide potential, its focus is not always global. For instance, a company selling holidays online may have a purely UK customer base. Therefore, it is valuable for that company to understand the socio-economic groups to which they belong. This can be of particular benefit when providing an email alert system. In such cases, the alert can be focused on the groups to which the vacations are most suited.

Psychographic: This is an analysis of the way an individual or group of individuals choose to lead their lives. This will focus on their social class, lifestyle type and personality, and will include an individual's feelings, needs, wants, desires and beliefs.

All these issues or factors tie into the aspects of buyer behaviour as discussed earlier in this chapter. What drives an individual's lifestyle is immensely complex. However, marketers attempt to gain greater understanding of this complexity through collecting and collating a wealth of information on current and potential customers. Online surveys can be used to profile an individual's purchasing habits, likes and dislikes. Thus, individuals can often be segmented from the mass population as a consequence of this information.

Ideal segments

Perreault *et al.* (2000) suggest that an ideal market segment should meet the following four criteria:

Homogenous (similarities) within the segment: Customers within the segment should be as similar as possible with respect to their likely responses to the marketing mix variables. For example, an online bookstore focusing on customers who like reading science fiction novels. This is, in actual fact, a large market segment as there are many different types of science fiction. Therefore, such an homogenous market can be sub-divided or sub-segmented.

Heterogeneous (differences) between segments: Here, the customers, within different segments, should be as different as possible with respect to their likely responses to the marketing mix variables. Again, we can refer to an online generalist bookstore. This caters for a wide range of different customers or segments. Some will read science fiction whilst others will prefer historical romance or 'chicklit' (novels such as the highly successful UK published *Bridget Jones' Diary* aimed at the younger woman's market). Whatever the preference, a generalist online bookstore must be able to cater for these different segments.

Substantial: Here, the segment(s) should be large enough to sustain costs and be profitable. Online bookstores such as Amazon.com and Barnes & Noble.com cater for large segments of the book buying public. Of course, there will be niche (or small) markets that will still generate the necessary revenues for the business. There are, for instance, specialist online bookstores who supply specialist academic texts or rare and out of print books. These could be described as micro-segments of the book market.

Operational: The segmenting dimensions should be useful for identifying customers and the most appropriate marketing mix variables. The segmenting dimensions would include lifestyle analysis. Such analysis would include various aspects of an individual's life style from their disposable income levels to their hobbies and shopping habits.

As Lerer (2002) suggests, the internet allows for 'real-time' segmentation of customers. He continues:

> Through questionnaires, click stream analysis and simple screening questions, it is possible to customize a web page for an individual. While online segmentation and the resulting attempts at segmentation may be somewhat crude (one need only recall some of the personal book recommendations from a site such as Amazon.com), visitors at some of the better pharmaceutical websites can have their questions reasonably well answered. Once individuals and their information needs are better identified, web application servers are powerful tools in delivering the appropriate content and customising the user experiences.

Targeting

Once a company has selected the most appropriate segments for its product and/or service, it needs to develop a strategy to target its specific audience(s). A company may discover that it can target several segments of the population with its particular product or service. However, the company will have to make the decision as to whether that is feasible or not. By targeting one or two key segments, it will be able to concentrate its marketing efforts to maximum affect. If it attempts to spread its marketing activity over numerous segments, it may deplete its marketing resources and reduce potential return on its investment. This is particularly the case where the company is using several different communications media (for example, newspapers, magazines and television) beyond that of its website.

Positioning

Ries and Trout (1982) called positioning the 'battle for the mind'. Here, the company is attempting to create a clear, distinctive and desirable place for their product or service in the mind of the target customer relative to any competitor. However, whilst the company attempts to 'create' such a place or position, it is the customer who eventually decides the position of that product or service relative to its competition. For instance, customers will use one online banking service over another because they believe that they are receiving value for money. If they start to believe that the online bank is not delivering value for money, they are likely to switch to another brand. If significant numbers of customers decide to switch, then the online bank's reputation can be damaged, if only for the short term. Nevertheless, it may affect how prospective customers perceive it in relation to the competitors. They may 'position' it lower than a rival online bank. Thus, they may be persuaded to join the competitor online bank.

STP models

Although discussed in isolation, segmentation, targeting and positioning are by no means drivers that operate in isolation – there are clear links. Various authors have developed enhanced STP schematics that illustrates the relationship between segmentation, targeting and positioning. However, we have opted for the schematic created by Dibb *et al.* (1997), which we have adapted slightly.

As you can see from the schematic, the end point is the customer's reaction to the segmentation, targeting and positioning. If the company has, for whatever reason, poorly segmented the market, then the targeted customer may receive promotional material for products or services that do not match their needs and wants. As stated earlier, this can be elevated through permission marketing and linked email alerts. However, numerous online businesses have opted for unsolicited emails/email alerts. These become 'spam', just as direct mail becomes 'junk mail' or unsolicited faxes become 'junk faxes'. Such spamming becomes an irritation for the receiver and highlights a lack of foresight on behalf of those companies distributing it. If they focused their resources on careful segmentation of the marketplace, they are more likely to reap greater rewards.

The future

We can argue that the internet and e-business are still very much in their infancy. Whilst we may continue to use 'modified' forms of traditional seg-

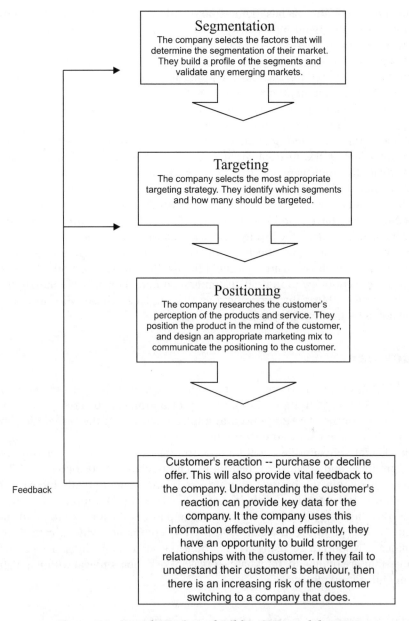

Segmentation
The company selects the factors that will determine the segmentation of their market. They build a profile of the segments and validate any emerging markets.

Targeting
The company selects the most appropriate targeting strategy. They identify which segments and how many should be targeted.

Positioning
The company researches the customer's perception of the products and service. They position the product in the mind of the customer, and design an appropriate marketing mix to communicate the positioning to the customer.

Customer's reaction -- purchase or decline offer. This will also provide vital feedback to the company. Understanding the customer's reaction can provide key data for the company. It the company uses this information effectively and efficiently, they have an opportunity to build stronger relationships with the customer. If they fail to understand their customer's behaviour, then there is an increasing risk of the customer switching to a company that does.

Feedback

Figure 6.1 **An adaptation of Dibb's STP model (1997)**

mentation, this will unlikely be the future. The development of ever increasingly intelligent software will change the nature of cyber-segmentation, targeting and positioning. As Louvier and Driver (2001) suggest, the 'ability to electronically track changes and re-segment reflexively offers superior adaptability and overcomes the problem of relatively longer delay times (marketing system lag) associated with the segmentation processes employed in classic and neo-classic direct marketing approaches' (Louvier and Driver, 2001). If this view becomes a reality, and there is no reason why it should not, then cyber-STP could have a much greater immediacy. Companies will have the opportunity to be both highly pro-active as well as reactive to changing customer markets.

In Chapter 5, we stated the role and importance of data warehousing and data mining. The development of new interrogative software will allow companies to mine their databases more efficiently, thus (ideally) understanding their customer's behaviour. We place the word 'ideally' in parenthesis because companies will need both the determination and resources to exploit the technology. It is one thing having the technology; it is quite another using it both effectively and efficiently. For several years companies who have provided their customers with loyalty cards have had the opportunity to use technology to focus on key customers and their needs. Few have successfully exploited this opportunity. Moreover, they have failed to understand the need to 'get close' to their customers. In other words, the loyalty card has been a public relations exercise – not a means of developing an effective and mutually rewarding opportunity. There is the risk that many e-businesses could follow this course of action. Those that do use the technology to mutual customer–company benefit will increase their survival rate within a hypercompetitive marketplace. Those who do not are unlikely to be first-tier players in the future.

Summary

In this chapter, we have covered the role and importance of segmentation, targeting and positioning to the marketing of products and services. Although 'traditional' forms of STP are used in e-business, there is the recognition that these will undergo some transformation in the future. With the development of intelligent software there will be opportunities to segment, target and position products and services in 'real time'. The tracking of customers and their behaviour (within the bounds of ethical standards) could greatly increase the company's understanding of their customers. This can be mutually beneficial. However, there must be an awareness on the part of e-businesses to build such mutually acceptable relationships. Moreover, companies will have to devote significant resources to using STP to build closer relationships. Those companies that are unable to, for whatever reason, risk their survival within a highly competitive marketplace.

Questions for review and reflection

Look at two websites for organisations in the same business. We suggest lastminute.com and opodo, as both of these are involved in the air travel ticketing business. However, you can choose whoever you wish, so long as they are in some way competitors.

1   From the evidence of the websites, what would you say are the key segmentation criteria used by each of these sites?

2 What targeting does each use to get to its chosen market?
3 What features of the sites help the organisation in question to create a sense of position in the customer's mind?
4 How well do the STP aspects fit together? Does the whole work effectively to get to and attract the chosen target market?

Notes and references

Day, G.S. and Montgomery, D.B. (1999) 'Charting new directions in marketing', *Journal of Marketing*, vol. 63, special issue, pp. 3–13.

Dibb, S., Simkin, L., Pride, W.M. and Ferrell, O.C. (1997) *Marketing: Concepts and Strategies*. Boston: Houghton Mifflin.

Kotler, P. (2000) *Marketing Management*. Harlow: Pearson.

Lerer, L. (2002) 'Pharmaceutical marketing segmentation in the age of the internet', *International Journal of Medical Marketing*, vol. 2, no. 2. pp. 159–66.

Louvier, P. and Driver, J. (2001) 'New Frontiers in cybersegmentation:marketing in cyberspace depends on IP address', *Qualitative Market Research: An International Journal*, vol. 4, no. 3, pp. 169–81.

Perreault, W.D., McCarthy, E.J., Parkinson, S. and Stewart, K. (2000) *Basic Marketing*, European edn. London: McGraw-Hill.

Ries, A. and Trout, J. (1982) *Positioning: The Battle for the Mind*. New York: Warner Books.

Yelkur. R. and DaCosta. M.M.N. (2001) 'Differential pricing and segmentation on the Internet: the case of hotels', *Management Decisions*, vol. 39, no. 4, pp. 252–61.

☑ 7 Marketing communications

Introduction

By the end of the twentieth century, the use of the internet could not be considered as just another 'add-on' to a company's marketing communications. Any company that took that view was just throwing money away. Such an approach was hardly likely to see a return on their investment.

Although marketing communications is often aggressively taught within business schools worldwide, it is surprisingly how ineffective the use of integrated marketing communications (IMC) often is! In this chapter, we investigate the use of the IMC within an e-business context. The aim is to show how the internet is now an integral component of any company's marketing communication, and that this is beyond the display of a website. The internet can clearly be used as an interactive marketing communications tool to promote a company's products and/or services.

Additionally, this chapter illustrates how the misuse of the internet, and email, in particular, can cause negative communication. This, in turn, can severely damage the reputation of individuals, companies and organisations alike, including governments.

What is central is that the internet can both enhance a brand's qualities and also destroy them. Thus, it must be handled with care and respect.

Before we proceed further, we should consider a brief explanation of internet and intranets. The internet can be described as an international open network of computers linked by modems, dedicated lines, telephone cables, microwave and satellite links. An intranet uses very similar technology. However, it is a closed link that connects a company to its various worldwide subsidiaries. Only staff within that organisation would have access via password protection systems. An intranet is used for specific internal communications, whereas the internet is for primarily external communication.

Learning objectives

On completion of this chapter you should be able to:

1 Define the purpose of marketing communications within an e-environment;
2 Link the purpose of marketing communications to individual communication elements;

Definitions and purpose of marketing communications

Perrault *et al.* (2000) have described promotion as 'communicating information between the seller and the potential buyer or others within the channel to influence attitudes and behaviour'.

Developing these individual themes further we can see that marketing communications can be used to achieve several different, yet linked, objectives. These can be defined as:

1   Creating, developing, maintaining and reinforcing brand awareness. This is clearly important within an often crowded, sometimes overcrowded, dynamic changing business environment. This is likely to be increasingly the case as companies and organisations cross national boundaries and become international, or indeed global, in their focus.

2   Creating, developing, maintaining and reinforcing a positive image of the brand in the mind of the customer. This is equally important within the B2B context as it is within B2C. Additionally, we must consider not just products or services within this equation but also celebrities and even governments. Since the late 1990s, the British Government has employed 'special advisors', often referred to as 'spin doctors' to create a 'favourable' outcome for difficult legislation. However, as we will see later, that has not always worked in favour of the government and has, in turn, lead to crisis management.

3   Influencing the views and decisions of key opinion formers. These range from government officials and politicians through to individual consumer and the business customer. The internet provides a potentially powerful channel to reach a 'public' with regional and potentially global issues. Later, we will report on the considerable use of the internet in the 1990 McLibel trial.

4   Creating the environment for the customer to purchase the product or service direct. Whilst we will deal with this in more detail in a later chapter, it is vital to recognise that marketing communications provides a critical link to purchasing activity.

5   Providing after-sales communication in order to create customer retention. Linked to this is the ongoing development of relationship marketing. Companies, such as Dell Computers (www.dell.co.uk) and Decca Classical Music (www.deccaclassics.com), provide customers with e-mail updates on new products, new releases, concert dates and special offers.

Integrating marketing communications

The marketing communication mix can be described as a combination of several promotional activities or elements. These elements can be either standalones or, to a greater or lesser degree, integrated. What must be realised here is that these activities operate both within an e-environment and external to it. Companies will use 'traditional' communication techniques in addition to those that operate via the internet. Thus, when we consider the individual elements in more detail later in this chapter, we will only be focusing upon those that operate within the e-environment. However, the reader must be aware of the links with more traditional forms of marketing communication.

Generally the marketing communication elements within an e-environment context can be considered as:

- company websites
- product or brand-only websites
- advertising
- direct marketing
- sales promotions
- sales force
- sponsorship
- public relations
- word of mouth – viral marketing

Due to the scale of some of these individual elements, we can only provide an overview.

Before considering the elements of the communication mix in isolation, we should appreciate the role of integration. Integrated Marketing Communications (IMC) is the coordination of the communication mix from the organisation through to the audience. The overall objective is to create, then convey a consistent, appropriate and complete message to the target audience.

There are both advantages and disadvantages to integrating marketing communications. Here we briefly consider these.

Positive aspects

1 IMC can assist in building a longer-term relationship with the customer. Companies and organisations (voluntary and charity, NGOs, for instance) seek to build a longer-term relationship, thus increasing the possibility of repeat purchasing, or better still, advocacy. Here, we mean that the satisfied customer recommends the company or organisation to friends and family. This requires the minimal investment by the company. However, it can produce maximised returns. Advocacy is what companies and organisations strive for – yet very few probably reach that pinnacle of customer satisfaction. If a company can optimise a range of communication channels, then they may be able to achieve competitive advantage over their immediate rivals.

2   There is an opportunity to increase sales by 'stretching' the brand message over several different communication channels. This assists in creating diversity and the opportunity for the customer to become aware and thus interested in the message. This could engender repeat purchasing, or indeed, create first-time buyer behaviour.

3   A consistency of brand message can be provided by IMC. This, in turn, can significantly aid brand awareness and identity – thus recall and retention in the mind of the buyer. This feeds back, to Point 1 above, thus helping to build that longer-term relationship and brand loyalty.

4   By focusing on an integrated message, duplication of marketing effort can be significantly reduced, or indeed, eliminated altogether; for example, several different communication specialists – advertisers, sales promotion, public relations, web designers and so on – working together on a consistent look and message. By seeking a 'commonality', there is a reduction of effort, cost and confusing mixed messages and standards.

Negative aspects

1   Resistance to change: IMC means that different groups within different agencies and consultancies must work together. In an ideal world, they would work towards the common goal of benefiting the client's aims and objectives. However, reality is not always so accommodating. People are afraid of change – usually because they have to think and act differently. Even with the next generation of marketing communicators, there is likely to a be resistance to change.

2   Organisational structures: Structure does not always permit organisations to work across functions and with other companies. In business, we can witness the rivalry between strategic business units within the same organisation. Take this a stage further and operate across different companies, who could also be rivals.

3   Restriction on creative freedoms: Often the issue here is 'Who is the real driving force behind the integrated marketing communications project?' From where does the creative brief emanate? Is it the advertising agency, the marketing consultants or the web designers? The answer is that it can really originate from any of these. But as with organisation structures stated above, there can be conflicts.

4   Difficulties of planning over time scales: Lead times can vary enormously throughout the different elements of the communication mix. Thus, careful planning is necessary so that all the elements gel at the given time to present a cohesive communication to the target audience. This may not always be possible.

5   Finally, but often critical to the overall success of IMC, is budget restrictions. Clearly, there cannot be an open-ended account. However, whilst major companies and organisations can 'stretch' their communication over several channels, SMEs may be heavily restricted financially. Thus, SMEs may have to focus on a much more narrow range of channels. Therefore, the

development of their own website, with appropriate links, may be the best targeted option for them.

As you can see from the above overview, IMC must be considered when developing marketing communications within and external to an e-environment.

Marketing communications techniques

Websites

We have divided this section to cover both company and product websites. This is an important distinction. Whilst company websites cover a multitude of issues from investor relations through to product range, the product-only websites, as the name suggests, focuses their energy on the product and the brand identity. In many cases, the consumer will not know, or be interested in, the parent company. The brand can thus standalone and reinforce its market position to current and potential customers.

Company websites

When the internet and world wide web started to gain popularity, many companies and other organisations were quick to 'jump on the bandwagon'. Many of them saw that this was a 'quick' way of gaining attention, building brand identity, and perhaps some sort of competitive advantage. The problem, however, was that many companies did not fully consider what was needed to create an effective website. True, it was another medium in order to promote the brand. However, bland, difficult to navigate websites are not going to attract an audience. The problem for many companies was that they did not fully understand the medium. Simply placing an online version of their brochure was not the solution. There had to be more.

To be fair to such pioneering companies, it was a new medium and technology had its limitations. Today, the situation is very different. A company's website cannot only be a vehicle to promote the company's products and services visually but can offer a much wider range of possibilities – company history, special offers, merchandising, employment opportunities and so on. It has become a gateway to the whole company. The case study below of Heinz Foods illustrates the range of communication opportunities.

☑ Case study Heinz Foods (www.heinz.com)

H.J. Heinz is a US$9.4 billion global food company selling 57 000 varieties in over 200 countries. For several years, Heinz have reinforced their strong brand awareness through their interactive website. Nor have they been complacent, their website has been developed and transformed over time, thus providing a wider range of facilities and information to customers and surfers alike.

The Heinz website covers the following areas:

- Consumers' FAQs
- Meal planners – recipes
- Special promotions
- Detailed information on their brand range
- History of the company
- Background to their advertising campaigns
- Careers opportunities
- Investor relations information – annual reports and stock marketing information.
- Information on corporate governance
- Press releases
- Downloads – screensavers
- Direct sales – Heinz-direct UK – where favourite UK Heinz products can be delivered almost anywhere in the world
- Email alerts – email updates on the company and its products direct to an individual's computer.

The screen dump below again helps to illustrate the range of information on offer to their audience that includes:

Consumers – purchasing products, discovering new food ranges and using their recipes:
Current and potential investors – details of the company's performance and future plans;
Students and tutors – material for projects and exercises: examples of internet sites, advertising, promotion and management.

The Heinz website is an example of how a site can build and maintain a brand identity and image. It also is a way of creating a customer relationship through providing extra benefits – for example, simple recipes using Heinz produce. This is a point that we will return to in the following chapter on customer relations management.

Source: The Heinz Company.

The global cruise brand Royal Caribbean developed an innovative website that provides an all-round communications platform. There is not only the types of cruise vacations, the range of ships and investor information, there is also the opportunity to book online as well. Royal Caribbean has taken the basic concept of placing information on web pages and created an 'interactivity' with its prospective and current customers. Many more companies are developing such websites. This clearly indicates that this powerful tool can be used for much more than just displaying a 'brochure'.

© 2003 The H.J. Heinz Company

Figure 7.1 **Opening page of the Heinz website**

▼ Case study   Royal Caribbean International (www.royalcaribbean.com)

Royal Caribbean is one of the world's largest cruise ship operators with 14 ships in service (2002). Among their fleet are the world's largest cruise ships, including *Voyager of the Seas*, which was the world's largest cruise ship until the launch of the *Queen Mary II* in late 2003).

The royalcaribbean.com website allows prospective passengers (or guests) to explore the ships and make travel arrangements. The company has created a virtual tour section on their web pages. This allows the prospective client to view the public areas, staterooms and suites, bars, lounges, conference facilities and onboard activities.

To quote Barbara Shrut, Vice President, Customer Loyalty and e-Marketing:

> We introduced this one-of-a-kind virtual access to the world of Royal Caribbean so that customers can experience a cruise vacation on our innovative ships from the comfort of their home. For those who are undecided about their vacation plans, we believe this dynamic site will help to transform many prospective cruisers into loyal guests.

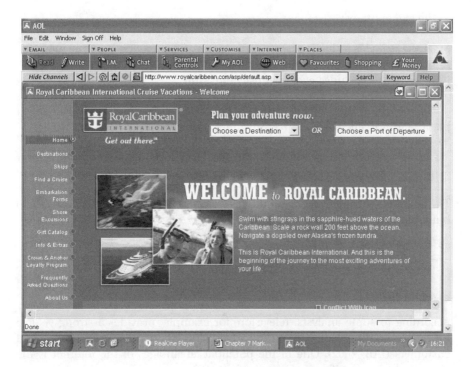

© 2003 Royal Caribbean International/Royal Caribbean Cruises Limited.

Figure 7.2 **Opening page of the Royal Caribbean International website**

In addition to the virtual tour, there is a web cam that allows live footage to be displayed on the prospective customer's computer screen.

Source: Royal Caribbean International

Product or brand-only websites

As stated earlier, such sites provide a platform whereby companies can focus their energies on the product's specific brand values, image and identity. Thus, their targeting is directed solely at their customer base. The following case study illustrates the point.

▼ Case study   Pringles   (www.pringles.com)

Pringles is a potato chip that is available in a variety of flavours from original through to Cajun flavoured. Whilst a Procter & Gamble product, the Pringles' website focuses, apart from a brief reference to Procter & Gamble, on it's own brand identity. The site is clearly aimed at a youngish audience, and aims to create interactivity with it's audience.

The site contains:

Meet the Pringles – this focuses on the various flavours that are available.
Pringles Zone – includes games, quizzes and activities.
Pringles Beat – includes events, music and 'stuff'.

There is also a Q&A section, details of how to gain pop-up news and a contact point. Additionally, there are feature zones. For example:

Cheese and Onion presents Tearjerker – Direct a tearjeaker – Move your friends to tears! Direct your own tearjerker movie and send it to your best buds!

This is a way of using word-of-mouth (as we will see later in this chapter) to help build brand awareness and image.

Source: Procter & Gamble

---

e-advertising

According to some analysts, television, for example, provides a strong vehicle for brand building. However, online advertising is a better generator of actual customers (IAB, 2002). One of the potential advantages of the internet is the ability to target specific customers, which improves overall cost effectiveness of internet advertising. However, there are possible downsides to internet advertising that should not be ignored.

At the time of writing (2003), it appears that few companies have launched a major brand via the internet, the exception perhaps being cigarette companies, who are increasingly being restricted in terms of their regional and international media outlets. The vast majority of other companies are still relying on television advertising (despite the downturn in advertising in 2001 and 2002). As several industry watchers have observed, television advertising is very much 'in your face'. If a viewer wants to avoid it, they have either to change channels or leave the room. Here, major brands, for example washing powders and food products, consistently bombard the individual's living room. On the other hand, even with animated banner advertising (see below) the viewer has to click on the advertisement to see the full 'offering'.

However, another point of view could be that if you are targeting a specific group or audience, the internet has specific benefits. It can also lead to a direct purchases via the internet. Advertising can take several forms on the internet. This is dependant upon the audience being targeted and the site chosen. There are several forms of internet advertising, including banner and classified advertisements.

The scope of internet advertising

The statistics for advertising on the internet often vary, dependant upon the sources used. Exactly the same applies to any form of media promotion or communication. However, according to the research company eMarketer™, online advertising spending in the USA alone would be (2001) US$8 billion rising to around US$13 billion by 2005 (eMarketer™, 2002).

According to eMarketer™ online advertising growth will increasingly emanate from traditional companies. This being a result of the internet becomingly increasingly mainstream, thus persuading traditional companies to use more cross-media campaigns (eMarketer™, 2002). However, as we consider later, advertising may not currently be as affective as the more traditional channels. This has led major companies to invest only a small fraction of their total advertising on web media. According to the international management consultants McKinsey, the top 10 corporations accounted for US$137 million or two per cent of the US$5.5 Billion devoted to online advertising in 2000 (Bughin, *et al.* 2001).

Advertising locations – internet sites

The following are the key areas where advertising can be incorporated. A company can use them individually or collectively if appropriate. The objective for the company or organisation is to gain exposure in front of the right audience at the right time.

Portals

As the word suggests, a portal is the gateway into the internet and the world wide web. However, as we will see, they are also 'destinations' for the surfer. The objective is that the visitor enters and decides to stay, using a range of services from free email facilities through to online shopping. However, the shopping experience is limited to the companies to which that portal has agreement.

An example of a portal is Yahoo! (www.yahoo.com). This site provides an extensive range of services from news updates, shopping, free emails through to a comprehensive search engine.

In addition to these large-scale mass market portals, smaller vertical portals have been created. Called *vortals*, these specialise in one or two specific areas.

News sites

Various newspaper companies and broadcasters have created their own interactive internet sites. Newspapers such as *The Financial Times* (www.ft.com), *The Times* (www.thetimes.co.uk) and the *Wall Street Journal* (www.wsj.com) have created extensive websites that not only cover today's news but also have archive facilities. The latter may require free registration; this provides the company with data capture and subsequent market research information on their target audience. As stated in Chapter 6, this is an ideal method for helping to segment the newspaper readership audience.

Broadcasters such as the 24-hour news channel CNN (www.cnn.com) and the British Broadcasting Corporation (www.bbc.co.uk) provide a range of services for both the regular and occasional user.

Consumer exchanges

These are online marketplaces that do not hold inventory; for example, ebay (www.ebay.com).

e-tailers

These are the internet 'retailers' who both hold and sell inventory. Examples include the online book and CD store Amazon (www.amazon.com) and the world's largest online grocery store Tesco (www.tesco.com). A key difference between Amazon and Tesco is that Amazon is purely internet based, whereas Tesco also have physical 'bricks and mortar' outlets.

Content service provider – specialist interest sites

As the name suggests, these are sites that specialise in a particular segment(s) of a market. Indeed, they can be single or multiple niche markets. In many ways, it is a replication of the physical world of magazines (for example, music and the cinema) and lifestyle-oriented stores. These B2C sites are supported by advertising that offers seller-affiliated content. An example of this is *i*Village.com.

▼ Case study *i*Village.com™ (www.ivillage.com)

*i*Village.com is organised into channels and communities across multiple topics of relevance to women aged 18 and over. It offers interactive services, peer support, content and online access to experts and tailored shopping opportunities. The major content areas includes Babies, Beauty, Diet & Fitness, Entertainment, Food, Health, Home & Garden, Horoscopes, Money, Parenting, Pets, Pregnancy, Quizzes, Relationships and Work. A look and feel is provided across content areas and the network to create a consistent brand identity.

Membership to *i*Village.com is free and provides customers with features such as personal homepages, message boards and other community tools. *i*Village.com has over 11 million members (July 2003).

*i*Village.com has built a reputation for developing innovative sponsorship and commercial relationships with marketing partners. The aim is to match the objectives of the marketers with those of the *i*Village.com members by providing relevant information and services.

Average monthly page views for the *i*Village network of web sites totalled nearly 353 million for the quarter ending 31st December 2003. According to comScore Media Metrix, *i*Village ranked 31 amongst the top 100 web and digital media properties within the US with nearly 15 million unique visitors (December 2003).

*i*Village.com is operated by *i*Village Inc a US-based women's media company that includes *i*Village.com, Women.com, gURL.com, Astrology.com, Promotions.com, *i*Village Parenting Network, The Newborn Channel, Lamaze Publishing, Business Women's Network, Diversity Best Practices, Best Practices in Corporate Communications and *i*Village Consulting.

Sources: *i*Village.com and *i*Village Inc.

Types of internet advertising

There are several types of internet advertising currently available:

- Banners
- Skyscrapers
- Pop-Ups
- Buttons
- Classified.

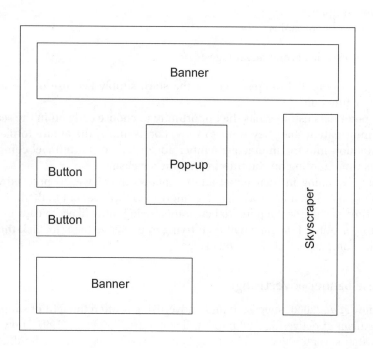

Banner advertising

This is a rectangular graphic that normally appears at the top of the page or along the bottom of the web page.

Banners can either be static or animated. As more consumers become comfortable with *Flash* and other animated technologies, companies will use banner advertising to create something different and eye catching.

Animated banner advertising

By using such technology as *Flash*, (which creates functionality for movement and related time dependent web features) banner advertising can comprise several different images in a sequence to attract the viewer's attention. The different layers help to build an image that can lead the viewer to a state of action – clicking onto the advertisement. This direct response mechanism leads them to the website. There are numerous examples ranging from online bookstores through to cosmetic companies and insurance companies.

Interactive banner advertising

This is one step beyond purely animated banner advertising. In addition to attracting the viewer's attention, the advertisement adds value by allowing the viewer to input information. This will then lead to a further, more personalised response.

Here are two examples:

- Travel company
- Credit card companies

These can provide several advantages:

1 Creates a potential interest right at the start, simply because of the inter-activity function;
2 The potential customer has the opportunity to choose early on in the search the information that they want to view. For example, the ability to place a destination into the interactive banner advertisement for a travel company saves time hunting on the travel company's website;
3 Simply by filling in their email address allows the viewer to proceed onto other websites in the knowledge that information will be sent to them. Again, it is time saving for the potential customer, being more likely to capture this customer's attention via email than trying to persuade them to click-though to the company's website at this stage.

Why use banner advertising?

As Chaffey *et al.* (2000) suggest, banner advertising is often thought of simply as a mechanism of delivering traffic to a website. Cartellieri *et al.* (1997), however, suggest that several objectives in using banner advertising can be identified:

- *Delivering content*: A click-though on a banner advertisement leads through to a corporate website, for example, a credit card company. Here, more detailed information is provided together with the opportunity to purchase directly.
- *Enabling a transaction*: A click-though to, for example, a travel company website allows the consumer to purchase online, a direct response activity.
- *Shaping attitudes*: If the banner advertising is consistent with the company's overall marketing and corporate communications, then it can assist in brand reinforcement.
- *Encouraging retention*: By positioning the company name prominently on a highly active website (for example, a portal), there is a high level of exposure. This can aid retention of the brand/company name.

There are, however, additional benefits that can be gained through the use of banner advertising. This takes the form of tracking. This can be subdivided into:

- *Click-through*: Here, the company can track the response to the banner advertisement; for example, how many people go through to the website, how many people start the purchase and do not complete, how many are browsers and lurkers,[1] why visitors may not complete and how many people do complete the transaction. This allows the company to modify the banner advertisements and links where necessary in a shorter time frame than many other media. This is relatively inexpensive in comparison to, for example, deciding that a TV commercial needs re-editing because it is not attracting the necessary awareness and product retention.
- *Cookies*: These are small identifying text files that some companies place on an individual's computer when they visit the site. When the individual returns to that site, it will note that they have returned and may add more information. Many companies use cookies to log an individual's personal preferences. This has particular benefits to both the individual, and the company concerned. Firstly, for the individual, the site will remember what they have bought before. Thus, it may be able to direct them to other products that they may like. For example, an online bookshop may be able to direct the customer to other types of books that may interest them. Secondly, it helps the company to build a profile of the visitor, and thus may be able to target specific advertisements and products to them. This can increase retention and build a longer-term relationship.

However, as discussed in Chapter 4, some people may be concerned that companies are breaching their personal privacy by gathering such data. There is

---

[1] In individual terms, a 'browser' is a person who occasionally views sites, like browsing the pages of a magazine. On the other hand, a 'lurker' is someone who tends to spend more time viewing the web page(s), usually on a regular basis. This is particularly the case where they are reading comments within chat rooms and newsgroups. However, they rarely if ever contribute to the discussions taking part within those forums.

a careful balance to be kept between commercial efficiency and the preservation of good customer relationships.

Skyscrapers

These are, in essence, a vertical form of banner advertising; the same interactivity and animation potential exists.

Pop-up advertising

Pop-up advertising is also known as *interstitials*. These are advertising windows that 'pop up' in between screens of information as a new page is displayed. Once displayed, the advertisement can only be removed by the viewer by closing the specific window. Thus, pop-up advertising has the advantage of being highly visible, and the viewer has to close it down.

However, the negative of this is that they are often deemed intrusive by getting in the way of the page the viewer wants to see. Equally, the physical action of having to close down the window costs time, if only a few seconds. Yet, it can still be irritating for the viewer, most especially if they appear on a regular basis.

Buttons

As the name suggests, these are small circular, oval, square or rectangular objects that display an image. That image is usually a company name and or logo. This provides a click through opportunity to the company's website.

Classified advertising

As with their print media counterparts, these are small, normally short text only advertisements that usually appear at the back of magazines and newspapers. They can cover everything from business opportunities through to individuals seeking friendship and marriage.

▼ Case study   *The Economist*
(www.economist.com)

The international business magazine *The Economist* has its own associated website. As well as displaying the range of internet advertising techniques described earlier, it also offers classified advertising. The classified advertising covers:

- business education
- recruitment
- business and personal.

Does advertising on the internet work?

At that time of writing (April 2003), the jury is perhaps still out on this issue. The business consultants McKinsey (www.mckinsey.com) have, amongst others, analysed advertising on the internet. In their findings, which focused upon the USA, the current major marketplace, they concluded that online media does not yet have the impact. They make the following comparison:

In 2000, while seven US television networks and 214 cable stations competed for US$16 Billion and US$13 Billion in advertising, respectively, more than 9,000 US web sites fought for less than US$6 Billion in advertising. Further-more, this revenue was concentrated in just a handful of properties: 76 per cent of the advertising went to the ten biggest sites (Bughin, 2001).

McKinsey contend that advertisers did not buy media space on the web for two key reasons (Bughin *et al.* 2001):

1   The average user clicks on only one banner advertisement per week;
2   The majority of consumers ignore web advertising.

In an earlier section of this chapter, we stated that that the top 10 corporations invested US$137 million in online advertising in 2000. Table 7.1 below illustrates the level of investment per company.

The internet research company Jupiter (www.jmm.com) stated that the vast majority of European companies would spend less than five per cent of their advertising budget on the internet (MediaGuardian, 2001). However, it tran-spires, according to Jupiter, that the main reason given for low expenditure on internet advertising was that the medium was not mass market. Thus, there is a concern that those advertisers might not reach sufficient potential customers

Table 7.1 Online advertising spending of the top 10 corporations in 2000

Corporation	Advertising spend US$ Million
General Motors	48.0
IBM	24.3
AT&T	18.5
Ford	16.1
Citigroup	11.4
General Electric	8.8
Philip Morris	6.6
Wal-Mart	2.9
Exxon Mobil	0.5
Boeing	0.2

Source: CMR: McKinsey Analysis (Bughin *et al.*, 2001)

(MediaGuardian, 2001). In response to that, Staffan Englegard, Jupiter's advertising and marketing analyst, commented that companies would have to adopt new marketing approaches for the web. He stated:

> They [the companies] should apply a targeted marketing model better suited to the dynamics of the Internet than the mass-marketing model that most are used to ... Companies cannot ignore online advertising if they want to sustain or increase the overall time consumers are spending with their brands (Media Guardian, 2001).

This view is reinforced by year-long research undertaken by a consortium of companies and organisations. The investigation on the relative effectiveness of and synergies between online and traditional media advertising found that online advertising's share of the media mix can have a significant increase in the effectiveness of an overall advertising campaign (IAB, 2002). The research concluded that (IAB, 2002):

- Consumer packaged goods (CPG) brands that increase their online advertising may result in increased key metrics, such as brand awareness, brand attributes and purchasing intent.
- Higher online frequency of advertising boosts branding effectiveness. In one example, increasing the number of online impressions from six to 12 impressions over a six-week period increased Dove Nutrium Bar's (a Unilever product) overall branding effectiveness by 42 per cent.
- TV, print and online advertising are each effective at branding. However, online advertising is generally more cost-efficient in terms of branding from the pre-campaign level.

This research is important in that it helps demonstrate that online advertising can improve a brand's return on investment when it is a significant part of the overall media mix (IAB, 2002).

Whilst, in the short term, McKinsey do not believe that there will be significant improvement, the longer term has more potential. In the past, other media channels have undergone low take up of both advertisers and consumers; television is a good example. However, today it is often the mainstay of many advertising campaigns. To some extent this is supported by research undertaken by the UK media company Emap in 2001 (Admap, 2002). Their research showed that 91 per cent of visitors revealed that simply because they did not click onto the banner did not necessarily mean that they had not seen it (Admap, 2002). Emap found that 60 per cent of men tended to click on advertisements, compared to 51 per cent of women. In addition, 62 per cent of those aged between 25 and 34 click onto internet advertising. Overall, the view was taken that the internet helps to raise awareness, understanding and, through appropriate content, helps to promote relevance (Admap, 2002). We could then argue that it will become a relevant component within an integrated approach to marketing communications.

Table 7.2   Global online advertising, 1999–2005

Region	1999	2000	2001	2002	2003	2004	2005
North America	3 509	5 390	7 444	9 768	12 237	14 623	16 913
Western Europe	434	906	1 535	2 258	3 118	4 111	5 263
Asia	225	502	880	1 375	1 922	2 556	3 324
Latin America	52	127	240	402	628	888	1 168
Australia New Zealand	24	74	135	208	288	373	462
Other	9	28	61	118	211	351	578
TOTAL	4 253	7 027	10 295	14 129	18 404	22 902	27 708

Note: All figures in US$ millions.
Source: *Marketing News* (2002).

However, we need to determine the size of the overall advertising market. This will help companies predict the possible click through possibilities of internet advertising for the future.

Table 7.2 shows the global online advertising for the period 1999–2005 (prediction). As perhaps expected, currently the largest percentage is generated within the USA. However, both Europe and Asia continue to make advance in this area and will, most likely, see strong growth in the coming years.

Anti-advertising

For a moment it is worth considering, for want of a better phrase, the anti-advertisement movement. In the early days of the internet and world wide web, the consumer was operating within an advertisement-free zone where they could surf without colliding with advertising. This is no longer true. Whilst it could be argued that most advertising is unobtrusive, it is not always the case. Nor is it necessarily regulated, except by ISPs and alert specialist sites. If it is seen as obtrusive, it may well dissuade the customer from pursuing further information simply because of this bombardment.

Just as with television, advertising on the internet can be annoying to many people. One of the major areas for criticisms is pop-up advertisements, as these can be seen as an interruption to reading web pages. Indeed, commercially available software has been developed automatically to prevent pop-ups from displaying onscreen. Both advertisers and ISPs may have to rethink the use of pop-ups. Otherwise, they may actually dissuade consumers from viewing the web pages/sites where there is a proliferation of pop-ups. This, in turn, will be detrimental to both advertisers and ISPs as consumers seek alternatives.

Direct marketing

Direct marketing is often considered as a one-to-one communication as outlined in Chapter 5, both the UK supermarket chain Tesco and the European low-cost airline easyJet have used the direct marketing aspects of the internet to win business. Tesco, for example, are able to build a profile of their customers by logging their purchasing habits. Thus, special offers can be directed towards particular segments of shoppers to whom they are most appropriate.

As indicated in Chapter 5, the introduction of the internet can reduce channel length. For instance, airlines are now able to deal directly with their end-user, the passenger. By placing ticket sales on the internet, airlines gained the opportunity to both lower costs and build stronger relationships directly with their customers. This is an area that will be explored in Chapter 8, Relationship e-marketing.

The real key in the direct relationship is 'interactivity'. This interactivity allows the customer to shape the product they want and for the supplier to learn from the customer. Companies such as the online book and CD retailer Amazon and the travel portal Expedia have developed this interactive exchange. They, and other e-tailers, have developed customer profiles based upon their previous purchases. For example, Amazon will suggest to a customer other books which are likely to be of interest to them. This is based upon what customers with similar tastes are buying, whether it is the latest in crime fiction or a classic novel. Equally, Amazon invite customers to submit reviews and comments on the books they have read. This, in turn, may attract customers to consider purchasing these books.

Processing as much data as possible on the customer helps the company achieve better understanding of their customer. That is the theory. In practice, it may be harder to do and it does require a commitment in terms of investment and people to process and act upon such data. If a company can successfully utilize such data, then the returns can be significant. More than 60 per cent of Amazon's business is generated through repeat sales (Willman, 1998).

One company that has built a successful online relationship with its customers is the Dell Computer Corporation. In the case study, the company's founder Michael Dell explains the importance of both clear customer relationships and efficient supply chain management (see Chapter 10).

⋎ Case study   Dell (www.dell.com)

In 1984, Michael Dell founded the Dell Computer Corporation. By 2000, sales via the internet reach US$50 million a day (approximately US$18 billion a year), and by the end of 2001 the company was generating total revenues of US$31.2 billion.

In 1994, Dell launched its website, introducing in 1996 e-commerce facilities allowing customers to buy their computers via the internet. By the end of 1997, sales via the internet sites had exceeded US$4 million per day.

The company was created on the premise that it would sell directly to its customers. By selling direct, the company felt that it could best understand customers needs and efficiently provide the most effective computing solutions to meet those needs. This direct model allows the company to build every system to order and offer computing systems at competitive prices.

At their website, a customer can review, configure and price systems within Dell's entire product range, then order and pay online, and track their order from manufacture through to shipping. In addition to their relationship with its customers, Dell are using their internet capabilities to build relationships through their supply chain. At www.valuechain.dell.com the company is able to share information with suppliers on various issues, including product quality and inventory status.

In a speech delivered in Washington, DC in June 2000 on the future of the internet, Michael Dell stated:

> Last year we shipped almost 12 million computers into about a hundred and fifty countries around the world. And the Internet has become not only a competitive weapon, but an essential tool for dealing with the volumes and the complexity of our business in an efficient manner.
>
> But the Internet is much more than just sales and online sales, although that seems to be something that people get attracted to as a headline. One of the real values of the Internet is that we've been able to use the support information that we gather from our customers. Our business is centred around these direct relationships with our users. And the fact that we deal directly with our customers means that we have perfect information about what they want to buy. We don't need to rely on inventory.
> . . .
> It's indicative of a fundamental value shift that's occurring, where physical assets like inventory are being replaced for information assets. This data and knowledge that we have from our customers gives us a fundamental edge. And this content really becomes the foundation for a successful online business.
>
> Today, instead of protecting this information, we go out of our way to put it online. Every day thousands of customers come to Dell.com and they receive support; support for the specific machine that they've purchased or are planning to purchase. They go to support.dell.com where they get specific information about their individual computer. And this allows us to not only solve these problems in a more efficient manner, but also to cultivate online communities. We have a forum called Dell Talk, where we have hundreds of thousands signed up. This ability to create an online community, which users find a real value, allows us to maintain greater customer relationships.

Source: 'The Future of the Internet', The Michael Dell address at the National Press Club, Washington, DC, 8 June, 2000. www.dell.com/us/en/gen/corporate/speech.

Sales promotions

This can be defined as an offer created to launch or re-launch a product or service. Effective planning is, therefore, essential as to whether sales promotion is to be used as a support activity for the organisation's long-term objectives, or as a short-term tactic.

The following is a list of criteria that illustrate the purpose of sales promotion. It must be emphasised that this list cannot be definitive as companies and organisations will devise and define their own style of promotions. There will always be numerous options and circumstances where sales promotions can make a significant contribution to the marketing of a company or organisation.

The introduction of new products: by motivating customers to try out a new product, or e-retail customers to accept it at point of sale. For example, either a music store or CD label website may provide musical sound bites from the CD single or album (see www.deccaclassics.com/johnbarry as an example).

Attract new customers: by motivating people to try out a new product, or e-retail customers to accept it for resale for the first time. Some companies, through their websites, may offer special discounts not available within their normal retail outlets. This is aimed to encourage prospective customers to use the website as their mode of purchase.

Maintaining competitiveness: by providing preferential discounts, or special low prices to enable more competitive prices to be offered. Some airlines, for example, may from time to time provide special discounts for those who book direct and online.

Increasing sales in off-peak seasons: by encouraging consumption out of season. An example here could be the last minute vacation through a host of websites that provide different types of holidays. Some will specialise in that last minute getaway and offer special incentives in order to fill the vacation slot.

Special limited editions: niche marketing-oriented companies can reinforce their market position by offering web-only based promotions. This is particularly the case with limited edition CDs. For example, the CD company Rhino Handmade (www.rhinohandmade.com) has a contract with Turner Entertainment Company/Turner Broadcasting Company (www.turner.com) to release original MGM soundtrack albums which Turner now owns along with an impressive catalogue of movies. Rhino release limited editions via their website only. They are not available in retail outlets, and are usually limited to pressings of 3000.

Sales force

As generally indicated throughout this book, the internet can be seen as a medium for customer relationship building. This can be delivered through online added value; for example, via web exclusive special offers.

Additionally, B2B companies, as discussed in Chapter 5, are seeking an environment where they can buy and sell via e-marketplaces. These can be described as online portals that function as an information broker and gateway to services. The e-marketplace offers the expertise of a particular vertical sector, the aim being to ensure that information and services are of a high value to the participants within that particular e-marketplace.

In theory, the efficiencies and greater transparency through the demand and supply chain lead to significant benefits. These include:

- Increased speed of transactions.
- Access to more information.
- Enhanced customer relationships.
- Optimisation of the supply chain – this can be achieved through the use of sophisticated planning and forecasting tools, which assist in the automation of the business processes.
- Improved overall branding of products and services.
- A reduction in processing costs.
- Increased speed in terms of settling payments.

However, changes are not only proceeding within the B2B marketplace. There is growing use of e-sales for consumer products and services.

▼ Case study   Prudential plc/Egg plc (www.prudential.co.uk/plc)

The Prudential was originally formed in 1848 as the Prudential Mutual Assurance, Investment and Loan Association. Today, it is one of the world's largest insurance groups.

In early 2001, the company announced that it would phase out its UK direct sales force by 2002. The company planned to focus its sales efforts via the internet and telesales. There would be a small direct sales team who would be retained to focus on specific affluent customers.

Prudential believed that it was increasingly uneconomic to retain a direct sales force as more than 90 per cent of customers/potential customers interacted with the company via mail, the Internet and the telephone. From 2002, the company expected to achieve annual gross cost savings of some UK£130 million.

This decision to move over to a combination internet and telesales base was probably also borne out of the experience of Egg (www.egg.com). Launched in October 1998 by Prudential, Egg is an e-commerce insurance company. In June 2000, it was listed on the UK Stock Market and by 2002 (Prudential plc continues to hold 79 per cent of share capital) had gained almost two million customers. Whilst the main focus of Egg is via the internet, it does handle accounts via telesales and interactive digital TV.

Egg plc provides banking, insurance, investments, mortgages and a shopping portal through its Internet site and other distribution channels.

Sources: 'Prudential Announces Restructuring of Direct Sales Force and Customer services Channels in the UK'. Prudential Media Department, Tuesday 13 February, 2001. 'Egg No 1 Financial services Website in Europe', Egg Media Relations, 21 March, 2002.

Sponsorship

Companies can also seek to sponsor sections within websites. This can provide a two-fold advantage:

1 A level of authority and knowledge on a subject area; for example, a bank sponsoring a page on currency conversion or beauty advice (see the Case Study on iVillage.com stated earlier);
2 A link to their own website. There is an opportunity to click through to a company's own website.

Public relations

Public relations, often abbreviated to PR, is concerned basically with the image of the company or organisation and the product or service they provide. Every organisation, even the most secretive, has an image – it may be a false one, but it is an image none the less. Increasingly, even the previously most secret of organisations such as Britain's Security Service (MI5) and the USA's Central Intelligence Agency (CIA) have easily accessible websites to promote their existence and their role in society to a wider community.

The Institute of Public Relations in the UK defines public relations as: 'the planned and sustained effort to establish and maintain goodwill and mutual understanding between the organisation and its publics'.

A company or organisation's 'publics' can be many and varied from local community opinion formers, suppliers and customers through to the Press and employees.

Public relations must provide a planned, deliberate and sustained attempt to promote understanding between the organisation and its audiences. In fact, it must promote not only understanding but it must also create a positive interest in the organisation that whets appetites for more information, prompts enquiries, re-establishes dormant contacts and reinforces image with existing customers.

▼ Case study   James Bond's 40th anniversary (www.jamesbond.com)

November 2002 witnessed the launch of the twentieth James Bond movie – *Die Another Day*. From the first outing *Dr No* (1962), the James Bond movies have attained a global following. Marketing has been a key element in the overall success of this movie series. Adding to that has been the development of the official James Bond website. From the opening gun barrel sequence, accompanied by the James Bond theme, through to video footage of amazing action sequences, the site encapsulates the Bond phenomena. The site features include:

- 007 frequently asked questions
- 40th anniversary screen savers and wall paper
- James Bond mobile news alert – US and European mobile phone users could sign up to receive the latest information on the making of *Die Another Day*
- Press releases
- Production news – including video sequences of the making of *Die Another Day*

- Questions for the production team. Run in an asynchronous format, this provides viewers with the opportunity to ask specific questions of the production team; for example, details of the Aston Martin being used in the movie.

Source: Official James Bond website.

Governments can use public relations for several reasons. The following may be considered singularly or collectively:

1 To provide information to the needy within the community; for example, communication information on new welfare schemes for the less fortunate in society and how they can apply for the benefits. This information can be delivered though computers in libraries and welfare offices. However, as we have seen, there are societal reasons why this may not entirely eliminate the social exclusion problem with the internet;
2 To publicise the vast range of activities that governments undertake. Within a democracy, this can be seen as communicating with its electorate;
3 To communicate the philosophy of an open government; that is, communicate the workings of the government and civil service and how they benefit the country. (See the case study below on MI5);
4 PR can be used to explain difficult, or unpopular, political decisions; for example, why it might be necessary to increase taxation substantially. Thus, an explanation of the reason why might alleviate taxpayers frustrations, and not affect the government's standing in the polls;
5 To provide educational information to school and college learners.

▼ Case study   The story of a security service – MI5 (www.mi5.gov.uk)

MI5 is the historical name for the British Security Service. Founded in 1909, MI5's role has been one of counterintelligence and counterterrorism operations within the UK. Until the late 1990s, it was generally cloaked in secrecy. Indeed, successive government ministers denied that it even existed, even though 'official' histories of the service during World War II had been written. Equally, numerous myths and high-profile double agents – namely Anthony Blunt – had racked the service.

Prime Minister John Major's Government and the then Director-General Stella Rimmington, who became the public face of MI5, took a more enlightened approach.

Indeed, the MI5 website has been developed to dispel many of the myths that previously surrounded that organisation, such as whether knowing the colour of the carpet was a national secret or not! – and whether such knowledge was a criminal offence!

Equally, it uses the website as a means of explaining the type of people – from all aspects of society – that it needs to recruit, how to join the service, its history, its function and its vital role within modern-day Britain.

The internet is instant and global. Thus, when things go wrong, they can have a sustained and damaging impact upon a company or organisation. Whilst many companies develop crisis management plans, they may not always be able to repel a sustained onslaught.

Today, we live in a global media world that is all pervasive. Companies and organisations know more about people than their own governments. Every box we tick, whether on the internet or on a piece of paper, allows for another record to be kept, another file to be maintained. With the rapid transfer of information between sites, information on us, our beliefs and behaviours, transcends national boundaries. For the vast majority of us, that is inconsequential. If we believe that relinquishing something of ourselves leads to our receiving benefits, then we are, normally, all too glad to make such information public. Think of every time you may have answered a questionnaire, either on paper or on the internet. You might be surprised how much you have actually revealed over the years.

As we have stated, the internet has not just become a vehicle for external communication, but one for internal communication. It is when undesirable comments from the internal communications break through the boundaries and are released into the external global environment that a crisis may loom. The next case study is a dramatic case in point. It not only led, eventually, to the resignation of a British civil servant, but embarrassed a government and, more importantly, insulted the victims of a tragedy that will haunt the world for decades.

⍚ Case study   A Thought Too Far

On Tuesday September 11, 2001, two passenger aircraft struck the twin World Trade Center Towers in New York. This deliberate act of terrorism lead to the collapse of both towers and the death of an estimated 3 000 people. Millions worldwide watched the horror of this unfolding event, images imprinted on minds and souls for generations to come.

In her Whitehall office, in London, Jo Moore, Special Advisor to Stephen Byers, Secretary of State for Trade and Industry sent an email to various civil servants. It allegedly stated 'it is now a good time to bury bad news'. A civil servant, shocked by what they had read, released it to the media. It caused a public outcry and pressure for either her resignation or dismissal. Ms Moore later issued an apology for her comments. However, in February 2002, it was alleged that Ms Moore sent another email, this time suggesting that the Government release any bad news on the day of Princess Margaret's funeral. Within days, Ms Moore tendered her resignation.

The point here is not just about the alleged 'tone' of the communications, it is that copies were quickly distributed to the media – not just in the UK, but globally. It not only illustrated Ms Moore's views, but portrayed a government as uncaring in the suffering and grief of others. The lesson, perhaps, to be learnt is that people in positions of responsibility must consider the ethics of their communication, whether it can be misinterpreted and how, if made public, it could be perceived.

In this case, the British Government survived. However, there could be instances in the future that a 'rogue' email could bring down a weakly placed government. And exactly the same issues are relevant to any corporation, large or small.

⊻ Case study   McLibel trial

The power of websites for PR purposes can be seen in the so-called McLibel trial. In 1990, two environmental activists, Dave Morris and Helen Steel, campaigned against the McDonald's fast food company in the UK. The activists distributed leaflets which McDonald's considered libellous and the company decided to sue the two protagonists. The case in London's High Court lasted 314 days (the longest libel and civil trial in UK legal history), and resulted in 20 000 pages of transcript and a 750-page judgment.

Morris and Steel alleged that McDonald's destroyed the environment, endangered their customers' health and provided poor working conditions and pay for their employees. Whilst they lost the case, it is widely viewed that they won the public relations war. Shortly after, Morris and Steel were served with writs to appear in court and a group of supporters launched the McLibel Support Campaign (MSC). Initially, they were focused on raising funds for the two accused. Eventually, though, they were to reach millions through the website www.mcspotlight.org. On 16 February, 1996 this website was launched from a laptop connected to the internet via a mobile phone. The website was accessed more than one million times in the first month. This site was to feature interviews, daily reports and transcripts from the trial. It was used to put forward their case and mobilise people in more than 10 countries around the world. This led to coordinated days of action against McDonald's outlets in those countries, as well as distributing the libellous leaflet.

Additionally, the case delved into a wider range of issues than most libel suits in a British court. These included human rights, animal welfare, food safety, the relation of diet to disease, the destruction of rain forests and the impact of advertising to children. All this was reported to the world through the McLibel website, as well as to the ever growing army of journalists who followed the case.

On the judgement day – 19 June, 1997 – the mcspotlight website was accessed over 2.2 million times.

Ritzer (2000) sums up the case as follows:

The judge found for McDonald's on most counts but on several matters favoured the position taken by the defendants ... But this was a pyrrhic victory for McDonald's, one that was widely seen as a public relations disaster. McDonald's spent around US$15 million on the trial, hiring the best lawyers, while the impecunious Steel and Morris defended themselves ... Several million copies of the original leaflet 'What's Wrong with McDonald's: Everything They Didn't Want You to Know' have been distributed around the world, and it has been translated into a number of languages. More important, a site created on the world wide web reports an average of 1.75 million hits a month – a total of 65 million hits by March 1999. It has become the heart of a worldwide movement in opposition to McDonald's as well as other aspects of McDonaldisation.

The McLibel Support Campaign, originally set up in 1990 just to support Steele and Morris, took on a life of its own. The McSpotlight website continues to campaign against McDonald's worldwide, receiving substantial daily hits.

In 2002, a panel of eight public relations professionals – brought together by the UK public relations industry publication *PR Week* – declared that the McLibel campaign was seventh out of a Top 20 of the most effective public relations consumer facing campaigns. The point to be made here is that McDonald's is one of the world's largest and most successful organisations with tremendous marketing leverage. The McLibel campaign, on the other hand, involved no PR firms, had no marketing budget to speak of and no backing from a large institution. However, the reputational damage of the McLibel trial to McDonald's due to the use of the internet has been estimated in millions of dollars worldwide. McDonald's may have survived; however, a less wealthy organisation may not have been so fortunate.

Sources: 'The McLibel Trial' (www.mcspotlight.org/case/trial/story.html); 'A Clash of Cultures: The McLibel Case' (www.globalexchange.org).

Word of mouth – viral or contagion marketing

Word of mouth marketing is nothing new. Both individuals and groups have, for centuries, expressed their views and thoughts on a range of subjects. Of course, those views may not have always been positive.

Yet, word of mouth marketing, or 'Buzz' as it has been called, is becoming increasingly important to marketers. As Dye (2000) suggests 'people like to share their experiences with one another ... and when those experiences are favourable, the recommendations can snowball, resulting in runaway success'. Dye (2000) has dubbed this 'explosive self-generating demand'. Yet, as we saw in the McLibel case study above, word of mouth can also have a negative impact upon organisations in terms of their overall public perception.

Today, though, it is not just a question of a company or organisation waiting and hoping that there will be positive word of mouth. Companies are actively seeking word of mouth actions through *viral marketing* (also known as *contagion marketing*). As the term suggests, word of mouth spreads like a virus or contagion through the community, infecting virtually everyone that comes into contact with it. Blackshaw (2001) suggests that 'these talkative' influential consumers will play a ... 'critical role in the future of your marketing schemes, loyalty programs, privacy policies and bottom line'. He continues to suggest that 'these [viral] ambassadors can be valuable, low-cost avenues for building existing relationships, recruiting new customers and keeping old customers happy for life' (Blackshaw, 2001).

Whilst there may be positives, we must also consider those customers who disseminate their bad experiences to others. People tend to be negative rather than positive. Thus, companies must consider that this is more than advertising; it encompasses a range of communication mix tactics.

☑ Case study   Lee Jeans (www.leejeans.com)

Lee Jeans is a leading international retailer and manufacturer of work wear, western wear and casual clothing sold in some 20 countries. Lee Clothing produces a range of branded products – Lee Jeans, Lee Dungarees and Lee Pipes. Lee Jeans is a subsidiary of the VF Corporation (www.vf.com), the world's largest publicly quoted apparel company.

By the late 1990s, Lee Jeans had rejuvenated its brand identity to appeal to the new youth market. They wanted to influence their target of males (17 to 22) who played video games and actively surfed the net. Lee Jeans created a list of 200 000 potential influencers within this target group and sent them video clips via the internet. (Khermouch and Green, 2001). The clips were not of jeans, but scenes supposedly from a series of low-budget thrillers that were of poor quality – perhaps reminiscent of some of those dreadful 1950s B-formula movies. Intrigued, the target audience sent them onto their friends, estimated to be six per person (Khermouch and Green, 2001). Lee Jeans, together with their advertising agency, created a web address where the influencers fed back their views. As a result, some 100 000 unique visitors logged on to the website (Khermouch and Green, 2001). This then linked into a TV and radio campaign, where the video clips were linked to an online computer game. To play the game at an advanced level, the target audience of 17 to 22 year olds had to buy Lee Dungarees in order to obtain the Product Identification Number on the garments. This viral marketing exercise increased US sales by 20 per cent in 2000 (Khermouch & Green, 2001).

Another example of Viral Marketing is the e-card. Increasingly, companies are using e-cards as a means of promoting a particular product, range of products or services. It works on the basis that an individual sends a friend an e-card from a particular website. Thus, this acts as a reinforcement, as it has been sent from one friend to another.

☑ Case study   e-cards Decca Classics and John Barry (www.deccaclassics.com/johnbarry)

In 2001, Decca Classics released the John Barry concept album *Eternal Echoes*. Recorded with the English Chamber Orchestra, it is an album of personal reflections on the composer's life. The music is inspired by the writings of

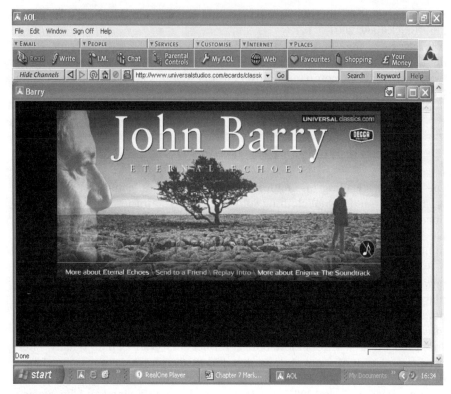

© Terry O'Neil/Decca 2003

Figure 7.3 **The Decca website for the John Barry album** *Eternal Echoes*

Barry's friend John O'Donahue and paints an image, to quote John Barry, 'of sounds, of places and objects that have always existed and always will exist. They are without beginning or end. They are infinite in our past and future.'

Decca employed various marketing techniques to promote this album. Beyond the traditional, it made effective use of the internet. On their website, they provided the following:

- Biography of John Barry.
- Video clips on *Eternal Echoes.*
- Video clips on John Barry's musical life – from the James Bond scores through to the Oscar® winning *Dances With Wolves* and his move into stand-alone classical albums.
- Extracts from the album.
- Links to other John Barry albums released by Decca Records – *The Beyondness of Things* and *Playing by Heart.*

Additionally, there is an e-card which shows a sequence of landscapes; these are combined with words to illustrate the emotion portrayed through the music. The objective is for those who have enjoyed the music to send this to a friend to alert them to the availability of the album, and direct them to the Decca/John

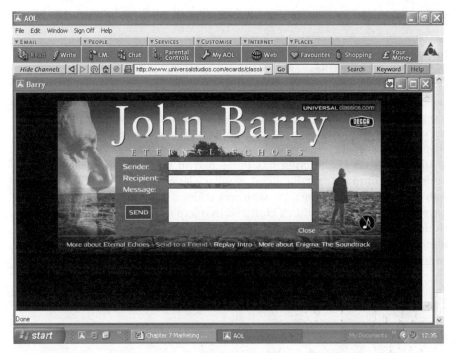

© Terry O'Neil/Decca 2003

Figure 7.4 **Opening page of the *Eternal Echoes* e-card**

Barry site. The e-card includes the sender's name and e-mail address as well as space to add a personalised message.

Those who send the e-card receive a combined acknowledgement from Decca Records and John Barry.

Figure 7.4 shows the opening pages for a web card that can be sent to friends and relatives. It is accompanied with part of a track from the album, providing some of the atmosphere of the music.

The future

In Chapter 1, we outlined the value and growth potential of the internet and world wide web. Clearly, if the analysis is valid, then these communication platforms will develop and spread significantly. In following that logic, the potential of marketing communications should also expand rapidly. However, there are concerns that internet marketing communications, especially advertising, may become as cluttered as other forms of media. Equally, the use of cookies provides ethical and security concerns. This is an issue that we will explore further in Chapter 8.

Technology continues to develop at a rapid pace. This, along with creative media planning, will provide opportunities to target specific customers with key information. This will increase relationship building with the potential to transact more goods and services.

Summary

In this chapter, we have explored a wide range of marketing communication techniques. Many of these are built upon traditional communication forms; for example, public relations. However, it is the technology that drives the physical communication potential. As we witnessed with the McLibel case study, the power of the world wide web is enormous in disseminating information. As in the case of McDonald's, the reputational damage is believed to have been significant.

Advertising via the internet has developed to become an increasing component of a company's media spend. None the less, it risks becoming a cluttered web page for the customer. As with most forms of media today, web based advertising finds itself within a cluttered marketplace. As with television advertising, companies that can create something different and/or integrate marketing communications successfully may gain a competitive position. However, within this dynamic environment, it may be a short-lived advantage.

Further reading

Michael Dell (with Catherine Fredman) (1999) *Direct from Dell: Strategies That Revolutionized an Industry*. London: HarperCollinsBusiness.

Questions for review and reflection

Go back to the two websites that you considered in the questions in Chapter 6. (We suggested opodo and lastminute.com but you might equally have chosen your own pairing).

1 How effective would you describe their communication strategy as evidenced within the websites?
2 What external evidence can you find about the two organisations? How effectively have they handled their public relations?

Notes and references

Admap (2002) 'Branding and internet advertising', *Admap*, 1 January, p. 16.
Blackshaw, P. (2001) 'Viral consumers', *Executive Excellence*, July, vol. 18, no. 7, p. 20.
Bughin, J.R., Hasker, S.J., Segel, H. and Zeisser, M.P. (2001) 'What went wrong for on-line media?', *The McKinsey Quarterly*, No. 4, web exclusive.
Cartellieri, C., Parsons, A., Rao, V. and Zeisser, M. (1997) 'The real impact of internet advertising', *The McKinsey Quarterly*, no. 3, pp. 44–63.
Chaffey, D., Mayer, R., Johnston, K. and Ellis-Chadwick, F. (2000) *Internet Marketing*. Harlow: Financial Times/Prentice Hall.

Dye, R. (2000) 'The buzz on buzz', *Harvard Business Review*, November/ December, vol. 78, no. 6, pp. 139–47.

eMarketer™ (2002) 'Online Advertising: Statistics, Strategies, Projections and Trends', *eMarketer Report*, April.

IAB (2002) 'Internet is powerful complement to traditional advertising media', Press Release, Interactive Advertising Bureau, 6 February, www.iab.net

Khermouch, G. and Green, J. (2001) 'Buzz-z … Marketing', *Business Week*, 30 July, No. 3743, pp. 50–7.

Marketing News (2002) '2002 marketing fact book', *Marketing News*, 8 July, American Marketing Association.

MediaGuardian (2001) 'Advertisers shun the net', *New Media Advertising*, MediaGuardian.co.uk., 14 August.

Perreault, W.D., McCarthy, E.J., Parkinson, S. and Stewart, K (2000) *Basic Marketing*. European edn. Maidenhead: McGraw-Hill.

Ritzer, G. (2000) *The McDonaldization of Society*, New Century Edition. Thousand Oaks, CA: Pine Forge Press.

Willman, J. (1998) 'Consumer profiles made to measure', *Financial Times*, 5 November, p. 16.

▼ 8 Relationship e-marketing

Marketers will increasingly be called upon to make more rapid decisions, acting on near real-time information. Changing the old style marketing organization to one that deals with real-time feedback puts marketing in the centre stage across the customer channels.

Erin Kinkin, CRM Analyst at Giga Group

Introduction

In the previous chapters, we have considered both the development of e-business, in the overall strategic sense, and e-marketing. In this chapter, we look further into the building of one-to-one relationships with the customer. The customer covers the full spectrum from the individual through companies to governments.

Without customers or buyers there is no business, that is basic logic. It is not rocket science but mere common sense. The difficulty, as stated in earlier chapters, is winning the customers and keeping their business. As we will see, there has been much debate regarding customer relationship management (CRM); now companies are having to adapt to *e-crm*. The word 'relationship' implies a continuing (and continuous, in some cases) involvement. Therefore, the relationship is an asset or resource to the organisation, and thus requires careful management. That is, perhaps, the real challenge for the twenty-first century. With globalisation, especially through the internet, companies face competition from all corners of the globe. Building valuable long-term relationships, both face to face and online, will be critical to survival, let alone growth.

Learning objectives

On completion of this chapter you should be able to:

1 Evaluate the role of data warehousing and data mining in building longer-term relationships;
2 Critically assess how e-businesses can win and retain customers within a global commercial environment;
3 Explain the value of mass customisation within an e-crm environment;

What is relationship marketing?

Relationship marketing (also known as one-to-one marketing, customer relationship marketing and customer relationship management) is about being
customer-focused so that mutual benefits are gained.

Before considering the contemporary views of relationship marketing in terms
of the internet, we should get back to basics. Read any book that introduces
the principles or foundation of marketing, and it will most likely outline its
overall development. Generally, it is agreed that marketing has evolved through
several orientations – production, selling and societal. Through these different orientations there have been varying and often complex relationships with
the customer.

It was in 1983 that Berry introduced the term 'relationship marketing' within a
services marketing context (Berry, 1983). However, we can argue that earlier
relationships were significant to the success of a business. Consider the merchants in medieval Europe who travelled from one town to another on a regular
basis. They were building relationships with a relatively local customer base.
It is only with the development of mass manufacturing techniques – a production orientation – that relationships (in some cases) became secondary to the
business and financial transactions. However, as Webster (1994) states, even
during the dominating production orientation phase some industrialists, such
as motor manufacturer Henry Ford, were conscious that 'building relationships'
with customers contributed to business success. Following Webster's view, we
must be careful not to assume that people's actions during a period of history
change because of manufacturing or selling technique changes. It is clear that
not all companies display a societal marketing approach today. Many are still
(especially when you look internationally) purely production and sales oriented.
Whether they have a long-term future is an issue for debate.

Berry (1983) views relationship marketing as a strategy to attract, maintain
and enhance customer relationships. Rapp and Collins (1990) go further by
stating that the goals of relationship marketing are to create and maintain
lasting relationships (our emphasis) between the company or organisation and
their customers that are rewarding to both groups. Blomqvist *et al.* (1993) provide a list of the key characteristics of relationship marketing:

- Every customer is considered an individual person or unit.
- Activities of the company or organization are predominately directed
  towards existing customers.
- The relationship is based upon interactions and dialogue.
- The company or organisation is trying to achieve profitability through the de-
  crease of customer turnover and the strengthening of customer relationships.

Here we should consider the term 'profitability' not only in the strictest financial sense of a commercial enterprise – but the profit or benefits gained by not-for-profit organisations. In this case, it may be an individual who denotes a fixed amount (for example, via direct debit facilities) to a charitable cause each month.

Grönroos (1997) suggests that many of the definitions or descriptions attributed to relationship marketing are too narrow. The view is that the relationship appears to be only between the supplier and their customer. It is clear that when a value chain approach is taken (refer to Chapter 2) and all parties are involved, the value added can significantly improve the overall marketing relationship.

Grönross (1997) and Rapp and Collins (1990) suggest that marketing communications is central to reaching customers, and the focus on relationship building leads to an interest in emphasising dialogues and creating, for example, advertising campaigns that facilitate various types of dialogues with identified and targeted customers. Reichheld (1993) states that 'building a highly loyal customer base cannot be done as an add-on. It must be integral to a company's business strategy'.

Hunt and Morgan (1994) contend that the process of relationship marketing lies in the development and growth of trust and commitment amongst partners. They define trust as a 'willingness to rely on an exchange partner in whom one has confidence and commitment ... as ... an enduring desire to maintain a valued partnership'. They suggest that trust receives positive support from communication and shared values. Relationship commitment is sustained through the same shared values together with relationship benefits and relationship termination costs (ending the relationship has a cost to be borne) (Hunt and Morgan, 1994).

The learning relationship

As Varianini and Vaturi (2000) suggest, what makes marketing via the web different is the incredible amount of real-time information that is available regarding the behaviour and interests of each customer. Peppers and Rogers (1999) believe that understanding the customer and the interactions they become involved in helps to build both a *learning relationship* and a loyal customer. To quote:

> Think of a learning relationship as one that gets smarter with each interaction. The customer tells you of some need, and you customize your product or service to meet it. Every interaction and modification improves your ability to fit your product to this particular customer. Eventually, even if a competitor offers the same type of customization and interaction, your customer won't be able to enjoy the same level of convenience without taking the time to teach the competitor the lessons your company has already learned (Peppers and Rogers, 1999).

Customer information, both real time and historical, is vital to the development of any relationship marketing approach. However, creating such information systems can be expensive, and as such may be prohibitive to new companies entering the e-business environment. The risk for such companies is that they fail to build the capabilities to monitor customer behaviour. Thus, they are in danger of failing to be in the position to nurture the relationship with their potential customers. Clearly, it is only by monitoring and incorporating such information that companies will be able to *learn* about their customers' *needs*. Perhaps the key words here are 'learn' and 'needs'. It is only by learning about customer needs that a company can react effectively.

▼ Case study   University of Texas research

A research team from the University of Texas surveyed more than 1 200 companies throughout America and Europe, representing a cross-section of business customers of all sizes. Respondents were questioned on their levels of internet integration. The team looked for true integration in several areas relating to customer business activities and objectives. The research highlighted that the more companies integrated the internet into the capabilities of their customers and suppliers, the greater the financial impact upon their business.
   The findings showed:

74 per cent of companies provided basic product information online,

but only

55 per cent of companies provided any online customisation capabilities,

and only

44 per cent of companies even notified customers of their order status.

In addition,

27 per cent of companies surveyed had some capability to report customer feedback and quality issues to their suppliers in real time. This 27 per cent displayed tremendous competitive advantages.
   However, of all the companies surveyed, only 14 per cent had online processes to share production-related information with suppliers.
   This goes back to earlier issues – (1) the importance of building relationships; (2) the importance of embracing the internet within a company's value chain operations; (3) that relationship building is more than a link between the supplier and the customer.

Source: 'Growing With the Internet: Worldwide and Direct', Michael Dell, key note address, Boston, 3 November, 2000.

In this section we have developed the theme of relationship marketing and its importance within contemporary business environments. As we progress through this chapter, the key issues discussed here will underpin our further analysis.

Table 8.1 Life time values

Potential and purchasing levels	Potential values
Mass population	This can be considered as the whole population within a district, region or, indeed, country. As globalisation develops through both the internet and 'bricks and mortar' environments, a powerful brand may consider the world as its 'mass population'.
Suspects	This is where companies start to focus on their target audience by targeting and positioning their products or services to their key audience. Companies also try and predict who will be buying in the future, what they will be buying and what are their potential motivators for buying.
Prospects	These are members of the segment who have made some form of contact. Within a web environment, the prospect may have visited the site on a couple of occasions (identified by a 'cookie'), registered a password for easy access, or requested further information to be sent via the postal service (for example, investment or insurance policy information). The aim of the company or organisation is to translate this prospect into a first time buyer. This could be achieved through introductory discounts. For example, an online bookclub may advertise 'Buy one book at full price, and choose any four books from our introductory list for UK£1.00'. This approach is not new – direct marketing companies have been using such mail based promotions for years. Now it is just translated to the internet.
First-time buyer or One-off purchase	This could be defined as a single purchase. For example, a car which may be traded in several years later but not at the dealership where it was originally purchased. This would not engender a life time value customer.
Repeat purchasing short term	This could be a few purchases over a relatively short time frame. For instance, a student on a three-year degree programme may use the same grocery store during the tenure of their programme. Once they have finished their course, they leave the university, the location and thus do not frequent the grocery store again. Whilst they may recommend the grocery store during their tenure at the university, they are most unlikely to do so after they leave – they simply have no further use for that service.
Repeat purchasing medium term	Here, we can consider a slowly emerging longer time span. In the medium term, we may be thinking of over five years. The retailer will be seeking to serve the customer on a regular basis and building upon their relationship. An example could be a book club whereby the customer purchases books that interest them, either via the post and/or over the internet. The book club may engender the relationship by offering established customers special offers.
Repeat purchasing long term (The potential for advocacy)	Ideally, this is the customer for the remaining life span of the customer. For instance, the customer may have a favourite restaurant that they frequent on a regular basis over a long period of time. The relationship that builds between the restaurant owner/staff and the customer can be a particularly strong one, even becoming friends in the process. This creates a loyalty that leads to advocacy – the recommendation to others. Of course, all things end in one way or another. The ending of this relationship may be due to several factors – the death of the customer, the death of the restaurant owner and closure of the restaurant, or the changing geodemographical landscape that leads to a major change in the location, and thus closure of the restaurant. This may, for instance, be changes in land values and property rents that force the closure of the restaurant.

Managing the relationship

As we have already seen, CRM is very much linked to creating customer reten-tion. Relationships have to be managed, and managed effectively, to have the longer-term benefits that companies seek. This becomes especially critical at times of economic slow down, reduced disposable incomes, greater price sensi-tivity and political uncertainty.

The customer life cycle

Marketers often discuss the values of product life cycle and industry life cycle. However, the customer can also be considered in terms of a life cycle. Com-panies seek to understand the life time value (LTV) of the customer, which can be varied in length. Table 8.1 provides a generalised illustration.

Table 8.2 illustrates the key positions of the cycle and their determinants.

Table 8.2 Key positions of the customer cycle and their determinants

Cycle positions	Determinants
Acquisition	An overall strategy and tactics are required to acquire the customer. This may the product or service offering and the associated marketing mix elements.
Development	The company has to understand the range of customer behavioural nuances – what drives customers' needs and buying decision making. By understanding and reacting to these, the company has the basis for building the relationship.
Retention	It is one thing winning a customer, it is clearly another being able to retain them as a customer. Customers have choice, they can be loyal to one, several or indeed no company. They can move at a moment's notice. Therefore, a company has to employ a series of actions to retain the customer's interest. Again, the need exists to add continuous value to the product or service. This could include targeted promotional campaigns, including special offers to loyal customers. An example would be an online grocery store that targets loyal customers with promotions related to the products they regularly buy.
	It should also be the aim of the company to build a relationship such that the customer becomes an ambassador or advocate for the company. Word of mouth recognition is often the greatest promotional tactic. You may want to reflect back to the previous chapter and Decca's use of e-cards to promote the composer John Barry and his CD *Eternal Echoes*. Here, it was asking customers, as well as site visitors, to email the card to friends. If you had purchased the CD and wanted to let others know about it, then this was a means of conveying both the music and the concept behind the CD.
Decline (and termination)	As in all life cycles, there is a period of decline. The customer may 'outgrow' the product or service; for example, teenagers who become adults and thus change/adapt their own lifestyles to a changing environment – family, work and so on.

Throughout the customer life cycle the company should be in communication with the customer. Continuous testing and learning is necessary if the company hopes to retain the customer over the longest time span possible.

According to Almquist *et al.* (2002), CRM encapsulates four basic principles:

1 Develop customer value growth strategies;
2 Capture and employ customer information;
3 Link value metrics to CRM initiatives;
4 Create a learning organization to accelerate value growth.

Develop customer value strategies

The objective here is to develop an effective strategy to acquire, retain and develop or grow profitable customers. The strategy needs to focus on several core values as illustrated in Table 8.3.

Table 8.3 Customer values

Core values	Requirements/outcomes
Customer selection	As with any marketing exercise, it is vital to consider the potential growth opportunities within customers themselves – the customer life cycle. An individual who buys on a regular basis over a period of years may be more profitable, over time, than someone who buys several items in one major purchase. It is not an easy analysis, as many marketers and authors would have people believe. It is often a value judgment – a critical one nonetheless.
Development of value propositions	Here, the company must consider how to add value to their propositions, and how to communicate that value. In Chapter 2, we discussed value chains (see also Chapter 9). Here again, the company must consider how to add value each step of the way. For instance, a CD store operating online can send an email to the customer stating that their order is ready for shipping and will be dispatched within two days. Therefore, the customer has been updated and knows that they will receive the CD shortly. This adds value in the relationship because the customer feels that they are an individual. Thus, if the delivery is successful, the customer may be retained.
Employee recognition of customer values	There is a perception often amongst customers that online means immediate responses. In many business areas, email has created an emotional impatience. By this we mean 'I sent you an email and now I want an immediate response'. When that response does not arrive immediately, there is an emotional aggravation. We could argue that this is becoming part of our 24/7 society. The problem or, indeed, the burden, falls upon the employee recognition of this emotional impatience. There are both human systems or strategies as well as software programs that can be used to add value here. On the basic level, a return acknowledgement email to the customer alerts the customer to the fact that (1) the email query has arrived; and (2) that it will be responded to within a set time frame.

Table 8.4 Building the service relationship

Questions	Values and requirements	Actions
What excites?	**Proactive service** Effective storage and analysis of information – data warehousing and data mining. Using information in a proactive manner. Email confirmations. As stated in Table 8.3, some companies send email confirmations when an order is placed and at the point of shipment. Advice – informing customers. A company may provide early advice or information; for example, when a particular service agreement is about to expire, with the opportunity to renew online. Also within this category is linking knowledge of the customer to their purchases. For example, an online bookstore can recommend new titles to customers on the basis of books they have previously bought and/or preferences they have stated within an online survey. **Value added service** Dynamic brokering – this is where there is greater customisation to meet the customer's own specific requirements. For example, Dell Computers offer their customers a range of options so they can build the computer to their own specifications. Where a visit to a website could be considered an 'experience' in its own right; for example, an online book store where extracts of books can be read prior to purchase. This browsing mirrors the retail experience.	**Value added**
What differentiates?	**Trust and confidence** There is an important need to create an environment of trust and confidence. The customer (wherever they are located) must have trust in both the site and the organisation behind it. Equally, there must be the confidence that the product or service will be delivered on time and to the quality standard required. If for any reason there is a failure in the system (for example, damaged goods), the customer must equally have the confidence that the goods will be replaced or money refunded. **Configuration and customisation** For some organisations, such as Dell Computing, their business is based upon configuration and customisation. Here, there is an interaction with the customer as they state the specification required. Whilst some buyers may go for a very basic specification, others may go for a complex one. It is all dependent upon current and future needs. **Information and status** The ability to provide the customer with updates on the state of their transaction (for example placing an order for a CD) confirmation of order, clearance of	**Customer centred**

Table 8.4 (continued)

Questions	Values and requirements	Actions
	credit card payment, date of shipping and (sometimes) estimated arrival time. In B2B scenarios, customers can track their deliveries by logging onto their suppliers web site. This is increasing the case in the freight forwarding industry which is a mixture of specialist and volume product driven.	
What is expected?	**Site responsiveness** Customers seek ease of navigation which includes: Limiting the information on any one page. Segmenting potential users so they can reach the parts of the site they want to read. Rapid downloads. (The problem here is that download time may be limited by the user's computer and telecommunication connections. However, overuse of graphic devices can also slow download times.). Allowing book marks at all levels. The quick and easy ability to return to selected pages. The ability to print information, both clearly and on the page. **Site effectiveness** Organizations need to test and monitor the following: How well the website meets user requirements, and suggestions for enhancements. Customer satisfaction (both objective and subjective) with the site. What is the level of quality of the outcome for the user? Task performance (for example, was it easy or difficult to order and pay for the groceries using the supermarket's online facilities?). **Fulfillment** What was the quality of the fulfilment? In a 24/7 society, many people increasingly expect rapid fulfilment of their order. In some cases, this is possible (for example, buying a ticket from the airline's website). Increasingly, the email confirmation will act as the airline ticket, being verified on arrival at the airport. In other cases, it may take several days to fulfil the order, especially where delivery of internet orders is increasingly global.	**Foundations of service**

Source: Adapted from Ward (2000).

Ward (2000) suggests that there are various building blocks that an organisation can employ to build the service relationship. Table 8.4 illustrates Ward's basic concepts. Whilst the values and requirements are compartmentalised for the purpose of this table, in reality they should be seen as integrated or blended.

Capture and employ customer information

Information is power is a truism in the twenty-first century. However, the focus of data collection, warehousing and mining must be on relevant data. Data capture must have a relevance to the customer, and not be data gathering for the sake of having as much data stored as physically possible.

Equally, there has to be a realisation that whilst historical data has a value, it can become irrelevant quickly. Both customers and markets change, thus it is vital that companies capture data that has currency.

Table 8.5   The relevancy of customer data collection

Data type	Relevancy to the customer value proposition
Value-oriented	**Revenue potential** The opportunity for cross-selling and up-selling of products and/or services. The potential to sell customer information to third-party providers (there are legal and ethical issues associated with such on-selling of information). The life time value of customer purchasing through the customer life cycle. **Cost involved in servicing value** There are variable and fixed costs associated with overall marketing spend. There is a cost involved in acquiring each new customer – from related marketing spend to administration and facility costs. The intensity of service – demands made upon the service function incur resource costs.
Forward-oriented	**Media** Use of experimental stimuli to test buying sensitivities to factors such as price, promotions, packaging, service and brand attributes. Analysis of problems associated with the website; for example, navigability. Analysis of the problems associated with current products and services. Unmet needs for products and services. People's attitude towards the brand(s). How do they perceive it?
Externally-oriented	The percentage of customer net income spent on the product and/or service. **Non-customers** Their needs and priorities. Their problems associated with competitor products and services. These might include, for example, convenient delivery times for the customer and the time span from online ordering through to delivery. Category, produce and provider usage. Perceptions of brand value and attributes. The reliability of life style data. The use and range of communication channels in placing product information in front of potential customers.

Almquist *et al.* (2002) state: 'companies must gather data that will allow
␣ to measure customer-level profitability, prioritise different initiatives and
␣ their success. Such data illuminates not only the current behaviour of
␣y's customers, but also the future priorities of current and potential customers'. Table 8.5 (adapted from Almquist *et al.*, 2002) illustrates the relevancy
of customer data collection.

As Almquist *et al.* (2002) point out, by creatively combining customer research
and behavioural, financial, and operating data, companies can identify which
elements of the customer experience – which specific touch points, service
interactions and channels – matter most to customers, and which improvements will cause the greatest lift to loyalty or value.

Link value metrics to CRM initiatives

Of course, a customer can be loyal. However, what is their value to the company
from which they purchase? Earlier we provided a generalisation of lifetime
values (Table 8.1). From that table, you can probably reflect on the potential
values derived from the customers. The one-off purchase may be in the region
of UK£20 000, for instance. However, it is a one-off purchase. For the dealership
to survive, they need several purchases of that value per week. For them, the real
return does not come from the single purchaser but from the likes of fleet car
purchasers. This type of purchaser will require a fleet of vehicles, say for their
sales staff, and with options to update models on a regular basis.

As Almquist *et al.* (2002) suggest: 'the goal should not be to increase customer
loyalty across the board, but rather to acquire, retain and develop the most
valuable customers'. There is an important link here to data warehousing and
data mining, which we briefly consider later in this chapter. What is important
to consider is the capture and analysis of the most relevant information to assist
managers in making appropriate marketing decisions.

As stated in Table 8.6, it is one thing collecting data; it is another analysing
and using the results of that data. Direct marketers have, over the years, refined
their expertise in this area. Companies within the e-environment must consider
the same or similar types of refinements if they are to maximise their growth
and development potentials. Table 8.6 further highlights the market factors that
companies should and should not consider.

The above perspectives deliver the view that companies must move towards
the analysis of customer value and that this has a direct correlation with the
management of the customer relationship over a variable time frame. However,
we must never forget that other factors can impact upon such relationships; for
example, the quality of the end product itself and whether or not the customer
believes that they have received value for money.

It is one thing to suggest that companies must take such an approach.
Such consideration may lead the company to re-appraise its approach to
the whole customer relationship issue. Now, some commentators may say that
young internet-based companies can quickly absorb such perspectives, but this

Table 8.6 Developing the most valuable customers

Stage	Actions
1	Analyse the cost of acquiring customers. Direct marketers for years have been analysing the cost of acquiring new customers whether they are in a B2B or B2C environment. The focus has been on generally developing improved revenue streams from current customers rather than seeking whole new groups. However, many factors impact upon whether people keep purchasing, including changing lifestyles and incomes. Thus, there does need to be a replenishment of the customer base from time to time, if only to remain stable.
2	Analyse the cost of maintaining individual and clusters of customers.
3	Create metrics such as life time values and customer level return on investment (ROI).
4	Identify from the metrics the most profitable or valuable customers.
5	Link this information to monthly management reporting systems to monitor values.
6	Continually review customer values and the means by which these values are measured. Within highly dynamic markets, companies must be both pro-active and reactive to changing scenarios. Within this, companies must seek to find the most effective ways to maintain customer interactions. Companies must not become complacent.

Source: Adapted from Almquist *et al.* (2002).

may not be the case. The fact that new companies may be purely internet-focused does not naturally mean that they are farsighted enough to embark upon becoming, in essence, a learning organisation in terms of customer development and retention.

One of the major reasons that so many dot.com companies collapsed in the late 1990s was not because of over saturation within the marketplace. Simply, many did not understand their potential customer base. Failure was created out of naïvety – a clear lack of understanding as to whether there was a market for their products or services or not, and how to build that market if there was one.

Whether it is a new internet-only company, or a traditional 'bricks and mortar' company expanding into the e-environment, both have to develop a positive learning organisation approach. Such an action can lead to a better understanding of customers, thus creating a potentially improved return on investment per individual customer or cluster.

Create a learning organisation to accelerate value growth

It has been suggested that in order to innovate, companies need to work towards developing learning organisations. Gavin (1993) suggests that a learning company is:

> an organization skilled in creating, acquiring and transferring knowledge, and at modifying its behaviour to reflect new knowledge and insight.

Table 8.7 Moving towards the analysis of customer value

Past analysis	Developing future analysis
This past approach to understanding business may lead to a failure to fully appreciate the complexities within the marketplace.	The objective here is to gain market and business information, effectively process that information and apply it within the realms of a dynamic environment. This may help the company foresee and react to changes within that environment.
Market share	The share of high-value customers buying from the company. Analysing how customers' purchasing may lead to changes in value delivered to the company; for instance, a customer who is an occasional purchaser may become a regular purchaser. Thus, the customer's value to the company increases – this could be significant.
	Customer acquisition rate. This is the rate at which potential customers become new customers. Of course, there is a cost in acquiring new customers. However, if they become regular long-term purchasers, then this cost is often quickly absorbed. Thus, they become profitable for the company.
	Customer retention – customer turnover rates – tenure. Here, the company needs to consider the level of customer retention and thus link to value generated. Equally, they need to understand why customers leave. This may be for various reasons, but companies are often poor at attempting to understand why. It may be a question of poor customer service or, indeed, a feeling of being isolated and not valued (a charged often levied at British banks). However, if companies fail to understand why, then the tenure of their most valuable customers may be short-lived. This will have direct results on their cash flow, long-term profitability and thus survival within the marketplace.
	Success of target programmes and promotions. All customer targeting programmes and promotions must be measureable. Whilst advertising, for instance, can be used to create brand awareness rather than straight purchasing activity, there must still be a measurement of awareness success or otherwise.
Number of customers	The level of return on investment from each customer and/or clusters of customers. The value of customers must be measurable.
	Customer lifetime value – an analysis of the life time value of each customer. Building long-term relationships may lead to repeated purchases over a longer time frame, thus delivering value to both the customer and the company.
	Depth of the relationship between the customer and the company. Relationships between customers and companies are often complex. It is important for the company and individuals to appreciate this complexity. The greater the depth of understanding between the customer and company, the greater the possibility of increased life time values being delivered to both parties.

Past analysis	Developing future analysis
	Level of spending from repeat customers. This links directly to the point above of the 'value' created by customers. The more the customer spends over a long-time frame, the greater the value to the company. Strong relationships often engender such levels of spending. Of course, the company still has to deliver value to the customer, otherwise the relationship may become strained and they switch allegiance. Customers can be unpredictable in their actions.
	Linkage to the marketing mix. It is important to analyse how customers react to the marketing mix; for example, how they react to such variables as promotion (onsite advertising and e-alerts) and price (cheaper online than instore, also the impact of postage and packaging surcharges. These surcharges can make the purchase of the product from an internet site prohibitively expensive).
	The marketing communication through the web pages may be poor compared to other sites. However, it may be the price of the product or service that actually captures the customer's imagination, and thus buying power.
Direct costs	Cost per acquisition. How much it costs to acquire a new customer against building relationships with existing potentially high-value customers.
	Conversion costs. This is often under-estimated. However, there is a cost involved in converting occasional buyers into repeat buyers. Depending upon the product or service, this may be marginal. However, building any relationship with the view to long-term value creates costs. These costs need to be considered and analysed.
	Campaign costs and efficiency. This reflects back on the point made earlier in this table about the effectiveness of any promotion. It must be measurable in terms of outcomes against costs.
	Channel usage and efficiency. With the internet, some companies have adopted a single channel approach. This may work under certain circumstances and conditions. However, it may not be replicable in all cases. Companies may need to seek a blended solution whereby several channels are developed to meet the needs of the marketplace. Once again, the analysis of these must produce measurable data. Equally, companies may need to change or mix channels depending upon market dynamics.

Source: Adapted from Almquist *et al.* (2002).

Perhaps the value of learning can be gained from this quote from Japanese management theorist Ikujiro Nonaka (1991).

In an economy where the only certainty is uncertainty, the one sure source of lasting competitive advantage is knowledge. When markets shift, technologies proliferate, competitors multiply and products become obsolete almost over-night, successful companies are those that consistently create new knowledge, disseminate it widely throughout the organization, and quickly embody it in new technologies and products. These activities define the 'knowledge-creating' company, whose sole business is continuous innovation.

We would add to Nonaka's quote that knowledge is not just about new technologies and products, although they are clearly important. The additional factor is knowledge about customers, and the dissemination of that knowledge within the organisation in order to maximise value for both the customer (primary objective) and the company (secondary objective). Get the first objective right and the second should flow from it. The issue of learning in organisations and its application to the internet is discussed again in Part Three.

Table 8.8 Commitment to learning

Level	Managerial and operational commitment
1	The leader to instigate, develop and continually support testing and learning – in terms of both motivation and resource investment. All too often a leader goes through a fad stage, then loses interest. The result is that others lose interest as they try and deal with the next CEO 'fad'. This inconsistency and lack of longer-term development can damage the business and the relationship with its customers.
2	Equally all levels of management must be committed to supporting such ideals and visions. It is easy for managers to pay 'lip service' to such visions. However, again, the lack of focus and commitment may lead to loss of customers, especially within highly competitive environments.
3	The creation and support for an organisational culture that encourages all employees to learn and share information within departments and across departments.
4	The creation, development and maintenance of training and compensation initiatives that empower and motivate employees to gather, analyse, share and learn from information. Such actions can help employees understand their customer's current and longer-term needs much more effectively and efficiently. Through such greater understanding, there is the potential to improve customer retention, and longer-term value to the business.
5	Organisations must have the flexibility to respond to, and learn from, dynamic changes within the market(s) or business environment. This flexibility may include the need to modify (to a greater or lesser degree) strategies or processes.
6	In addition to being reactive, organisations, though market research, customer analysis and competitor intelligence gathering should be proactive. Organisations must be continually monitoring both the micro and macro environmental factors and how they 'may' impact upon the business and industry. If some of the dot.com business had been proactive in such areas, they may well have prevented their own demise.

Source: Adapted from Almquist *et al.* (2002).

Later in this chapter, we discuss the value of information in building tionships – through data warehousing and data mining. The key in build customer value is aligning all the units within the organisation to the sam organisational goals. This is far easier said that done. Almquist *et al.* (2002) quote one executive as saying:

> Several divisions often have the same customers, but each one wants to have it their own way. Getting them all on the same page is like pulling teeth.

This problem is far from new. Since the Industrial Revolution of the eighteen century and dawn of mass production in the early twentieth century, there has been conflict within organisations. Additionally, it is a fallacy to think that it only happens within large monolithic corporations, micro and small businesses are equally prone to it. People in organisations need to feel comfortable in sharing information in order to grow the business. However, this is all dependent upon the leadership and management culture that infiltrates the business. Whilst it is beyond the scope of this book to consider management cultures fully, it is important to remember that such issues do impact, often critically, on the success of the organisation. Many an organisation has been brought to its knees due to failure of management to create a supportive culture, learning and sharing environment.

Table 8.8 illustrates that a company or organisation requires commitment to transform itself into a learning organisation that systematically gathers and acts upon customer information.

Permission marketing

Godin (1999 and in Nicolle, 2000) suggests that a key to successful relationship building is through permission marketing. This is where a company regularly communicates with a customer because the customer has given their 'permission' for the company to do so. This reinforces the communications process and the notion of shared values. This is not a totally new concept. Several direct marketing companies have built solid reputations through regular supporting communication. In the case of permission marketing, there is a reinforcing mechanism. By asking the prospect or customer directly, for example, 'Would you like email alerts on a weekly basis?' the company has gained the interest of that person. Additionally, and importantly, the prospect or customer wants that information.

We saw in the chapter on marketing communications that the marketplace is crowded with millions of messages. Virtually every moment of our waking lives we are bombarded with one message after another. Often these messages are unwanted and conflicting. Thus, if companies could gain:

1   Our permission for communications from them to the customer on a regular basis.
2   Elicit relevant information from the customer.

in a better position to:

and the customer

respect across the customer group, including transaction

sition to reach out to the customer with relevant informa-
and services
websites that fulfill customer needs
• Increase their return on investment per customer transaction.

∑ Case study e-mail alerts

A company can promote through its website an email alert facility whereby details can be emailed to the customer/potential customer on a regular basis. At a basic level, the website visitor may only have to input their name and email address to receive such email alerts. A company may use this basic type of information gathering as a means of updating people with the latest company news through the public relations function.

On the other hand, a publishing company, for instance, may ask the visitor to tick a range of boxes. This can provide valuable customer information way beyond the type of books they like reading; for example:

• Educational background.
• Income levels – thus potential purchasing power.
• Size of the family – if there are children, for instance, there may be an opportunity to email the parents with appropriate books.

This approach focuses clearly on the visitor's particular preferences. This has enormous potential to both publisher and customer alike. The customer knows that they will receive information on the type of books they prefer, even down to specific genres. For the publisher, there may be the opportunity to sell directly to the customer.

The value of information in relationship building

Data warehousing and data mining

In Chapter 5, we introduced the concepts of data warehousing and data mining. In this section, we expand these concepts further.

Information is critical to a company's success. For most companies, information is stored – but not analysed. However, with the right tools and techniques, it is possible to tell where a customer has been on the website, their footprint, whether they looked at something (such as a book) and did not buy it. In the future, a company will be able to make offers to individual customers in real time. But the key will be the company knowing and understanding their customers – who they are, their needs and requirements.

The advantages of data warehousing and data mining

1 Enables organisations to profile potential customers, thus reaching specific valuable sectors of their market with precisely targeted communications.
2 Enables the company to track their customers and their purchasing habits/history/preferences. Thus, the profitability of each customer or group of customers can be analysed and – importantly – calculated over time.
3 Can be used to develop and sustain repeat business through the effective and efficient use of marketing communications, thus developing the opportunity for the creation of a virtuous circle of loyalty. This, in turn, may lead to advocacy.
4 The company's decision makers can access data without affecting the use of the company's operation systems. The normal day-to-day transactions can take place whilst, for example, customer buying habits are analysed.
5 The availability of a wide range of data, which can be queried easily and quickly, can encourage users to view problems from a different perspective.
6 Data warehouses have been used successfully by organisations to, for example, (1) quantify the effects of marketing initiatives; (2) improve the organisation's understanding of its customer base; and (3) identify the organisation's most profitable revenue streams.

Kelly (1997) states that there are four business concepts that have the potential to exert substantial influence on data warehouse development. He contends that these need to be incorporated into any data development and extraction processes. These are outlined in Table 8.9.

Building a relationship marketing programme

Peppers *et al.* (1999) suggest that there are four key stages in developing a one-to-one or relationship marketing programme. In Table 8.10, we have adapted their key stages in response to e-marketing.

Relationship marketing fatigue

Earlier in the chapter we outlined the concept of emotional aggravation from the perspective of the immediacy of response. In this section, we consider the potential of fatigue generated by too much relationship building, the point where the customer is overwhelmed, and thus needs to seek escape.

Companies need to act with caution in building relationships with their customers. If the objective is to maximise the opportunities from the relationship (to mutual benefit), then the company must not burden the customer with information, or indeed special offers. Of course, under certain circumstances the customer may want daily e-alerts. This will most likely be the case in B2B scenarios with daily financial news updates.

Table 8.9 The four business concepts influencing data warehouse development

Business concept	Action
Value exchange	The concept of value exchange holds that increased profitability can best be achieved through a better understanding of the profitability of individual customers. Profitability is enhanced through the acquisition and retention of high-value customers, by leveraging the relationship with these customers to sell them a wider range of products, and by extending the period that these customers remain loyal to the enterprise. (Reflect back to Table 8.1, Life time values)
Disintermediation	This concept is based upon the principle that organisations with direct access to end-customer data will have a significant advantage over organisations that service customers through intermediate channels. Disintermediation is the process of removing the intermediary and dealing directly with the end customer. Avon cosmetics, for example, built their reputation of dealing directly with their customers through direct marketing campaigns. Today, they have added web based purchasing to enhance their blended direct marketing. Increasingly, manufacturers are providing, through the internet, the ability for their end-customer to purchase online directly from them.
Disaggregation	This is the process of breaking down mass markets into separate discrete segments and niches. Each of these segments requires a separate response from the organisation in terms of the full range of the marketing mix. (Reflect back to Chapter 5 and the development of the marketing mix.)
Mass customization	This is the logical conclusion of the process of disaggregation, in which the organisation finally deals with each individual customer on the basis that they represent a unique segment of one. Dell Computers is an example of a company that asks their customers to tailor their own products. Thus, the customer chooses the computer to match their needs and wants, rather than the computer retailer.

Source: Adapted from Kelly (1997).

We need, however, to consider this beyond just the realms of the internet. If companies have opted for integrated or blended solutions, then emailed alerts are not the only channel of communication. Here, it is critical that the company marshals that information effectively so that the customer is not just receiving emailed information – but also via the postal services and telephone (see the section 'Create a learning organisation to accelerate value growth' on p. 163. Here, it demonstrates the need for companies to pool information (data warehousing) and for departments to work together.

Permission marketing goes some way towards alleviating the risk of relationship fatigue by empowering the customer (to some extent at least). However, this 'permission' should not be taken for granted. There needs to be a process whereby the customer can reduce or increase the level of contact to suit their needs, on an ongoing basis. However, the Catch 22 here might be that the

Table 8.10 The four key stages of an e-marketing programme

Stage	Driver	Commitment – action
1	Identifying customers	'Bricks and mortar' retailers or established direct marketing companies who are developing a website may already have a database of segmented customers. For them, it is relatively easy to present customers with the added value of purchasing via a website; an example would be a book club. For companies launching purely as websites, the task is much greater. However, potential customers provide a source of valuable information. They can also become first-time buyers, then repeat buyers. The customer needs to be recognised each time they log on to the site – this is the value that cookies and/or passwords offer in terms of understanding customer behaviour more effectively.
2	Differentiating customers	Customers are generally different in two key ways: they represent different levels of value and they have different needs. This is where the company needs to reflect upon the customers potential life time value, thus allowing the company to focus its resources effectively; for example, some B2B information sites have different levels of entry onto the site. Level 1 may be free. This provides a basic level of information, perhaps the week's business news. Level 2 may be charged at a basic rate. This provides the week's news in addition to archive searches. Level 3 may be a premium rate that not only provides the above information – but research data as well. Customers can choose the level best suited for their needs. The company can then marshals its resources to focus on the premium level customers.
3	Interacting with customers	Whilst companies need to interact with their customers, this must be both cost efficient and effective. Peppers *et al.* (1999) believe that every interaction with a customer should take place in the context of all previous interactions with that customer. Therefore, the company needs the database facilities to warehouse (store) and mine that information. Dell Computers, for instance, seeks to develop a highly interactive dialogue with customers in order to find the right product options for them. Other companies working to create online communities and enhancing customer identification with the brand are Disney and Nestlé's Nescafé.
4	Customising the product and/or service	This is where the company needs to put the learning relationship into practice. Tailoring the product or service to match the customer's needs and wants (1) increases the learning relationship; (2) builds loyalty and the customer relationship; and (3) firmly links the customer to the company. These three points should be considered as a reinforcing loop, rather than singular independent issues. Again, Dell Computers has been successful in mass-customising their products to meet customers' needs and wants. (Refer to Table 8.9).

Source: Adapted from Peppers *et al.* (1999).

company has to contact the customer directly in order to seek that knowledge, thus adding to the potential for fatigue. The remedy, when it comes, may be in the form of software, placing the control firmly in the hands of the customer. When that day arrives, companies will have to be both proactive and reactive to maintain their customer base, especially their profitable one. What they will also need to do is be truly sensitive to the customer, rather than paying lip service. Those who are not 'sensitive' to the customer's real needs, concerns and desires risk going the way of the dot.com companies.

The future

The combination of

- management techniques
- improved computing power
- improved technical communications (through broadband or similar systems)
- improved customer relations software (including data warehousing and data mining systems)
- the development of learning organisations building upon internal knowledge and
- a customer-focused organisational culture

should deliver meaningful customer relationship management or one-to-one marketing. The technology is the tool by which this relationship is operationalised. But, whatever medium is used, it is people who eventually communicate. That needs to be the focus for the future – that it is still a 'people business'.

Summary

Arnott and Bridgewater (2002, referring to Reichheld, 1996) state that the:

> Creation of a loyal and satisfied customer base is an important determinant of marketing success, as research shows that loyal customers buy more of a company's products, are cheaper to serve, less sensitive to price and bring in more customers by word of mouth.

This is nothing new. It has perhaps been the backbone of marketing for generations. Some authors (Furash, 1999 and Walsh and Godfrey, 2000) have focused upon the interactive potential of the internet, even suggesting the feasibility of targeting a 'segment of one'. Arnott and Bridgewater (2002) suggest that if that is possible, then that would allow marketers to build stronger relationships with customers, for mutual gain. This is already possible. The key, as we have studied, is understanding the volatility of the environment that the internet operates within.

As Peattie and Peters (1997) suggested, marketers can now engage customers on a global scale, in real-time, two-way interactions. The internet has moved significantly since then in terms of global reach, and being part of a company's operational strategy. Strong 'lock-in' relationships can be created to create a virtuous circle of loyalty. However, this can only be maintained if the company understands the customer's needs and wants and actively seeks to serve those needs and wants.

Whilst there are enormous gains to be made by building such relationships online, equally, companies need to be cautious that they do not create relationship fatigue as a result. There are times when the customers may be burdened by the sheer input of information, whether it is via the computer, mobile phone or both. Such overload can place at risk the long-term relationship with the customer. That could spell disaster for the business.

Further reading

George Day (1999) *The Market Driven Organization – Understanding, Attracting, and Keeping Valuable Customers.* New York: Free Press.

Questions for review and reflection

1 What might be some of the potential drawbacks in data warehousing and data mining for a company with a sizeable internet presence?
2 Are there any ethical issues relating to e-CRM?

Notes and references

Almquist, E., Heaton, C. and Hall, N. (2002) 'Making CRM make money: Technology alone won't create value', *Marketing Management,* May/June. pp. 17–21.

Arnott, D.C. and Bridgewater, S. (2002) 'Internet, interaction and implications of marketing', *Marketing Intelligence & Planning,* vol. 20, no. 2, pp. 86–95.

Berry, L.L. (1983) Relationship marketing in *Emerging Perspectives on Service Marketing.* Berry, L.L., Shostack, L. and Upaih, G. (eds). Chicago: American Marketing Association.

Bloomqvist, R., Dahl, J. and Haeger, T. (1993) *Relation-Smarknadsforing. Stategioch Metod for Servicekonkurren* (Relationship Marketing Strategy and Methods for Service Operations). Goteborg: IHM Golag.

Furash, E.F. (1999) 'Why banks may be getting it wrong – and how to get it right', *Journal of Retail Banking Services,* vol. 21, no. 2, pp. 37–43.

Gavin, D. (1993) 'Building a learning organisation', *Harvard Business Review,* vol. 71, no. 4, pp. 87–92.

Godin, S. (1999) *Permission Marketing.* London: Simon & Schuster.

Grönroos, C. (1997) From marketing mix to relationship marketing – towards a paradigm shift in marketing. *Management Decision,* vol. 5, no. 3–4, pp. 322–40.

Hunt, S. and Morgan, R. (1994) 'The commitment-trust theory of relationship marketing'. *Journal of Marketing,* vol. 58, pp. 20–38.

Kelly, S. (1997) 'The Future of Data Warehousing', *Monograph 20*, Data Warehouse Network Monograph Series.

Nicolle, L. (2000) 'Selling is easier if you ... gain permission', E.business Review, *Computer Weekly*, June, vol. 1, no. 4, p. 31.

Nonaka, I. (1991) 'The knowledge-creating company'. *Harvard Business Review*, vol 69, no. 6, pp. 96–104.

Peattie, K. and Peters, L. (1997) 'The marketing mix in the third age of computing', *Marketing Intelligence & Planning*, vol 15, no. 3, pp. 142–50.

Peppers, D. and Rogers, M (1999) *Enterprise One-to-One*. London: Piatkus.

Peppers, D., Rogers, M and Dorf, B. (1999) 'Is your company ready for one-to-one marketing?', *Harvard Business Review*, vol. 77, no. 1, pp. 151–61.

Rapp, S. and Collins, T. (1990) *The Great Marketing Turnaround*. New Jersey: Prentice Hall.

Reichheld, F.F. (1993) 'Loyalty-based management', *Harvard Business Review*, vol. 71, March/April, pp. 64–73.

Reichheld, F.F. (1996) *The Loyalty Effect*. Boston: Harvard Business School Press.

Ryan, C. (2000) 'How disintermediation is changing the rules of marketing, sales and distribution', *Interactive Marketing*, vol. 1, no. 4, April/June.

Varianni, V. and Vaturi, D. (2000) 'Marketing lessons from e-failures', *McKinsey Quarterly*, no. 4, pp. 86–98.

Walsh, J. and Godfrey, S. (2000) 'The Internet: a new era in customer services', *European Management Journal*, February, vol. 18, no. 1, pp. 85–92.

Ward, R. (2000) *Managing Complexity*. London: Economist Books/Profile Books.

Concluding case study to Part II

The following case study examines the launch of J.K. Rowling's book *Harry Potter and the Order of the Phoenix* in 2003. This became a mega-sales hit within a matter of days. However, the marketing behind the scenes included effective and efficient use of the internet. The case study illustrates the various functions of marketing that have been discussed within this section of the book. Moreover, it demonstrates the power of e-marketing and e-business in generating sales for a product or service.

⚄ Case study   Harry Potter™

Since the launch of J.K. Rowling's first book *Harry Potter and the Philosopher's Stone* in 1997, the Harry Potter™ series has become a global publishing and movie phenomenon. The subsequent books (five in all) have sold a staggering 190 million copies (as of June 2003) worldwide. Merchandising as a result of both the books and the two movies (as of July 2003) has generated an estimated £1billion in revenue.

Harry Potter and the Order of the Phoenix (also known as 'Harry Potter 5') was launched simultaneously in 150 countries on 21 June, 2003.

Below, we outline several of the key e-business and e-marketing issues that have help propel J.K. Rowling's books into the global marketplace.

Web sites

A random, non-scientific survey suggests that there are over 3 million sites related in some way or another to Harry Potter™. However, many of them will be 'repeated' sites; these are sites that are listed several times within any one list.

Generally speaking, the websites can be sub-divided into direct and indirect websites. The direct focus purely on the Harry Potter™ books, whilst the indirect include the Harry Potter™ books as part of their wider portfolio of discussions, perhaps on literature.

Direct

Various web sites has been developed to either market or discuss the Harry Potter™ character and stories. These range from the Bloomsbury site (the publishers) to the BBC and their Harry Potter™ Phenomenon site. Moreover, there are a vast number of Harry Potter™ supporter sites. Bloomsbury's website (www. bloomsbury.com/harrypotter) contains an array of features including:

Interviews
Message board
e-Cards
News
Frequently asked questions
Competitions
Screensavers

Indirect

These will include book review sites such as www.cool-read.co.uk that focus on children's literature.

Both the direct and indirect sites include a growing number of user communities where like-minded people can discuss and debate issues. The Harry Potter™ books have probably become the most talked about books in the history of publishing. This is ideal material for user communities who will reinforce the books' promotion through word-of-mouth or viral marketing. (See Chapter 13, Developing user communities.)

Internet promotions and sales

Online retailers such as Amazon.co.uk heavily promoted *Harry Potter and the Order of the Phoenix*. Prior to the launch, Amazon.co.uk reported advanced orders of more than 300 000 of its half-price copies in the UK. Globally, it is believed that Amazon received some 1.3 million pre-orders.

The recommended retail price for the hardback of *Harry Potter and the Order of the Phoenix*, in the UK, was £16.99. However, a fierce price war developed between supermarkets, books shops and online retailers. As can be seen from the following listing, there was significant discounting.

Online price plus postage and packing

Amazon.co.uk	£8.49 + £2.75
Blackwell.co.uk (online division of the retailer and publisher)	£13.99 free p&p
Sainsburys (supermarket)	£9.99 + £2.75
Tesco.com (supermarket)	£7.64 + £2.75
TheBookPlace	£10.99 + £2.75
WHSmith.co.uk (online/bricks and mortar retailer)	£11.89 + £2.99

It is evident from this table that Tesco.com were selling this as a loss leader, thus using it as a vehicle to gain other purchases from customers at the same time.

On its first day, over 1.7 million copies of the book were sold in the UK alone. However, with heavy discounting amongst both bricks and mortar and online retailers, it is likely that few actually generated significant margins for their bottom line. According to Nielsen Bookscan, the USA saw first day sales totalling some 3.9 million copies.

Web cast

On Thursday, 26 June, a live web cast was held at London's Royal Albert Hall before an audience of some 4500, mainly children. Actor and broadcaster Stephen Fry, who introduced J.K. Rowling, hosted the web cast. During the event, Rowling answered questions and read from her new book. This web cast, presented amongst others by MSN, provided the opportunity for a global audience to see Rowling and hear her views on Harry Potter™. The web cast remained available for downloading for a week after the event. Those unable to see it as a live event could then view it offline.

Associated logistics

It is, of course, one thing to order a product online and perhaps quite another receiving delivery of that product by a certain date. Physical distribution of *Harry Potter and the Order of the Phoenix* remained a critical issue for online retailers.

Amazon.co.uk's aim was to fulfil all its orders on the morning of 21 June (launch day). Some 420 000 books were despatched on Friday night by Amazon. co.uk for delivery by the Royal Mail the next morning. It is estimated that all online pre-orders in the UK totalled some 500 000 for delivery on the Saturday morning. This operation became the largest distribution of a single item in e-business to date.

Harry Potter is the copyright and trademark of Warner Bros., 2000™.

Sources: *The Sunday Times* online; Rich List 2003; Lewis, R. and Rickett, J. (2003) 'Harry fever reaches peak: The biggest launch in bookselling history holds challengers'. *The Bookseller*, 13 June, p. 9; Lewis, R. (2003) 'Chains reveal their Harry Potter prices', *The Bookseller*, 13 June, p. 1; Finlay, J. (2003) 'JK, 4000 kids and me. The Harry Potter Phenomenon', BBC News Online, 26 June; 'Potter deliveries disappoint few', BBC News Online, 23 June, 2003.

Part III

▼ Implementing e-business

In Part I, we looked at the key impact of the internet on business in broad strategic terms. In Part II, we looked specifically at marketing, as this is probably the area which offers the greatest potential for internet driven change.

In this part, we shall look at the main areas related to implementation of e-business strategies, those of operations, human and organisational behaviour, and lastly finance. In each case, we shall take a non-specialist perspective, addressing the issues that general managers are likely to want to have answered, rather than dealing with specific IT technicalities. In keeping with the over-all theme of this text, we shall try to minimise the amount of time-critical information, which might be overtaken by new developments quite quickly, in favour of longer-term trends and potentialities.

☑ 9 Operational implications of the internet

Introduction

An organisation can be viewed in many ways. One of these is in terms of finance, where the organisation is conceived fundamentally in terms of capital, costs and revenues. An alternative perspective is that of the impact of the organisation's activities on the customer, where every element of the organisation and its work is evaluated in terms of how it might add to the customer experience. Operations is another overall perspective on organisational activity. This looks at what an organisation is doing in terms of how and where it brings in its key inputs, how and where it stores items of value until these are needed, how the value relocates to the appropriate points (that is, how the organisation brings the various elements together to create products or services) and how that ensuing service or product is then delivered to the customer or beneficiary.

Within this sequence the impact of the internet is likely to be highly differentiated, depending on issues such as whether or not the service involved is digitable, and how far the consumer has sufficient resources to benefit from internet delivered services or products. Amongst the various areas of operational management, perhaps the biggest transformation has been in the supply chain. Much of the development so far relating to supply chain management is bound up with the processing of transactions. Towards the end of the chapter, we shall also look very briefly at other aspects of the way the internet is changing business, such as the potential for distant controls on processes alluded to in Part 1.

Learning objectives

On completion of this chapter you should be able to:

1 Identify the key features of supply chain management that are affected by internet operations;
2 Describe some of the key issues that pertain to the processing of transactions on the web;
3 Describe the differences between specific types of internet marketplace;
4 Evaluate the current and potential future roles of trading intermediaries.

The supply chain

Within the supply chain we can identify a number of distinct elements:

- Preparation of purchasing requirements and specifications.
- Identification of potential suppliers.
- Negotiating/agreeing deliverables – specification, volumes, price, delivery and timing.
- Completing transactions.
- Receiving and holding supplies.
- Ensuring timely location of supplies to the appropriate places for operations to run as planned.
- Long-term monitoring of the relationships with suppliers and the value that they deliver to the organisation.

What we will find is that the internet creates greatly expanded opportunities in just about every one of these areas, but the greatest area of development so far has been in the area of *procurement* [1] – the process of purchasing materials and supplies (which includes not only actual transactions but the identification or *sourcing* of potential suppliers, evaluation of different sales packages, negotiation of terms, delivery and invoicing). The focus of this discussion is primarily the B2B sector. This sector has seen an explosion in internet commercial activity in recent years, and in value by far outweighs the other kinds of internet relationships, such as B2C, G2C or C2C. Much of this activity is related to the procurement of so-called *MRO* goods (maintenance, repairs and operations). The prime reason for this is that such goods allow for both detailed specification and high volume transactions, which is one of the areas which can benefit most from the increases in speed and geographical reach that the internet can bring.

The context of supply chain management

The internet is transforming the management of the supply chain for many organisations, but it would be misleading to regard this series of changes as solely *driven* by the internet itself. The development of the management of supply and/or logistics in the last few decades has demonstrated several themes, which the introduction of the internet has accelerated tremendously, but the themes themselves are generic business issues. These include:

- Continuing pressure on costs of supplies (thus influencing market prices), both as investors seek improvements in ROI and as increased competition drives prices down.

---

[1] We have already encountered e-procurement in Part Two. The thrust of the current discussion will be on the operational aspects of this phenomenon.

- Continuing pressure on the costs of procurement – the sourcing and purchasing of supplies (thus creating a demand for greater efficiency in the procurement process).
- Demands to reduce the costs of physical storage and warehousing.
- (Related to the previous point) the corporate financial implications of large quantities of stock raw materials and work in progress (for example, effects on balance sheets and on volumes of working capital needed).
- Increasing degrees of quality needed as specifications of products and processes become more precise.
- Time-to-market and time-to-delivery (as reflected in the concept of just-in-time operations) becoming ever more important components of competitive advantage, and thus requiring products and services to be developed more quickly, and delivered more quickly.
- The general trend of large manufacturers and retailers to want to exercise greater control over the quality, cost, and delivery times of their supplies.
- Growing preferences for working in partnership with a small range of suppliers, to avoid the twin disadvantages of overreliance on one, or failure of influence over many.

These and other trends are not in themselves *about* the internet or directly internet generated, but they have all been affected by the opportunities offered by the internet. What is clear is that many of the largest firms that have been able to develop and enhance their competitive advantage in the area of logistics have done so in virtue of their internet strategies. The web has *facilitated* developments that have been happening in any case.

Supply chain networks and upstream/ downstream B2B

The term 'supply chain network' means more than simply those organisations that deliver services to a business; for example, by selling them raw materials. It really refers to the whole of the primary value chain, covering not only the direct suppliers to an organisation, but the *internal* movement of goods and services between one part of a business and another, and the *onward* delivery of goods and services to the customer – who, in a B2B context, are also businesses, using your products as supplies to their own process, just as your suppliers have received goods and services from other organisations. The concept of *supply chain management* refers to the overall processes of supply in this broad sense and the activities that managers need to undertake to make sure these work effectively and help to provide competitive advantage for commercial businesses.

It is convenient to refer to the supply chain that leads into an organisation as its *upstream* supply chain (on an analogy with a river or pipeline – the goods and services that flow into the business) and to the supply chain that leads from the organisation to its own customers as the *downstream* supply chain. Strictly speaking this can be endless, but taking an example of a physical product to be retailed to the public, the visible elements of the supply chain are:

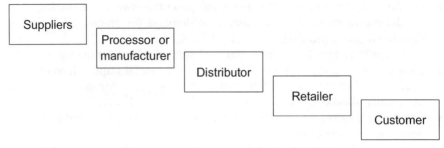

Figure 9.1 **Production oriented supply chain**

For a service organisation, the basic linear model still works, but in this case there is less of a 'processor' or 'distributor' element, hence the sequence looks rather like the following:

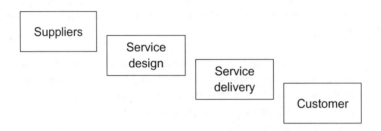

Figure 9.2 **Service oriented supply chain**

The whole nexus of what goes on in order for a company to receive stocks of, say, metal staples, then, is the *upstream* supply chain, and the linkages that flow on from the sale of, say, student writing or exercise books (which use the staples) are the *downstream* supply chain. In some cases, the real level of strategic importance of the downstream supply chain may end quite quickly – supplying a group of schools with durable exercise books that are non-toxic is probably as far as an organisation might need to consider in this particular market. But in other cases, this line may extend further, for legal as well as for customer relationship reasons. For example, the producer of radioactive materials may be required to ensure that their customer not only has adequate safety procedures for handling the goods, but also has clear policies on what they will do with the material, how they will dispose of waste, to whom they might sell on the materials, security procedures to prevent theft by terrorists, and so on.

Supply chains will differ depending on the nature of the activities that they supply. One can distinguish between production modes that involve continuous, or more discrete, responses to the customer. Many organisations will work on a *continuous replenishment* or stock building basis. This clearly is efficient where the product involved is standardised and sales, although fluctuating, have a degree of constancy. Where, however, there is a demand for a more customer specific product, or where the product or service does not sell on a rolling basis, then an organisation may adopt a more *customised* strategy, building to order or even adopting a distributed or channel production process (the latter being where a number of different locations are involved in preparation of different elements of an item that are then brought together subsequently for the customer).

In keeping with the comments made at the start of this chapter, these are all generic supply chain issues, but they underline some of the challenges for any internet based approach to the management of the supply chain, in particular these three related questions:

How much *trust* to place in a particular supplier?

How much *shared information* between supplier and customer?

How much *control* to exercise over the supplier's activities?

What we will see is how different approaches to electronic operations resolve these questions.

Intermediaries

Figures 9.1 and 9.2 of this chapter greatly oversimplify the actual supply chain, but even here we can see evidence for parties other than the supplier manufacturer and customer being involved in a transaction. For the average sale to take place, there are often several intermediaries, providing services that help facilitate the transaction, such as:

Brokers: finding buyers and sellers and often conducting the negotiations for each party, sometimes also finding the finance and handling the physical handover of money or goods.

Wholesalers: holding goods for a specific industry in bulk, from which the retailer can then purchase what they require in smaller volumes than the manufacturer usually ships, reducing the amount of research an organisation might need to do to identify and evaluate potential suppliers of a certain item (often called *sourcing* activity).

Distributors: transporting goods from manufacturer to wholesaler, retailer or even customer (often an organisation may offer both warehousing as well as distribution services).

Retailers: providing a range of goods for the consumer, in effect therefore relieving them of the burden of sourcing suppliers and evaluating each individually.

In addition to these agents that may help facilitate the sale of goods between one party and another, in the internet environment there has grown up an additional type of intermediate service, one of providing information on customers to trading firms. These *infomediaries*, as they are called, collect information from sources such as online questionnaires, and then sell their databases on to retail companies who may use the data to trigger advertising or even to generate specific leads for sales. Clearly, in some cases this can be regarded as an abuse of privacy, and violates the idea that one should have the opportunity to exercise some control over the way an organisation presents itself to you. Nevertheless, it is a major form of intermediation over the world wide web currently – whether it will remain so is a matter of how far such an approach may respect or abuse the rights of the consumer.

These intermediate activities add significantly to the costs of any transaction. Consistent with the impact of internet developments on the role of intermediaries has been a general recognition of the importance of managing their role in commercial processes to reduce correspondingly some of the costs of trading (sometimes called transaction costs). This trend towards limiting the role of intermediaries is known generally as *disintermediation*. In some cases, the internet has facilitated a complete elimination of these, in others a realignment of their role and function.

It is important to recognise that although intermediaries add to the direct costs of any transaction, this does not mean that they are economically undesirable. Turban and King (2003) have identified five distinct benefits that an intermediary may bring to a transaction, whether electronically or physically facilitated:

- *Search costs*: For an organisation to trawl through directories and catalogues finding out who supplies, say, metal staples is a long affair that consumes significant administrative and sometimes managerial time; an intermediary, such as a broker or a wholesaler, does all this as part of their role.
- *Lack of privacy*: In some cases, a buyer or seller may wish to remain anonymous (it may be that if it becomes widely known that the Virgin Group, for example, is trying to buy cruise ships, then the industry immediately knows they are trying to enter this market and the main players will be able to take advantage of the start-up times to take action to minimise the impact, so the new entrant is at a competitive disadvantage); a broker can act for an *anonymous* buyer or seller and thus protect their privacy.
- *Incomplete information*: Any buyer or seller will carefully manage the information they disclose to the other party relating to the sale; a specialist intermediary can have access to a wider range of sources of information that they can provide to help one or other (or both) parties to conclude a transaction.
- *Contract risk*: One or other party to a transaction may fail to honour their commitment; this may be a refusal to pay or supply at all, a failure to deliver the goods safely, so that they are lost or damaged in transit, or a failure to meet specifications; intermediaries such as carriers and payments agencies (such as credit card companies) reduce these risks for the parties to the transaction by taking these risks themselves.
- *Pricing efficiencies*: Generally, an intermediary has a much better understanding of the market they operate in day-to-day than the supplier, or

especially the purchaser who may well enter that market much less frequently; hence, intermediaries can help both parties to reach mutually advantageous trades more easily.

All these are important functions that different intermediaries can and do fulfil. Nevertheless, it is understandable that any organisation will take advantage of any facility that enables them to achieve the same benefits without having to pay a broker or wholesaler or whoever. A number of the initiatives that we describe in this chapter represent ways in which organisations can reduce or restructure the use they make of different agents that smooth the path between producer and ultimate consumer.

One of the simplest forms of disintermediation is direct selling from a website. For example, most major publishing houses today have a website from which one can order books. In practice, only a small number of sales come from this channel. There are several reasons why this approach does not always work well. In the case of a relatively simple consumer good such as a book, one disadvantage of ordering from a single publisher site is that there are no alternatives to make comparisons against – 'if I am not sure whether I like one publisher's celebrity cookbook, I may have no other to consider and compare with. If I just want to browse, then it is clear that I will do better with a large general bookseller (and, in fact, many people feel that browsing for books is usually more effective in physical bookshops than on the internet)'.

In the case of more complex services, then it may be necessary for the seller to engage in some process of identifying and understanding the buyer's needs before attempting a transaction. In some cases, such as financial investment services, it would be illegal in the UK (and many other western countries) to conduct a sale directly without an attempt to protect the interests of a private investor. In other cases, it may be that the kinds of services are too specific to be resolved automatically.

One area where the supply chain is beginning to erode is with large food supermarkets, several of whom have developed online 'malls'. In the case of the big UK supermarkets which have gone down this route, the mall is really no more than a lists of items and their prices. It seems to work for well established customers who order repeats of their weekly core family purchases (milk, butter eggs, bread, and so on) but this approach loses out tremendously on the elaborate psychology of impulse buying that the modern physical supermarket design is intended to stimulate, with the result that the general expenditure per head in online supermarkets is lower than that in physical stores (quite apart from the fact that some people simply do not trust their choices of apples to someone else).

In practice, when these are successful, online supermarket sites are less a matter of reducing reliance on third party intermediaries, as the major supermarkets are highly integrated operations that in some cases involve farm to store supply chains, including food processing, packaging, warehousing and transportation. So, these supermarkets are aiming basically at reducing their own costs by transferring some of their customers over to a non-physical presence. This can be done successfully; witness the transfer by the (then)

Midland Bank (now part of the HSBC group) of many of their retail banking customers over to branchless banking via the FirstDirect subsidiary – originally a telephone bank but now including a telephone and online channel. But in the long term, an online site will only work for a retailer if they can reduce physical costs – in Midland's case, there was a branch closure programme that operated more or less alongside the growth of FirstDirect.

So, whilst the reduction in the use of intermediaries is a significant motivation for the development of online sales systems and supply lines, it is by no means the only way in which an organisation can reduce its transaction and trading costs.

As one preliminary example of how the internet changes the role of intermediaries to a transaction, interestingly one which covers B2C and C2C activities, consider the process by which someone would have sought a job pre-1994 or so:

- Deciding what kind of job they want.
- Gathering information about which organisations want to employ people to do that job (generally via newspaper or journal advertisements or employment agencies).
- Comparing different jobs as advertised.
- Making an application.
- Being selected.

Consider too the supply side of this, the process that the organisation would have gone through in order to employ someone:

- Decide on the kind of job and the qualities the person needs to have, as well as salary and so on.
- Advertise the role, perhaps internally as well as externally, through agencies or newspapers.
- Send out further information and respond to enquiries.
- Receive applications and sort these.
- Make a selection using methods such as interviews.

Now compare one characteristic approach that someone might adopt today:

- Go on to 'Ask Jeeves' and ask 'How can I find a job?
- Select one of the options that Jeeves offers ('I can answer the question "How can I find a job in London?" ')
- The enquirer then finds themselves on a proprietary website – in one case conducted as an illustration on the 1 April, 2003, one of the authors found themselves directed to a site called 'This is Jobs', a sub-site of the 'This is London' website, which is the internet arm of the main London post-breakfast daily newspaper, the *Evening Standard*.

  A banner navigation bar indicates that there is a jobs, homes and travel section of the site – in effect, the site is an electronic version of the copious small ads section of the newspaper. Inspection of the central frame indicates that the person seeking a job can search by region (all London, London

Central, West, North and so on) by salary and by job type (including an additional keyword as well as a range of site-supplied categories such as 'education and training' or 'catering'). But also there is a wide range of additional services. The job-hunter can have their own 'profile' section where they can save results of searches, they can submit their CV, they can receive advice on job hunting, they can ask for email alerts of suitable vacancies, they can be linked through to a separate site for a psychometric assessment. With the exception of the last of these, the rest is free. Once one accesses an advertised job, there is a contact telephone number or email address – many of the advertisers, incidentally, are recruitment agencies.

- There is also a page for 'employer services' which will help an organisation design and place advertisements, for example.

What has happened here? The *Evening Standard* has long been a place where Londoners could look for jobs – often short term or lower level jobs were advertised there. The website has expanded this by *integrating* both upstream and downstream in the job hunting process. The individual finds that a large amount of the work they formerly had to do themselves has now been taken over by the website – in a similar fashion to the way a physical recruitment agency might give candidates advice on CVs, interview technique and so on, as well as actually sourcing jobs. The organisation finds that some of the work they formerly had to do themselves, or pay a hefty commission to an agency to do, such as designing job adverts, receiving applications, searching lists of CVs, and so on, is done by the website for them.

Online recruitment services of this kind are now common on the web. Some (such as Monster.com) cover every industry and almost every level and grade, and include services such as online submission of applications using a stand-ardised format. Others may be functionally specific – for example, for secretarial roles – and others may be industry specific – for example, as mentioned before, the site www.jobs.ac.uk deals with posts at all levels in higher education insti-tutions in the UK.

Is this 'disintermediation'? In one sense, the employer is reducing the number of different agents they might use in order to employ someone, though not all of these are intermediaries in the traditional sense of the term (for example, some of the activities undertaken by online recruiters might, in some circumstances, be done by human resource consultants). But in some cases, all these activities would have been done internally, with the job advert placed in a newspaper being the only use of any kind of intermediate element in the process. What has happened is not necessarily a reduction in the use of intermediate agents, but a change in the degree and depth of these, and in this case a reduction in the number of intermediate agents. One could as easily call this *re-intermediation* as disintermediation.

The point about this example is to indicate one example of how online facilities can change the nature of the transaction, increasing the possibilities open to the parties concerned. But it also indicates that the impact of this change is not necessarily to reduce or eliminate certain functions and tasks, but rather to reconfigure them. Recall the points made earlier, that intermediaries fulfil a range of functions. Unless an organisation can cost effectively take these on themselves, then there remains a value in using external intermediaries for some or all of these. What may change is not the fact that intermediaries are used, but the manner in which they are used and the range of services that they can provide.

Not all such re-intermediated services are welcomed. Some employers do not wish to relinquish control over job applications or job trawling activities, for example, even though it can be done extremely quickly via an online facility. The argument here is that sometimes an unusual candidate can appear who does not quite meet the set criteria but would strike the person experienced in a specific industry or looking for a specific kind of role, when an automated facility might simply cast them aside as outside the specification. In other areas, an organisation may feel that to share information with an infomediary (which can bring the benefits of receiving information back from them relating to the whole industry) may result in the loss of competitive advantage.

At the end of the last section, we presented three interlinked questions relating to the potential internet based operational or supply chain initiatives; these related to trust, information sharing and management control. The trend towards reducing intermediaries is, as we have seen, as much about reframing the packages of services that an online intermediary can provide as it is about eliminating them. The decision to disintermediate as opposed to what we have called here re-intermediate does not by itself *resolve* those three questions, so much as *relocate* them directly in the supplier–customer relationship, rather than with a third party. Whilst this may afford both parties a greater degree of control over the transaction, as well as allow a wider spread of information sharing, it does place a larger burden of trust on both sides, which of course increases the contract risk of the relationship.

Re-intermediation, on the other hand, where intermediary agents offer a wider range of services, often integrating up or down stream, is likely to result in structured information flows (which can leave out as much as they tell) and an exchange of direct management control of a process in favour of third party control. Depending on the range of services involved, this can often lead to a reduced dependence on mutual trust, and therefore a reduction in the risks of entering into a contract.

We shall see in the following sections further examples where online B2B trading systems restructure or even eliminate some of the 'middle men' – a question to be considered is whether this is beneficial in all cases. Having looked at the potential cost advantage of reducing or eliminating intermediaries, in the following section we shall look at the potential advantages of communicating data electronically.

Data exchange

Electronic B2B interaction predates the internet by some decades. Since the 1960s, there have been various attempts to automate the purchasing process, using electronically driven order systems. In the 1970s standardised methods of sending electronic order forms, invoices, purchase orders and similar documents evolved, using formats known collectively as *electronic data interchange* (EDI) which were regulated internationally. EDI systems involved the transmission and receipt of such documents entirely by electronic means, without direct human intervention. So, one organisation could transmit a purchase order for metal staples with a supplier, receive a confirmation of purchase, later have delivery documents and invoices sent to them, all without a hand putting pen to paper. The platforms which enabled EDI to operate were usually provided by specialist third parties (sometimes called VANS (value added networks)).

The pre-world wide web version of EDI is a good example of what is today called an *extranet* – that is, a system that is private to its users but operates outside of one organisational boundary. Extranets have retained their appeal in many contexts, even outside of standard EDI, as they are often perceived to be more secure than direct internet based platforms. For example, a company may directly transfer data from a computer linked sales till via an extranet connection to one of its suppliers, generating orders for fresh stock to replace what has just been sold. This is facilitated by the use of what is sometimes called *enterprise application integration* software – programs that enable one company's applications to 'talk' to those of another meaningfully, so that the sales records of one can be used to generate the stock replenishment orders of another.

Traditional EDI suffered from several disadvantages, but perhaps the greatest was simply that when the internet developed, it was not easily integrated into the world wide web. As a result, the approach has been re-developed in recent years to operate through the web, using internet specific platforms called *VPNs* (virtual private networks, which operate over the web, often in encrypted form).

EDI is specifically an ordering and order fulfilment tool. As such, its impact in terms of operational enhancement is limited to:

- Improvement in order times (added value for the customer).
- Reduction in order handling costs by eliminating paperwork and human interventions (added value for the seller).

In terms of the three questions raised earlier, we can see that there needs to be a high degree of trust between the parties to the transaction and, naturally enough, the whole system is based on a certain level of shared information (albeit highly structured and regulated), but control, except in the sense that all parties use the same document formats, is not so important an issue.

There are many other approaches to the acceleration of sharing of information between different partners to a transaction. One interesting (and potentially far-reaching) example of how the internet continues to develop more effective ways of moving data around effectively is the emergence of *extended mark-up language* – generally known as XML. XML arose out of some of the shortcomings of the standard website language HMTL. Primarily, HTML is a set of *presentational* instructions – sometimes, it is true, this might be supplemented by Java routines that do a little bit more, but essentially it is about how text and images look on a screen. All the operators in HTML (called 'tags' and recognisable by being enclosed inside half-diamond brackets: ⟨ and ⟩) are set by international standard, and although they behave a little differently on different browsers, the meaning of them is not user-controllable at all. As such, HTML is not geared up to enable users to acquire or transmit data between them quickly and efficiently, and interpret what it signifies. There are ways that this can be done, but they involve programming in other languages that are relatively complex, in stark contrast to the ease with which HTML can be picked up by people with a fairly low level of computing expertise.

XML, on the other hand, allows the individual to define what different tags mean, and therefore enables a web page to become much more closely customised to the purposes of the organisation. Data entered into one website is thereby more meaningful and thus more easily assimilated by another that uses the same tag definitions. The implication of this is that rather than rely on the international standardisation of EDI, or on the development of customised programs to read in or out data from one organisation's applications to another's, the partner organisations can agree – privately, if they wish (which can be a significant potential benefit in itself) – on the meaning of the tags they will use in their XML web pages.

The applications of XML potentially have been loudly trumpeted, though at the time of writing this is still in its infancy and has only had a limited take up by browser software – the key to success for any web language. Still, a number of different applications have been developed using XML, such as Microsoft's *Biztalk* which creates an environment where different organisations can define XML protocols and post these for public knowledge. This means that any customer or supplier can access these to see what format they will need to use for any files they want to transmit to the receiving organisation. A more specific application is the *Open eBook* standard, which uses XML to enable different book publishers to work on common bases to publish electronic books in standard formats that will be realisable by different pieces of hardware, such as handheld virtual bookreaders. XML has also been used to great effect in financial systems, and in developing systems for transmitting medical records of patients from one health authority, with its own information systems and data formats, to another, with, in turn, its own idiosyncrasies of data formating and processing.

How far a development such as XML is the future is hard to say – we will come back to it in the Part IV of this book. But, at the least, it indicates some of the key trends with internet technologies today – applications across several different physical forms (PC, handheld, mobile phone), increased opportunities for collaboration between trading partners, and a reframing of existing commercial activity, rather than a replacement of it.

The electronic marketplace

By far the most visible manifestation (though not the largest by volume or value of trading) of the impact of the internet on trading, and especially on B2B trading, is the marketplace phenomenon discussed in Part II. Many people will be familiar with C2C marketplaces such as eBay. Although some B2B marketplaces operate slightly differently from e-Bay, which is an auction space, the basic principles are apparent in a marketplace such as e-Bay, as they are in more specialised e-marketplaces, as well as in physical markets.

Not all internet trading, by any means, occurs in an electronic marketplace. Chaffey (2002), amongst others, has categorised electronic procurement as consisting of three distinct forms:

Sell-side: This is where one supplier sells from their own website to many buyers; whilst we have seen that this is not an optimum for the B2C market, it can be of greater value in a mature B2B market – it clearly assumes that there is high demand for the supplier's goods or services, and that buyers either are easily able to make appropriate comparisons or do not feel that they need to.

Buy-side: This is where one buyer, usually a major manufacturer or retailer with vast purchaser power, buys from their own site, using many suppliers; this sometimes works by means of the interesting idea of a 'Dutch' auction. Here the buyer specifies a certain product and then the suppliers bid downwards from a maximum until a bid is made that the buyer is prepared to pay.

Marketplace: This is defined as many-to-many trading, where the control is in neither the buyer's nor the seller's hands, but is maintained by the third party that provides the marketplace.

The key elements of any marketplace are:

- A group of people offering a variety of goods or services for sale.
- A group of people looking to purchase goods or services.
- The opportunity, within the marketplace, to scrutinise the goods offered by several different vendors before making a purchase.
- A regulator of the marketplace.

In any marketplace, the regulation of the operation is usually intended to be as invisible as possible – the higher the profile of the regulation, the more this can inhibit and even prevent trading, which is after all the main purpose of having a marketplace of any description. Buyers are expected to make the payments that they commit to, and sellers to deliver goods in the condition people are led to believe from the webpages. e-Bay allows buyers the opportunity to rate the vendors on a staff scheme, and to leave comments, so that future potential purchasers from that seller can view these and decide how much risk to take. The body that provides the marketplace and regulates it is clearly a form of intermediary. In some cases, such as financial electronic marketplaces, government legislation requires a high degree of regulation to protect private investors and to inhibit money laundering, fraudulent trading and other illegal financial activities.

Laudon and Traver (2002), amongst others, have categorised B2B net marketplaces into four types, based on the two dimensions of what businesses buy (direct or indirect inputs to the production process, which more or less

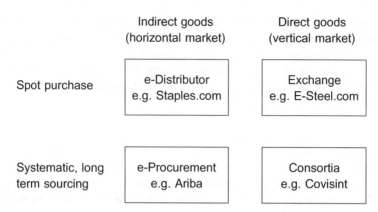

	Indirect goods (horizontal market)	Direct goods (vertical market)
Spot purchase	e-Distributor e.g. Staples.com	Exchange e.g. E-Steel.com
Systematic, long term sourcing	e-Procurement e.g. Ariba	Consortia e.g. Covisint

Figure 9.3 **Types of net marketplaces**
(from Laudon and Traver 2002, p. 676)

correlate with vertical or horizontal markets) and how they buy (spot v. long-term sourcing), as illustrated in Figure 9.3 below:

e-Distributors: These are more or less online catalogues, where a wide range of goods from many suppliers are listed and can be purchased on an as-needed basis.

e-Procurement : These are also many-to-many environments, but the difference is that here a wider range of services is available enabling longer-term strategic purchasing, as opposed to the tactical immediate purchase that is characteristic of the e-Distributor.

Exchange: Where a relatively small number of major purchasers can source goods and services from a wide range of suppliers, usually on a short-term tactical basis.

Consortia: Where major players in a specific industry invite approved suppliers, for the purpose of developing longer-term supply chain relationships.

In practice, although these may look like distinct types of marketplace, they might be better viewed as different *functions* of these, as some trading environments combine more than one of these types, and thus are hybrids.

In a consumer oriented environment, the main revenue opportunities come from advertising based on large volumes of hits to the site. In a B2B environment, there are wider opportunities for revenue – commissions on trades, or licensing for membership of a market, for example. But also there is a much wider range of potential additional services that may be provided, by infomediaries for example. Where a B2B e-marketplace includes a small number of major purchasers, then there is the development and dissemination of specifications for goods and services, as well as general market data such as trading volumes, prices, current delivery times and so on.

The success of a marketplace is measured by the volume of business carried out within its confines. In this respect, it is worth noting that an industry with a large number of markets will be splintered and fail to develop the efficiencies that the marketplace can offer – for the simple reason that if there are many marketplaces, then they are each likely to have only a small number of players. The smaller the number, the less useful it is to operate in the marketplace. Marketplaces live off volumes of access – if buyers know that is where the supplies are, then they will visit the site, and equally if the buyers are there on the site, people will enter it to sell to them. If the site has low volumes of visitors, then it will remain flat – there is a self-perpetuating quality about the size of a marketplace. Generally, there will be a trend towards reductions in the numbers of marketplaces for any one industry. Certainly, in the late 1990s and early 2000s, there has been a voluminous growth in third party marketplaces, some of which hardly facilitated trades at all! Unsurprisingly, many of these have closed or been taken over by other marketplaces.

The image of a marketplace suggests an open area where agents can freely move about. Interestingly, several writers use the terminology of the *hub* as a leading metaphor for the electronic marketplace. Why is this so?

The idea of a hub is of a central mass, from which radiate spokes linking the central component to the peripheral members. For internet marketplaces, the main point is that there is a high degree of control located in the ownership of the market platform. In some cases, the platform provider will use the marketplace as an opportunity for cross selling. In others, a single purchaser may develop an auction based site (as described above), leaving them with the complete control over specifications, lead times and so on. For an organisation with a great deal of purchasing power (such as a food supermarket chain), this increases the opportunity for them to dictate terms by specification rather than having to negotiate these face to face. This is not always healthy for an industry, as it can lead to an imbalance where a small number of very large players can act almost like monopolies, and eventually inefficiencies will creep in to the industry as a whole.

Covisint is a characteristic example of a hub-style marketplace. This is a marketplace for auto components, originally set up by three of the major motor companies (General Motors, Ford and Daimler/Chrysler) though now catering for others as well, to facilitate their purchasing of key components without the uncertainties of supply and with a clearer and more transparent view of the length of the supply chain, tracing back through their direct suppliers to their more remote ones. It is clear, however, where the power for this marketplace lies, which reflects the traditional dominance that the major motor companies have had over their suppliers.

Although, strictly, Covisint is a consortium, it is clear that this kind of development is only available for a restricted range of industries. Consortia usually work when there are a small number of partners. Hence, there needs to be a large imbalance of either supplier or customer power in order that one side or another of the transactions is sufficiently few in number that they can agree on a common set of rules for the marketplace to exist at all. Where there is a more fragmented market, such as may be found in the more generic MRO field, then it is misleading to think of this kind of marketplace as a hub, it is more like a flat arena where buyers and sellers meet on more even terms.

Covisint is also interesting because it exemplifies the trend towards *vertical* marketplaces, where the goods for trade are all related to a single industry. This contrasts with the other possibility, of *horizontal* marketplaces, trading more generic goods that may have applications in a wide range of different industries.

There is a wide range of different forms of marketplace, though they all share the basic features of trying to attract buyers and sellers to a relatively safe, well regulated environment. And they are all based around the need to develop a large volume of interest quickly enough to create a self-fulfilling prophecy of success rather than failure.

Going back to our three questions (trust, control and information sharing) the trust is placed primarily on the market regulators, control passes from the individual parties of a sales negotiation to the key players in the market, and information is shared in a relatively formalised way – or facilitated by additional infomediary services.

Having said all this, although electronic marketplaces and auctions are interesting developments, the potential loss of control can be a disadvantage for the major purchaser, which is generally used to having a much greater influence on any transaction. Trading in an open environment does mean that a significant amount of information needs to be publicly disclosed, which some may prefer to hold back to give them greater leverage. In addition, there is a constant question about whether these markets are in compliance with anti-trust style legislation, which aims to provide a fair trading opportunity for all within that market. For these and other reasons, where the very largest firms are concerned, the electronic marketplace has not found as much favour as the private trading network, which we shall look at in the final section of this chapter.

Private networks and collaborative commerce

A private network takes the thinking behind consortia marketplaces a step further. Now the marketplace is that of a single buyer, who brings in a range of suppliers, some of whom will be in competition for certain goods and services. It is, however, a vertical market, dealing with all the needs of the buyer, and thus there will be many participant organisations that are not in direct competition. It might be thought that the benefits here are for the buyer, in that they can set the specifications and prices without suppliers being able to make comparisons, and it can have a dominant influence over any negotiation of deliverables. But there are benefits also to the suppliers, most notably that they have direct access to a major customer, and whilst they may still have to compete with other suppliers of the same goods, the risks of new entrance or substitution are much lower.

However, there are significant differences between private networks and marketplaces, even though there may be marketplace style activities, such as auctions, carried on within the network. The marketplace is essentially a trading arena – whilst we have seen that some of these involve a richer relationship than simply handing over money and taking delivery of products, the basic orientation is to bring numbers of potential commercial partners together for the sake of trade. The basic purpose of a network is quite different. It is there more directly to help a specific organisation carry out its business, and therefore its structure and operations are designed around this asymmetry of power and purpose.

A private network is therefore a strong form of vertical integration, where a company with really large purchasing power can achieve the same benefits of ownership of up- and downstream integration, without the major corporate implications that acquisition of up- or downstream suppliers and distributors would carry. In itself, this is not a new phenomenon. The largest purchasers in many countries are their governments, who have long operated preferred supplier status and other mechanisms to create a closer relationship with suppliers.

The internet version of the private network concept can be seen as a development out of EDI, in that, in many cases, there will be a commonly agreed set of documentation formats and data exchange protocols. But whilst EDI involved specialised systems, the modern private network is designed to run through desktop computing power, so that a supplier of metal staples can log on the system and see that their customer has sold 10 000 school exercises books (each using two staples of such and such specification) in August, and that the demand for exercise books in September normally doubles the August figure (as schools start back again). So, the staples manufacturer can access their customer's warehouse system directly and identify how many staples they will need and when, and proactively manage the ordering process rather than wait passively for the customer come to them. What is more, through the same network they may also be able to source a transport firm that will carry the staples at the right time to the customer's warehouse, and may also be able to coordinate delivery times with the suppliers of paper and covers.

This kind of deeply integrated activity across different parts of the value chain, involving several partners working together to support the activity of a major customer, is often called *collaborative commerce*. Generally, this is seen as a valuable kind of set up for both the purchaser and the supplier organisations, in that there is a degree of stability in the relationship, there is a greater than usual flow of information, there is a high degree of trust between partners, and there is a clearly agreed set of controls and procedures that operates to the benefit of both parties.

A particularly effective and rich form of collaborative commerce is so-called *CPFR* – collaborative planning, forecasting and replenishment of resources. This involves the partners within the network sharing information about matters such as stocks, sales and supplies, so that inventories can be kept to a minimum, and the host companies operations can operate on a more just-in-time basis, with the clear cost advantages of reduced storage space requirements and reduced risks of over- or underproduction, as well as the small but significant improvement in stock holding risks (for example, theft, or loss from fire).

There are, however, surprising risks to the host company in collaborative commerce. For example, the host has to trust that two or more of their suppliers do not enter into private agreements to their benefit, but at the expense of the host. A road transport participant in a network, say, and a warehousing partner, might both agree on a specific packaging format that suits them but is not necessarily cost-effective for the host, and might each try to limit the options or the relevant technical information for the host to specify alternatives. Whilst it has been a common feature of procurement through the ages that suppliers will try to sell what is easiest for them to sell rather than what the client is actually asking for, the extent of networking, and the corresponding degree of information sharing and high levels of trust, can create an exposure for the host organisation. Of course, trust is an ethical business concept and should at all times be encouraged, but it would be rash for any business to assume that because they would like to trust their partners entirely, then they do not need to hedge against the possibility that this is violated.

In this chapter, we have looked at one aspect of the way in which the world wide web has affected and will continue to affect the operations of the firm; namely, that of acquiring the necessary supplies of material equipment and other goods that a business needs to carry out its own business. Supply chain integration has been closely bound up with certain features of the way that B2B e-commerce is transacted, including the net marketplace and private network phenomena. But it would be unwise to conclude that the benefits of the internet will stop there. In the future, it is likely that we will see a growth in remote processing, as detailed data on operations will be transmitted across distances in the same way that currently details of sales and inventory lists are transmitted. In many cases, this will come with the diversification of internet devices, such as handheld computers and mobile phones, which will enable much more localised inputting of data. So, for example, it may not be too long before we may see the farmer testing the acidity of apples using a handheld device or mobile in the field, which then sends this data to a partner organisation, which in turn adjusts the dissolved gas content of the sparkling water which is combined with the juice from the farmer's apples to make a fizzy apple drink.

We have seen along the way here, as well, that the three questions of trust information sharing and controls each have an influence on the nature and structure of the electronic supply chain mechanisms, with some solutions emphasising the trust element, others the control, others the information sharing. However, all three are dimensions of each such solution, and are an appropriate way for a manager to estimate the kind of risk and kind of implementation methods that need to be used in this field.

Having looked at just one aspect of the operational impact of the internet on organisations, in the next chapter, we shall look at what is generally seen as the most critical area of any business – how its people are organised and work.

Questions for review and reflection

1 Think of an established physical business that you are familiar with, that now decides to set up an internet arm of its activities. What are the operational implications of this?

2 What kind of net marketplace, if any, would be suitable for this organisation?

References

Chaffey, D. (2002) *E-Business and E-Commerce Management*. Harlow: FT Prentice Hall.

Laudon, K. and Traver, C. (2002) *E-Commerce: Business, Technology, Society*. Boston, MA: Addison-Wesley.

Turban, E. and King, D. (2002) *Introduction to E-Commerce*. Harlow: Prentice Hall.

■ ⋈ 10 Managing people and organisation in e-businesses

Introduction

Much of the current literature relating to the internet has been concerned with its vast opportunities for increased and more dynamic commercial activity. Consequently, there has been limited attention to how the internet changes the way that people work, how they are organised, how they are developed, how they contribute to strategic capability and to organisational performance (though Chaffey (2002) provides one notable exception to this). Nevertheless, as for all economic activity, the organisation and management of people is a critical area that can determine how successful the enterprise will be.

Learning objectives

On completion of this chapter you should be able to:

1 Identify the key structural pressures on organisations with an internet operation;
2 Evaluate the main strategic approaches to people management implicit in e-business activities;
3 Identify and appraise the requirements for strategic competences that a developing internet operation requires.

Structure and people

It is important to recognise the role of the organisation and management of people in the achievement of any strategic imperative, whether it be internet related or physical in nature. Figure 10.1, adapted from the work of Bowman (1990) illustrates the inter-relationship of key elements of an organisation and where people management stands in relation to these.

The point of the following diagram is that business decisions, such as the choice to move a certain part of an organisation's activity online, are directly linked with formal organisation-wide factors affecting such aspects as reporting lines, but also with the actual skills and capabilities of individuals, and with the

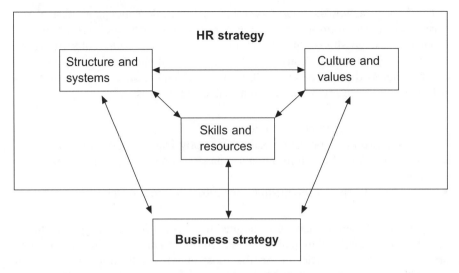

Figure 10.1 **Strategy and people management**

less formal cultural norms and values that are prevalent in the business. At the most basic level, an internet set up requires not only a workforce with a certain skill set, but also a degree of flexibility in the way people respond to the tasks and roles they are required to fulfil. When one looks at the established business that chooses to develop an online operation, then a significant change in culture is required on top of formal people targets such as acquiring the appropriate skills and developing commitment towards the new departure. The language of business models and business plans often obscures this reliance of commercial decisions on human related implementation factors. What we will see in this chapter is the manner in which decisions about how an organisation will operate on the internet is linked with the nature of the organisational structure and the manner in which people behave and are managed.

Business models and organisational structure

It is customary to distinguish between pure e-businesses – dot.coms – and those organisations that combine a physical operation with an internet one – the so-called 'clicks and mortar' approach. In reality, this is a grave over-simplification: every business, however electronic, has a physical presence, and in the western world it is fast becoming a truism that every business, however much it operates in physical terms, is acquiring an electronic manifestation, whether it be through email, the world wide web, dedicated networks such as EDI, or other formats. So, the depiction of how organisations interlink their physical and electronic forms is better thought of as a scale that runs from extremely electronic firms down to extremely physical ones (strictly speaking this, too, greatly over-simplifies, since there is the added dimension of how far the actual work of the organisation is digitisable, as discussed in Part I).

The idea of a *business model* is, roughly, the basic concept or idea of the business – so, for example, the business model of Amazon is to sell the widest range of books possible online. There are as many different ideas of the range of e-business models as there are people to ask about them. But, in essence, there are four factors that will determine the way in which people management issues will relate to the internet based operations of a business:

- The depth of customer interaction.
- The proportion of the value chain that is physical as opposed to virtual.
- The extent to which internet and physical operations are integrated or differentiated.
- The onward plans of the business for future internet development.

These factors do not in themselves define business models, but they provide the key elements which will help an organisation both to determine the appropriate structural form and to decide on the most effective HR strategies. We shall return to them, therefore, in the following section when we look at HR strategic responses to the internet.

How do particular structures come about? Principally, they are determined by the manner in which the business model affects and is affected by a range of different organisational factors, including:

- Size
- Geographical spread of operations
- Extent of dispersion of staff
- Degree of risk inherent in the operation
- Nature of the ownership (for example, family owned, shareholdings, partnership)
- Degree of flexibility required
- How quickly changes need to be made
- How many different stakeholders need (or are in a position to demand) information about the operation.

The fact that an organisation has some internet presence does not in itself drive either the nature of the structure or the whole package of underlying factors, but inevitably there is a reciprocal influence between these factors and the particular kind of online operation involved. For example, a traditional medium sized non-electronic business is likely to operate in local or national markets. Once it develops a website, then automatically it has a much wider geographical reach – clearly, someone can view the site from anywhere in the world. So, it becomes important either to ensure that the site guards against this inadvertent inter-nationalisation or to gear staff up to deal with international enquiries.

Similarly, the structure of a dot.com start-up will be heavily dependent on the nature of its ownership – the typical example of such a company will most likely have a small group of highly motivated and highly skilled entrepreneurs plus, in some cases, a major funding source such as a venture capitalist. These two groups will apparently have similar interests – for the business to succeed – but their longer-term interests are different, and this will have an impact on the culture of the firm, as well as on its structure, which will need to represent both sets of interests.

People tend to think of an organisation structure as simply being the way in which different parts of the organisation are linked together, though actually a structure fulfils a number of different functions, not all of which are officially intended. As well as issues such as the application of authority and defining lines of communication, a structure can provide workers with a guide to their potential career progression, a map of the status of different areas and individuals, an indication as to salary differentials, and other functions. Again, the sheer fact that an organisation is operating, in part, on the internet does not of itself determine specifically the different ways in which an organisational hierarchy will impact on people's consciousness and motives, but it will indirectly contribute to this, in virtue of the operational and strategic choices that will be made in relation to the internet strategy adopted.

For example, take an established producer of goods previously sold through independent retailers that now chooses to sell directly to the public via a website. As often as not, this can be an unsound choice, since it requires an organisation that has previously been good at, say, making toys, to acquire core competence in areas such as customer service and packaging and dispatch. In order, therefore, for the business to do this successfully, they will have to bring in competence from elsewhere, initially at least – in the physical aspects of this decision at least as much as in the virtual. This is as one would expect but, then, the redesign of the structure creates, potentially, new territorial disputes, new players in the constant competition between different parts of the organisation for resources, and new potential sources of status and career progression.

In general, the internet operation of a firm presents particular difficulties for organisation design. Many of the people working on the development of online services will be so-called 'knowledge' workers, employed for their high levels of expertise. A much smaller proportion of the workforce will be employed for lower level skills than would normally be the case in most physical operations. True, the online retail operation still has a large number of people in warehouses, offloading the goods, packing them up and dispatching them, but this is the limit of the lower skilled work in an internet based operation.

Such a skewing of the workforce creates a degree of distortion in the traditional hierarchical image of organisational structure, because the 'pyramid' does not continue opening out further and further as one goes down the structure, but widens at the point of the professional knowledge workers, and then narrows again at the point of the lower skill workers. (As a complete tangent, it is worth recognising that many people employed to do lower skilled work are often capable of much higher levels of operation).

Mintzberg (1979) developed a more useful, all-embracing, model of organisational structure, and explored the various ways in which this model might lead to different specific forms in response to different strategic contexts. His model takes the idea of the value chain and turns this out into what it would look like structurally. The basic framework of this model is shown in Figure 10.2.

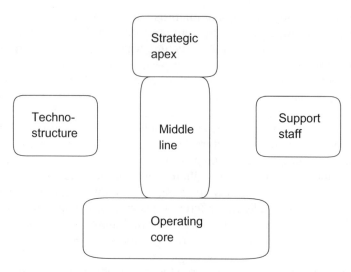

Figure 10.2 **Mintzberg's model of structure** (after Mintzberg, 1979)

The main roles of each of these elements are as follows:

- Operating core is the segment that actually does the core business of the organisation – assembling cars, flying aeroplanes, shelving library books.
- The middle line is the direct supervisory element for the operating – core line managers, in fact.
- The strategic apex is the policy forming and corporate governance component – the senior management team.
- Techno-structure is the support function that provides information, performance measurement and analytical services.
- Support staff include HR, administrative and clerical workers.

Mintzberg (1979) uses this analysis to present different kinds of structure that fit different kinds of organisation, such as:

Simple structure: Essentially no more than a strategic apex and an operating core, this characterises businesses in the earliest stages of development.

Machine bureaucracy: Here, there is a large operating core and line management component, and a relatively small strategic apex; this kind of structure, according to Mintzberg, fits large processing operations; what is interesting is that as well as a large line management function, there may also be a large body of technical and administrative support staff as well.

Professional bureaucracy: A flatter form, with little line management and often little in the way of technical support though there is likely to be a large administrative and support function.

Divisionalised: This structure has almost a fractal form, where each division has its own miniature 'Mintzberg' shape within the overall structure; usually this is a product or market driven form of organisation rather than an internal operational requirement.

Adhocracy: A jargon term for the idea of a highly flexible organisation that can reshape itself swiftly as circumstances change; this is highly effective when it can be achieved, especially in contexts of great volatility.

Each of these forms has a different balance of the elements depicted in Figure 10.2. But when one considers a business with an internet component, then there are different forms that need to be considered. Perhaps the most obvious aspect is that the 'techno-structure' elements will be greatly expanded in comparison to the operating core. Note that in this context techno-structure does not simply mean IT specialism – though this is certainly an important part – it will also cover customer capture systems, and market research functions. In addition, however, there is a much less clear form of middle line control, for there is much less that is directly delivered to customers. If one considers the organisation with a highly developed degree of integration with their supply chain (as discussed in Chapter 10), moving towards the notion of the 'virtual organisation' in the fullest sense of the term, then there is likely to be a high degree of administrative and HR support in addition to the techno-structure.

So, the general trend of an internet firm is to change the shape of the basic Mintzberg model as depicted in Figure 10.3.

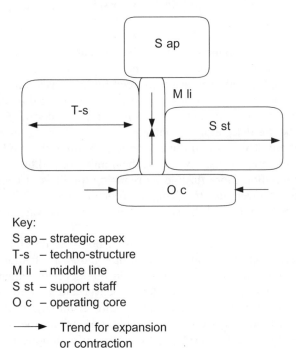

Key:
S ap – strategic apex
T-s – techno-structure
M li – middle line
S st – support staff
O c – operating core

———▶ Trend for expansion
or contraction

Figure 10.3 **The structural trend for internet operations**

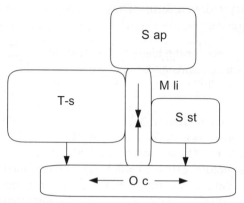

Key:
S ap – strategic apex
T-s   – techno-structure
M li – middle line
S st – support staff
O c   – operating core

→ Trend for expansion
or contraction

Figure 10.4 **Structural implications of modern operational efficiencies in physical businesses**

This is further complicated by the fact that, in many cases, this trend towards swelling the volume and importance of the staff functions, as they have sometimes been called, stands alongside the continuing development of physical operations for, say, a producer that chooses to start selling their goods directly online. One of the developments that such an organisation might be likely to adopt could be the delegation of managerial responsibilities further down the line of operations. This is often done for one or more of three related reasons: (a) to reduce operational costs by cutting the number of middle managers; (b) to make an organisation more flexible by reducing the lines of communication; and/or (c) to empower staff by giving them greater responsibility. But such a development is likely to pull the structure in yet another way, as illustrated in Figure 10.4.

Whilst there are some common themes in both the developing structural trends of internet operations and physical operations, as illustrated in Figures 10.3 and 10.4, most notably the reduction in middle management, in respect of the parts of the organisation that design deliver and support production or services, there are significant differences. The most important of these is that for the internet there is a growth in specialisation, whilst the trend for many physical operations is to develop greater expertise amongst front line or customer facing staff, with a view to reducing the dependence on specialists in favour of having a more flexible and generically skilled workforce.

This is not a problem for the dot.com style organisation. The number of lower level staff doing relatively unskilled jobs in an organisation such as lastminute.com is likely to be small relative to the overall workforce, which will have not only a lot of people designing and maintaining websites, but also a substantial number of people buying and selling tickets (the basic business model of lastminute.com is to acquire tickets for events, concerts, flights and so on, at very short notice – almost at the last minute, in fact, hence the name). The latter will have specialist sourcing, purchasing, negotiating and selling skills.

But it *is* a structural issue for the larger pre-internet organisation that decides to move into some form of online operation. The cultures implicit in the two forms shown in Figures 10.3 and 10.4 are quite different – the former is likely to manifest a high degree of what Handy (1993) calls a 'task' culture, where people get on with the job, and do not spend too much time fretting over rules and status. On the other hand, the structural type in Figure 10.4, whilst moving in some direction towards a greater task focus, is likely to retain a close attention to rules and procedures as a means of ensuring consistency in the absence of traditional middle managers.

This form of organisational expansion gives a fresh twist on a well known model. Greiner (1972) argued that as an organisation develops, it acquires structure through a series of stages of organisation, each of which is outgrown as the business expands. Each period of growth results in a critical challenge for an organisation, which it resolves by means of a rethink of its structure. The small, young organisation (such as the start-up dot.com) has little formal organisation, and grows via its creativity and personal dynamism, until it reaches a state of crisis where leadership based on technical excellence and drive is no longer sufficient. It then moves to a more directed formalised structure, including the appointment of specialist staff such as HR and finance managers, which creates the capacity for growth by pure expansion, until it reaches a crisis where some of the creative people who started it all up feel that they have lost the opportunities for self expression that helped the organisation grow so well originally. This crisis is resolved by delegating managerial responsibilities further down the line, and so on, through a crisis of central control, resolved through a more coordinated structure (building in cross communication mechanisms) through a bureaucratic crisis, where there are too many procedures covering all the different coordinating devices, which is resolved through a more flexible approach taken to coordination.

Greiner's model does make several assumptions:

- That growth or expansion is a natural force that moves organisations from one stage to the next.
- That each organisation learns in a linear fashion.
- That each organisation has to learn afresh the same lessons as others that have preceded it.

In the context of the development of the internet, it is plausible to see these as justified. Certainly, the dot.com explosion and implosion closely mirrored the explosion and subsequent dramatic contraction in the early railway era.

In Britain, for example, in the middle of the nineteenth century, a vast number of small railway companies grew up extremely quickly, but by 1870 power rested in a very small number of major players, the others having been bought out or forced out.

But the twist to this is that whilst it may be a reasonable description on its own of the growth of a pure internet firm, starting from next to nothing and expanding into a multi-million dollar enterprise, it is less helpful to explain the condition of the physical pre-internet company, which may already have a highly developed culture and set of organisational systems and procedures, as it chooses to diversify into some form of online operations. The implication of the Greiner model is that a mature firm that attempts to develop the entrepreneurial type of operation that the internet would normally require is caught between two conflicting imperatives – the one to take the organisation towards greater co-ordination, order and control, and the other to take the internet wing towards greater freedom and flexibility. Not that these two are intrinsically contradictory, but they will generally lead the physical and virtual parts of the organisation into a loosely jointed relationship that is likely to need continual monitoring to avoid a steady divergence of strategy and activity.

To sum up this argument, then, internet operations tend to require a high degree of expertise in both technical knowledge and in organisational support and coordination. A physical firm in the current era will require high levels of technical and coordinative expertise, but it will also be subject to pressures to shift management responsibilities down the organisational hierarchy. This creates a permanent point of conflict within an pre-internet organisation that attempts to move online.

We have not isolated every possible organisational form that may be appropriate for internet organisations. Rather, we have here looked at one characteristic strategic context – that of the firm that is already established in physical terms and then attempts to move into an internet environment as well. And there we have seen that there are significant difficulties with achieving this.

What, finally, of the idea of 'virtualisation'? How far is this a structural issue? In many ways, the move from a unitary organisation that physically does what it is especially good at, and then draws in services from elsewhere to complement its own core competence, has been disappearing for some years without the assistance of the internet. The Japanese concept of the *kieretsu* (a sort of vertically integrated conglomerate) is one piece of evidence for this. What is also true, though, is that many of the facilities offered by the internet create the opportunity to take this feature much further.

Quite literally, it is possible for an organisation to have an online auction, say, which results in it purchasing components from south-east Asia, which are then transported to selected external assembly firms in eastern Europe to be put together to make the organisation's own products, a sample of which are tested and the test data is streamed through to analysts in India and France, after which the products are packaged up and sold to the US market. The key issues here, it must be emphasised, are not those of data transfer and online procurement – these are tools which we have discussed earlier when considering internet operations. Rather, the key aspects of such a sequence are (a) physical transportation; and (b) liaison and control of operations to ensure that these work in tandem. Whilst there are digital coordination tools (*Lotus Notes* has been used for years to help geographically dispersed workforces to coordinate their activities), the most important feature of such communication and control is the human factor, to which we shall turn in the following section.

This discussion, ostensibly starting with organisational structure, quickly became as much about the management of change and the fundamental strategic choice of moving on to the world wide web. In doing so, it underlines the point of the model of HR strategy mentioned at the start of this section, linking together structure, culture and skills as partners with overall strategic choices.

The key people management issues

In the previous section, we saw four overarching factors that play a major role in the way in which any organisation, whatever the degree of its internet activity, organises its people to help achieve strategic objectives:

- The depth of customer interaction.
- The proportion of the value chain that is physical as opposed to virtual.
- The extent to which internet and physical operations are integrated or differentiated.
- The onward plans of the business for future internet development.

The discussion in the previous section was not a systematic look at the influence of each of these or at the specific business models and structural forms that these lead to, so much as an illustration of the kinds of issue that are likely to challenge an organisation intending to operate online. The subtext of that discussion was that these four factors create a greater degree of opportunity as well as a threat for a business when there is a strategic intent to develop internet operations, but these opportunities and threats are not of radically different nature, just specified for the online operation, and thus often more intense in their impact.

These four factors also, though, indicate the areas where management attention needs to be directed to make the most effective use of the people of the organisation. There are five key aspects of human activity that will be most directly affected by the internet strategy of a business: the management of knowledge, the management of quality and performance, the design of the work, the forms of innovation that are encouraged and rewarded, and the manner in which different key skills and strengths are put together to form strategic competences. As the argument of the previous section has indicated, the really key issue where the management of people, as much as the structural organisation of the firm, is concerned, is how the virtual and physical aspects of the business hang together.

Knowledge and expertise

The most obvious change in any organisation's knowledge profile when it implements an internet strategy is the technical knowledge necessary to deliver the implementation. However, like most technical knowledge, it gets easily 'ghettoised' where a small number of people become the computing 'magicians' of the business and everyone else stands around amazed when they do the digital equivalent of pulling chewing gum out of the works. This is not specific to the internet – it is a feature of all computing technology and many other areas of high tech as well.

A first and critical task where the management of knowledge relating to e-business is concerned, is to take steps that will ensure that at least, some, of the technical knowledge is spread round the organisation. This is not so much a matter of training more than one person in a certain specialist area as it is one of making sure that decisions made in different parts of the business are taken with a clear understanding of the implications for the organisation's e-business approach. Further, when different parts of the organisation are developing new solutions to issues, it is important that these are informed by an appreciation, at least, of the e-business opportunities and implications.

e-Business can, it is true, relieve some of the key challenges of knowledge management. For example, detailed understanding of specific market segments can, in some cases, now be based around material provided by third party infomediaries. How far this is a satisfactory solution will depend on the degree of current and planned internet operation, and on the degree of integration of physical and virtual parts of the business. But a far greater proportion of the import of the concept of knowledge management lies in the development of cultures of sharing knowledge and in the role of dialogue and reflection to help people recognise and identify elements of knowledge of which they may not be fully aware. In other words, knowledge management is a cultural and developmental concept at heart, for which technical solutions provide only a small contribution.

Quality of performance and particularly customer service

All businesses are crucially affected by the perception of their customer service. It builds and destroys customer loyalty. There is a temptation to think that an internet based business does not need to spend so much time on this area, as the automated aspect of the business can take care of customer problems, and can often deal with them more efficiently than when a human is involved. There are several flaws in this argument. Perhaps the most obvious one is that whatever system is set up to deal with customer problems, it still has to be designed and maintained by people, and their implicit assumptions about what is a justifiable customer complaint, for example, will in many ways determine the quality of response that the system delivers to a customer. Another key issue here is the sheer fact that retail customers tend to have a preference for some human interaction at some point in a dialogue with an organisation, especially if it has become problematic. Not surprisingly, many retail organisations will ally their website with a call centre, or will offer an 'email us' option somewhere on their site, as a means of allowing the customer an opportunity to have a human to human dialogue.

In all these cases, the perception of customers by the staff, the appreciation of the customers' needs, and the motivation to address these will have a determining effect on how any customer's problem is resolved and how they will perceive the organisation subsequently. This is a generic issue, common to all business activity. But the nature of the e-business component of an organisation's activity will present these challenges in novel forms. For example, if an employee is face to face with a customer (say, making a complaint), then they can clearly perceive any degree of annoyance or irritation. On a website, even with emailed communication, it is a greater demand on one's ability to empathise with a 'faceless' customer, and thus it can be easy to be impervious to a customer's feelings, which can often be central to the issue.

Indeed, it is arguable that the greater speed and reach of the world wide web means that, in time, customer expectations of efficient operations will rise above those for face-to-face transactions. In such cases the organisation will need to develop staff to raise their sensitivity to electronic signals of customer dissatisfaction.

A common issue with many websites, especially where an organisation has its own server, is downtime, where a machine crashes or maybe is taken out of service for upgrading or maintenance. In the eyes of the consumer, the loss of service is a major shortcoming of the service. On the inside of the organisation, of course, there may be high levels of activity whilst the server is down, so it is all too easy for the staff to overlook the fact that from the outside it looks as if nothing is happening (indeed, from the only perspective that the customer generally has, nothing *is* happening). How an organisation handles this – the virtual equivalent of the store making an unscheduled closure – is a telling measure of the customer orientation of the workforce.

Job design and patterns of working

If we think of the traditional store – whether it is engaged in physical B2B or B2C trading – one major difference with internet operations is the handling of *time*. The customer can choose what time they log on to the site, they can come and go as many times as they like, they can make a choice and then change their mind (constantly). The physical store represents as much a means of processing customers as of processing orders. The customer in the typical supermarket, for instance, is subtly led along a series of aisles each of which is intended to address needs in a perceived order of importance – fresh fruit and vegetables always first, alcohol last. They are then placed in a queue, and they wait whilst bar codes are read and a bill produced. The customer, in short, is controlled. On a website they are not, which raises a whole new cluster of issues about staff working.

One of the simplest of these is that the business needs to have some-one around at 3am just in case there is a major problem with a customer. Another is that the organisation needs a higher proportion of people working on development, rather than on day-to-day operations. The natural pattern of front line operational staff in a traditional store is that they turn up at a specified time, they work in customer facing roles for a specified time, and then they go home and the store closes – typically this was the archetypal '9 to 5' type job in the past, though contemporary shopping tastes have led to a gradual broadening of shopping times. The patterns of development staff are very different. For one thing, they are much more measured on outputs rather than on processes. A development worker is usually left to their own devices to achieve a certain result by a certain time, be this a new design for a web page, a new system for gathering customer data, or a new specification for linking website orders with physical delivery of goods. The standard role of the human resource in a physical store is to be present, facilitating a sale – either by discussing and showing the goods or by concluding a sale and collecting up the money. Hence, the latter requires a process orientation with a close control on physical presence – you have to be at your till or counter in a retail store. For the majority of staff, you do not have to be *anywhere* at a specific time with an online store. Differences in the basic business model lead to differences in the kind of strategy adopted for human resources. The Israeli writers Bamberger and Meshoulam (2000) identify four different kind of basic archetype of human resource management, as depicted below in Figure 10.5.

The traditional retail store, then, will tend to adopt paternalistic or secondary (that is, casualised) human resource strategies, where there is a high focus on controlling the details of processes and the use of time. The internet store, on the other hand, will tend to focus on commitment strategies – giving people wide areas of control over the operational details of their work, and rewarding them for committed service.

For an organisation to be successful in operating in either channel, it is essential that there is a consistent response not only for all staff, but across all people management areas – so that if there is a paternalistic strategy, then this is manifest as much in the reward and payment policies as it is in the training

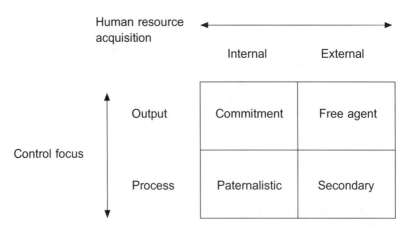

Figure 10.5 **Bamberger and Meshoulam's dominant HR strategies**

and development activities. In effect what these archetypes describe could as well be considered as an *HR business model*, paralleling the general business model. For the idea of an archetype or HR strategic type is really the basic conception of what people are there in the organisation to do or achieve – in a retail store it is to sell goods, in an educational institution it is to teach people, in the internet department of a food supermarket it is to facilitate the processing and dispatch of orders. Each organisation has its basic image of its activity, and corresponding to this is its basic image of how people contribute to this. Of course, there are many other roles that people play in the organisation, but the point here is that the core business defines the activity of the core worker, with all that this implies for how they are recruited, trained and developed, rewarded and so on.

What makes the HR business model especially challenging with respect to the internet is that, as we observed in the previous section (with major implications for structural choices), for most organisations there is some degree of hybridity about their physical and internet activities, so that the organisation has two different clusters of staff, with two different sets of needs, and for whom two different kinds of approach are often called for. It is notorious that even in traditional physical production and sales, development staff are often seen as higher in status than operational staff, simply for the fact that they have a higher degree of control over their day to day activities. True, they may therefore have to shoulder a greater amount of risk, but for most people that is seen as empowering (until it all gets too much for them).

This discussion underlines that there is a significant change management issue involved in the development of an integrated 'clicks and mortar' type operation, where different parts of the operation require different people responses, though the basic products and the basic markets may remain the same. Integration, then, whilst desirable for many reasons to do with overall organisational continuity, can prove a big challenge for the organisation wishing to extend its internet activity or integrate physical and web based operations.

Innovation

There are several components of innovation in any organisation:

- Creative and opportunistic thinking by staff.
- Space within the business to experiment without fear of getting the sack.
- A readiness to draw inspiration and ideas from all and any sources.
- Resources are available for new ideas to be developed.
- Time is available for ideas to be developed.
- Structural and cultural conditions within the organisation coordinate to encourage, to test and champion innovations, and also to cut out any that do not show promise.

How do these differ for an internet firm? Essentially they do not especially, but here is one place where there is some good news – internet firms are not that bad at innovation! They have to be good at this to some extent, as the external environment changes so quickly. Any that do not manage innovation effectively fall quickly and are unable to survive. However, the other side to this is that the sheer fact that they are surviving or prospering in virtue of their internet operations does not mean that innovation is protected forever. The current innovatory aspect of the word wide web is primarily a response to its sudden and unprecedented explosive growth, which has not just spawned many different firms operating in more or less the same industry, but has also created industries to manage the complexity involved – the search engine being one of the more obvious manifestations of this tendency. But when the growth slows, it is as likely that in each industry there will be some players who base a lot on the internet, and others who place less emphasis on this aspect but still survive as primarily physical commercial organisations. And the level of innovation in the former group is likely to dwindle as the competitive positions of key players become more predictable and more settled – and thus competitive advantage is likely to be based less on genuine novelty of product and more on cost leadership, promotion, and perceived quality of product and customer service.

The factors listed above will inevitably be affected by the degree of development of the business. If a firm is just starting up, then there will be lots of space for experiment, lots of resource available, and thus people will naturally try new ideas out as the business gets off the ground. The prospect of developing a 'killer app' that garners colossal profits for the organisation, even for just a short time, is worth the effort expended on such inventiveness. It is in later stages that the issue of innovation becomes problematic.

The Greiner crises of bureaucracy and control place great strain on the willingness of the firm to allow innovation. For many primarily physical firms, the cost of innovation – in strategic and managerial terms, as well as financial – is often seen as prohibitive, as traditional management styles need to change to encompass a more innovative style. In practice these second (or sometimes tenth) move players are likely to have limited innovative ambitions where the internet is concerned. Take the food supermarkets – their prime driver has been solely to develop their existing markets via online ordering. The idea that the weekly shopping list could be a vehicle for other sales opportunities seems to have been by-passed by these firms. The real danger with these kinds of firms, especially where, as in food retailing, they operate on narrow margins, is loss of existing revenue, not the prospect of increased revenue through fresh trading opportunities.

The people management issues for encouraging innovation are reasonably well known, and include requirements such as:

- Encouragement to experiment, avoidance of blame.
- Acceptance that not all staff are natural innovators, and rewarding people for what they contribute rather than punishing them for what they do not.
- Ensuring that staff do not have targets that leave them no room for manoeuvre; for example, by being so demanding that they have to work flat out on operational tasks.
- Ensuring that staff and managers are clear about the criteria by which innovations, both large and small, are tested and evaluated, and ensuring that these are applied consistently.

What is less well recognised is that the structure of the organisation can encourage or inhibit innovation, and indeed many of the most successful organisations are able to innovate, not by direct creation of new products or techniques, but by *innovative assembly* of existing competences and capabilities, as detailed below.

Dynamics of how strategic competences and capabilities are assembled

A core competence may be defined as a set of skills or capabilities that conjointly provide a distinct source of competitive advantage. We will leave aside in this section the issue about whether this says anything about non-competing or non profit-oriented organisations, but the reader should remember that issue is still there as a background theme.

Such advantages may derive from a variety of factors, including the following:

- Unique market-relevant knowledge.
- Moving knowledge around an organisation quickly.
- Coordinating factors that enable an organisation to respond more quickly to market opportunities than rivals.
- Deploying elements to provide qualitatively superior customer experience to that offered by rivals.
- Efficiency.

These examples illustrate that the idea of a core competence is not so much about just having some one distinctive element that is better than your rivals, such as more knowledgeable staff, a better set of machinery, a better location. All of these could provide a distinctive competitive advantage – and thus can be core competences in their own right. But the bulleted list given above is much more about the *management of the resources* that the organisation possesses. These may not be individually any better in themselves from those possessed by the competition, but they may be utilised and brought together in a more effective way. In effect, this concept is partially about which organisations are better managed.

With an internet operation, a business is likely to think of its primary value chain, schematically, as:

$$\begin{matrix} \text{Production} \\ \text{of physicals} \end{matrix} + \begin{matrix} \text{Internet platform} \\ \text{and orders, etc.} \end{matrix} + \begin{matrix} \text{Physical fulfilment} \\ \text{of order} \end{matrix}$$

Much of the innovatory activity is likely to be located in the central element of these three components. But it is essential that the internet business continues to seek ways to improve the physical side of the business, even where the value they deliver to customers is mainly electronic. In addition it is essential that the three components are effectively coordinated, so that a change in the product specification is not merely put onto the website, but that its implications for the website and for ordering are thought through and are managed in a consistent manner. For example, the website of the music software group, Emagic, includes not only software updates but also user group links and details of training and development on newly developed products. The site is an adjunct to the physical operation, and thus facilitates customer satisfaction.

For a business to be able to deliver an effective and seamless service to its customers, it is necessary that the structure of the business allows those people who develop new products to communicate sufficient information about these to enable fresh add-on or back-up services (such as manuals and training) to be developed alongside – there would be nothing worse than releasing an upgrade of software only for customers to find that the relevant online manuals have yet to be updated.

In addition, it is important for an organisation to make effective use of its core competences in different applications. Xerox have managed to redeploy their expertise relating to the basic copy model of business, so that now they see themselves involved in a much richer business model, that of document production. The central core competences of good copier design, production, performance and maintenance are still there, but have been linked to a far-reaching approach to sharing operational knowledge and common solutions to problems. Much of this has been facilitated by internal internet driven communications. The result has been that in an era when the copier business has been beset by licensing disputes, and a number of new players have come into this market, thus reducing the potential for each of the main firms, Xerox has subtly shifted itself from being the mass producer to being a more specialised and higher quality copier company. Sales are down in numbers – that was always going to happen – but the quality of customer satisfaction is much higher, which is at least as important for long term prosperity. The point here is that this strategic evolution has been directly facilitated by the firm's ability to take its existing capability, and add fresh services on to it, and in some cases use that capability in other ways, applied to other situations or in combination with other resources. This is in no small part due to the structural features of that company in facilitating shared information around the firm.

Culture too is an important aspect, as it can drive along or inhibit the strategic realignment of core competences such as expert knowledge:

- In tough guy macho cultures, people are sometimes too oriented towards blame avoidance to share information.
- In power cultures, knowledge is just that, and therefore jealously guarded.
- In process cultures, knowledge may sit around without being harnessed.
- In task cultures, the focus on results may assist transmission mechanisms.
- In some types of people culture, the collective examination of professional issues by group discussion directly contributes to the dissemination of ideas.

Again, these are just a smattering of the different ways in which culture might be relevant to the management of knowledge. The point is that this is one example of a resource that provides competitive advantage. It is clear that the structuring of the organisation and its cultural norms can make or break that competence.

This emphasises that the HR business model is as important to a strategic development as the general business approach.

In this chapter, we have looked at the *strategic* implications of structure and people management. The underlying assumption of our argument here is that the operational issues, such as recruiting and paying staff working on internet activities, are not an especially problematic cluster of issues. The differences between internet businesses and physical firms over the manner in which people are hired and rewarded is based not on the basis of the specific job they are doing, so much as on the design of the job, the tightness of the relevant labour market and therefore the degree of bargaining power candidates have over issues such as salary when they are appointed, and the general culture of the organisation and the industry they operate in. The interested reader is referred to specialised HR process texts should they wish to pursue this area, though our view is that the HR business model, as we have called it, and how it contributes to the overall business model, is the more important field to focus on.

Questions for review and reflection

1 What are the key HR challenges, in strategic terms, for a business such as a social housing association to develop an internet site to assist its operations with issues such as allocating applicants to housing, receiving and processing requests for maintenance and repairs, and so on?
2 What do you envisage the key crises and subsequent structural resolutions will be for the surviving original dot.coms such as lastminute or amazon?

Notes and references

Bamberger, P. and Meshoulam, I. (2000) *Human Resource Strategy: Formulation, Implementation and Impact*. London: Sage.

Bowman, C. (1990) *The Essence of Strategic Management*. Harlow: Prentice Hall.

Chaffey, D. (2002) *E-Business and E-Commerce Management*. Harlow: FT Prentice Hall.

Greiner, R. (1972) as discussed in Handy, C. (1993) *Understanding Organisations*. London: Penguin.

Handy, C. (1993) *Understanding Organisations*. London: Penguin.

Mintzberg, H. (1979) *The Structuring of Organisations*. Harlow: Prentice Hall.

⚛ 11 The financial implications of e-business

Introduction

In the previous two chapters, we have looked at the operational and people aspects of running e-businesses. We have focused mainly on the issues arising in these areas for established physical businesses wishing to develop an internet element to their work, rather than the dot.com phenomenon, which is relatively limited in its application, and may have already become a thing of the past. It is certainly true that e-business start-ups will continue for as long as there is e-business, but it is unlikely that we will see any replication of the particular circumstances of dot.coms – extraordinary perceived growth potential, the promise of access to volumes of customers unheard of for all but the most established firms and, relatively speaking, huge capital structures for their actual size. (It was said of lastminute.com that at the time of floating on the London Stock Exchange, raising something like UK£45 million for their founders, they were selling as many airline tickets as the average high street travel agency.) In the main in this chapter, looking at the financial aspects of internet business, we will continue this focus, though in some parts there will be reference to e-business start-ups.

Learning objectives

On completion of this chapter you should be able to:

1 Identify some of the key issues involved in measuring the performance of an e-business;
2 Describe some of the key revenue models and methods of revenue collection for an e-business;
3 Identify some of the key issues affecting the profitability of e-businesses;
4 Identify some of the key issues relating to the financing of and investment in e-business.

Identifying and measuring the key financial elements of e-businesses

A key part of the management of the finances of any organisation, be it e-business developed or not, is how the overall value of the business is identified and measured. In this section, we shall look at one way to achieve this, derived from an approach to finance sometimes called *value-based management*, which has been applied directly to e-business by Diese *et al.* (2000). These writers develop a very useful model that can frame the key financial implications of e-businesses, as illustrated in Figure 11.1.

In Figure 11.1, the left hand column lists a series of key business drivers – features of the operation of a business that will have a critical effect on the generation of value for the shareholder. The top two rows identify the key features of a business from the customer's perspective, and the key capabilities of the business that can help it develop competitive advantages. Each point where a 'tick' has been placed is where, in the opinion of Diese and his collaborators, e-business can create an improvement in shareholder value.

Take as an illustration of this a relatively typical physical B2B operation, such as a company that provides in-house catering facilities for offices and factories. There are a number of opportunities for e-business here, including areas such as cataloguing, auctioning the company's services, using auctions to procure supplies, stock management procedures (such as electronic reordering), and

	Customer value proposition				Competitive capabilities		
	Service	Price	Quality	Fulfilment time	Agility	Time to market	Reach
Revenue growth	✓	✓	✓	✓	✓	✓	✓
Operating margin	✓		✓	✓	✓		✓
Working capital			✓	✓	✓		
Capital expenditure					✓	✓	✓
Cash tax rate					✓		
Cost of capital							
Competitive advantage period	✓		✓	✓	✓	✓	✓

Figure 11.1 **Driving shareholder value** (adapted from Diese *et al.*, 2000)

even electronic capture of customer satisfaction. Whilst this is a fairly standard physical business, it is an unusual example of an e-business supported firm, being based on a business model that includes a multiple customer network – the primary customer being the company that brings them in to provide the catering services, and then the secondary customers being the staff who use the facilities and meals provided.

How far, then, can e-business activities enhance shareholder value in this example? One of the most important drivers for a business of this kind is its operating margin – the surplus of revenue over the costs of providing its direct operational activities. Catering services of all kinds tend to work on very tight margins – hence, cost control is crucial, and there are rarely the opportunities for a large scale of overheads that one might expect for, say, an auditing company.

Take the example of how electronic procurement can affect operating margin – this can have an impact on improved order fulfilment for the primary customer (the firm that commissions the catering services) through the reduction in time taken to source supplies and, potentially, even staff. E-procurement can reduce costs such as storage of one set of goods whilst waiting for others to arrive. It also increases the agility of this company to switch from one location to another, or to switch from one kind of catering service (say, light refreshments, supported by vending machines) to another (say, a kitchen with a full range of hot meals). With greater speed of sourcing and acquisition of supplies equipment and expertise, the firm can start up in a new location or with a new range of services promptly without the need to hire temporary equipment to ensure the start happens at the time specified by the customer, whilst waiting for the permanent equipment to be sourced and supplied.

One could expand on this example and indicate in more detail how different e-business initiatives can have a positive effect on each of the key value drivers, and so enhance shareholder value, but the point should be clear enough that each financial aspect of the business has the potential to be improved via the appropriate introduction of e-business activities. What is interesting for the discussion of the financial aspects is that the Diese *et al.* (2000) model uses a fairly standard – but not for that reason unimportant – set of value drivers such as working capital, cost of capital, revenue, and so on. The argument of Diese *et al.* (2000) is that e-business can have an effect on profitability and shareholder value in a variety of ways – but not necessarily in every single direction. Whilst the impact of e-business on agility – the ability of an organisation to realign its resources quickly to develop and deliver new services and products – has an effect on all aspects of shareholder value, the price of the service or product has, rather surprisingly, little direct impact as such (though it can be manifest in different ways, such as the perception by the customer of value of services or quality of delivery time 'for the price paid'). What is also clearly implied by Figure 11.1 is that there is little, if anything, that an e-business can do about the costs of capital – its activities have little direct impact on the money markets, for example. We shall draw on this model in several places in this chapter.

There are, however, two points that need to be made about the model as it is formulated above. Firstly, it is a depiction of how e-business can create shareholder value, and as such it is framed in terms of the impact on that stakeholder group alone. But one needs to bear in mind, in the measurement and evaluation of any organisation, that each different stakeholder group – the staff, customers (though these are catered for within the table already) suppliers, strategic partners, and so on – will all have different perspectives and different interests, so that in the grid above there would be a different left hand column, indicating a different set of causal factors affecting the interests of that group. For example, key drivers affecting the benefit to staff might include: health and safety, growth in the reward package, increased development opportunities, and so on. For suppliers, the key drivers might be factors such as working capital, delivery-time expectations, precision of specification information, and so on.

It is, of course, not customary to go into such detail on the value of a business in non-financial terms, let alone on the value of the business seen from the perspectives of different stakeholders, but the point is that e-business is not just a benefit to shareholders, but rather an overall social benefit, as it is creating a new economics, a new bundle of communication and occupational forms, a new dimension of living in a market economy and therefore, whilst here the financial aspects are well measured from the shareholder perspective, in general the real success of the internet – which we may only really get to recognise in twenty or more years' time – will be its overall impact, not just on shareholders, but also on customers, on workers, and on other organisations.

The second point that needs to be borne in mind here is that this is a PLC style model, essentially. It identifies the potential benefits for paying customers and the resulting impact on those who own the organisation. Clearly, some rethinking of this would be required to make it work for not-for-profit sectors. But it would be naïve to suggest that such a framework needs to be thrown out altogether. For many state activities, especially in western countries such as the UK, there has been a concerted effort to make them operate more and more like private companies. For this reason, if one were to use a similar model to identify financial aspects of, say electronic government, it is reasonably appropriate to keep a similar, but amended, set of drivers and key value proposition elements, something like the local council example given in Figure 11.2.

Similar grids to Figure 11.2 might be developed, with slightly differing categories, for other elements of public service, such as health service provision, or specific services provided centrally by national governments. What we can see here is that although some of the components of the grid are similar, the impact of the value proposition as experienced by the citizen combined with the capabilities of the authority creates quite a different pattern of influence on the overall impact of a local council as providing value for its citizens. It is also important to recognise that voluntary organisations, though still part of the not-for-profit sector of the economy, would have a quite different set of elements of their value proposition, and a different set of value drivers.

Two points need to be noticed from this discussion. Firstly, although we have not spoken much about the impact of e-business on government in this book, it is a potential major growth area. The discussion in the main part of this chapter will be focused on B2B and B2C e-business, but the point of this digression is to remind the reader that the phenomenon of G2C (government to citizen) has hardly really started yet.

	Citizen value proposition				Service capabilities		
	Consistency of sevice delivery	Price – direct or through taxation	Quality	Involvement in service design	Agility	Time to delivery	Needs identification
Revenue collection		✓			✓		✓
Revenue expenditure	✓	✓	✓	✓	✓	✓	✓
Working capital		✓				✓	
Capital expenditure					✓	✓	✓
Cost of capital raised		✓					
Level of funding from central government		✓		✓			✓
Government assessments such as Best Value	✓	✓	✓	✓	✓	✓	✓

Figure 11.2 **Driving public service value: local authority example**

Secondly, whilst a diagram such as Figure 11.2 may look visually similar to that of Figure 11.1, there are significant differences – one of these is that in a PLC the use of financial information creates an elegant language whereby inputs, outputs, activities and even the purpose of the business can be expressed in monetary terms. (This also has its downsides, as it can lead financial managers to view a firm solely in monetary terms, which inevitably misses some of its best features.) This is not possible for a local council or other public sector body, where there is a significant degree of financial management and control, but the objectives and outcomes of the organisation can and should be expressed in qualitative terms.

Revenue management

We shall look at three key management tasks with respect to the management of revenue:

- Collection and disbursement of revenue items
- Debtor management
- Revenue growth.

E-business, can in various ways, provide different facilities and services that will help with all of these, though in practice the collection and disbursement elements can draw a more direct operational benefit, and the growth of revenue tends to result from enhancement to the basic business model. The management of debt is currently underexplored as a specifically e-business area, though there are some initiatives that pre-date the world wide web that can easily be transferred or converted into internet based services. The main focus in this section will thus be the collection of payments.

Revenue collection

As always, there are two key dimensions to bear in mind here: the physical to virtual scale, at one end having almost completely electronic operations and services, and at the other having almost completely physical ones; and secondly, the B2B v B2C markets, the latter of which receives a vastly larger number of hits on websites, but it is the former that actually generates the larger amount of sales revenue.

By far the largest method of payment for retail items over the internet is by credit card. Facilities such as Secure Sockets Layer discussed earlier mean that the basic mistrust that the public has had over disclosure of their card details is gradually disappearing. An important development that provides a range of payment functions, linked to credit card payments, is the idea of the *digital wallet*. This is a software package, sometimes placed by a company on individuals' PCs and sometimes held on servers, that contain payment details, verification of identity (often using digital certificates), sometimes other consumer information such as spending patterns, even dispatch addresses in some cases.

One particular value of some digital wallets is the facilitation of so-called *micropayments*. These are sums that are too small in themselves to merit collection. Standard credit card transactions below UK£5 are often regarded by traders as uneconomic, given the premiums they pay to credit card companies. A micropayment might be even smaller – pennies in some cases, such as a temporary download of an image or snatch of music. Clearly, without some mechanism for aggregating these together into a sum that is cost effective to collect, the viability of the internet for small-scale transactions would be greatly diminished. Digital wallets, such as Microsoft's *Passport* system, are an interesting example of *reintermediation* as discussed earlier – they have found a role facilitating payments riding on the back of the credit card system.

Digital cash is a favourite of many internet theorists – the idea that money will cease to have any kind of physical manifestation, even symbolically, and be transacted and moved around entirely in electronic form. In reality, the proportion of financial value that moves electronically has increased dramatically in the last two decades, using pre-internet systems such as BACS (the clearing banks' automated clearing system). Their disadvantage is that they are generally transfers carried out by the bank as an intermediary, and naturally enough do not favour micropayments. In contrast, several systems of virtual currency have been proposed and adopted on the internet to a limited extent. Most of these have not survived more than a couple of years, mainly due to the difficulty of balancing out security with ease of use, and of keeping the cost of the financial transaction down to a minimum, to facilitate micropayments.

Wallets and digital cash systems tend to favour B2C interaction. One successful form of electronic transaction in B2C and also C2C (in this context often called person-to-person or P2P) is the *PayPal* system, where individuals can use supplied software to send money direct to another individual or to a business supplier. This is clearly an advantage in an electronic auction, and some e-auction rooms encourage and even supply *PayPal* or similar software to their users.

Stored value systems are another form of internet payment process. In this case, an individual makes an up-front payment and, as they make use of certain services or acquire certain goods, the value of their stored value is reduced stepwise. Clearly, this is one way round the micropayment problem. The idea has been around for a considerable time in non-internet areas. For example, the UK's Royal Mail postal service requires up-front payments of this kind for the use of business reply paid envelopes, which are generally paid for in physical form (cheques or even cash). One online version of this, *eCount*, links the idea back to digital wallets and credit cards (it functions almost as a virtual MasterCard™ in some contexts).

Smart Cards go one step further here. They store the financial value on a chip on the card itself, so that an individual can load it in a special reader at times, and then use it to make payments, again using a reading device. Despite the apparent simplicity and elegance of such an approach, the various experiments have not come up with a 'killer app' for this kind of product that has established itself in the cash movement market. One of the best known experiments, *Mondex*, can be loaded with cash from phone systems – which gives it a clear advantage over other systems, many of which require a specialised reader. Despite this, and despite ten years of development and piloting, *Mondex*, supported by MasterCard™, still only has 150 000 users, a paltry number in mass retail terms.

All of the above are B2C or C2C systems, and thus are designed to deal with the retail customers' standard requirements – quick, simple and easy to use, ideally transferable between different media or platforms, and to cover payments from the pence up to the thousands of pounds. These particular and somewhat demanding ideals are less relevant for the B2B transaction, where (outside of online financial trading) the payment time is not generally measured in seconds, where the amounts are large and therefore security is of a higher order of importance, and where transferability is still important but in order for transactions to be carried out at remote locations, rather than to enable junior to buy his trainers over the mobile phone.

Not that B2B transactions are free of specific difficulties. One of the most problematic is so-called *repudiation* – where a customer refuses to pay for a service (for example, claiming that they have not received goods dispatched). Related to this is order dispute, where the recipient claims that goods received are not in the specified condition, or damaged and so on. Larger B2B transactions (for example those involving the supply and delivery of goods on a just-in-time basis over several months) may require a line of credit to be agreed, so ideally the electronic transacting method needs to give some degree of assurance about credit-worthiness. And most businesses will want to link a payment process with their own internal reporting and documentation systems. Lastly, of course, where international payments are involved, there are financial risks involved, particularly with aspects such as money crossing a border from one regulatory system to another (risk of tariff barriers, or regulatory infringements), and converting from one currency to another (exchange risk).

There are several approaches to electronic B2B payments, though again none has become established as the leading method, partially because none provides a seamless linkage of all the various sub-services involved in e-transactions:

Electronic letters of credit: where a bank or other authority guarantees the payment, and therefore takes the risk associated with repudiation or order dispute.

Internet based EDI: although less standardised than more traditional EDI, this approach has the benefit of integrating payment details with other organisational systems.

Electronic billing presentment and payment (EBPP): this is a more amorphous category, including B2C consumer financial management services and payment service bureaux, as well as B2B billing systems that have evolved out of EDI.

To sum up, the key theme here is that payment – apparently a simple action of exchanging money for goods or services – in fact admits of a bewildering range of variants, involving credit, pre-payment, accumulation of small payments, and requirements for speed, convenience, security, direct billing and integration. As a result, although many products and systems have been developed that deal with some of these features, none as yet has achieved the ideal of a seamless and easy combination of the majority of these needs. As a result, payment is certainly potentially a lot faster and more efficient than pre-internet times, but still retains its own idiosyncrasies and blockages.

If we look back at the value drivers model depicted in Figure 11.1, we can see that ease of online payment can have an impact on such areas as order fulfilment or customer service and satisfaction (partially because the more efficient the payment handling, the less chance of awkward complaints at a later stage concerning over- and underpayments and similar issues) as well as indirectly on price due to the possibility of reduced costs. In practice with the latter, however, it is worth noting a general trend with the impact of computing that it has not only reduced operational costs significantly but improved quality – whether with old mainframes or with desktop PCs people have realised that the real potential of greater computing power is to enable higher quality of documents, of payroll systems, of data analysis, rather than simply allowing older flawed systems to run more cheaply. But all the same there is a likely impact on the price–quality combination.

Revenue models and revenue growth

Whereas the collection of revenue is an operational issue that admits of a range of specific systems, the *growing* of revenue is potentially a much wider issue that brings forward the whole range of marketing sales and branding issues already discussed. Here, it is simply worth noting some of the more specific features of e-business activities that can have an impact on the development of higher revenue income. But before that, it is important to be aware of the range of different *revenue models* that may apply to e-business. A revenue model is a part of the overall business model, and is essentially the underlying concept of how the e-business will attract and collect revenue, which can take at least three different forms:

- For a private sector company – sales.
- For a public sector service organisation – taxes (local or national) or individual service user payments (such as dental charges).
- For a voluntary organisation – financial contributions from the public.

We will focus as previously on the private sector, but the not-for-profit areas should be noted at least, for the future.

Laudon and Traver (2002) identify five different kinds of revenue model for an e-business:

- Advertising – income from, for example, banner ads, and linked to volume and quality of hits.
- Subscription – in effect a membership charge for the ability to receive services for a specified time; for example, instantchess.com charges a fee (this can be monthly or annual) for people to access their site and play chess against each other, analyse well known games, read news about chess players or a chess event: the point is they make one payment at one time to receive as many or as few of these services as they wish.
- Transaction fee – in effect, a broking fee for facilitating a sale between two parties.
- Sales – may be of goods or services, which can include information (for example, market information) or provision of web services themselves (such as server space for websites, or hit counters); sales packages may themselves come in diverse forms, such as forward payments for a series of services or deliveries of goods, or agreements to purchase a number of as yet unspecified items (for example, on a book club model) or basic sale plus discounts on add-ons, and so on.
- Affiliate – referral fees when one website leads a party on to another where they conduct a transaction – and the original site therefore gains a cut of the fee: a referral type model.

The largest original share of internet B2C revenue was advertising based, as the market itself was a classical problem child with huge growth potential but as yet very little actual volume. As it has moved into a rising star condition – still lots of growth but also now lots of existing business – sales and transaction fees have become much more important (and with good reason, for the earlier state could not have persisted for very long, and in some ways contributed to the dot.com boom–crash). It is likely that as more distinctive and web specific services are developed, the subscription segment will become a significant minority component.

An example of one aspect of the internet that is likely to have a major impact on sales volumes and revenue generation is the gradual convergence of different technological media discussed much earlier. The advent of T-business (television receiver related) on top of M-business (mobile phone based) means that doing business on the internet in the B2C field will become more diversified. Methodologies such as mobile phone text polling have already become a standard mechanism for reaching the teen and twenties markets, which exhibit to a more exaggerated degree the retail customer's desire for quick and convenient communications, selling and purchasing activities. But older customer groups are gradually being captured by means of interactive cable and satellite television commerce, and by sophisticated mobile devices such as intelligent hand held phones – which may rely not on the 'thumb and thumb' styles of mobile phone texting but on miniature keyboards on a more 'qwerty' format resembling the standard desktop computer layout, and supplemented by the now standard handheld computer electric pen and screen facility. These represent straightforward market development opportunities – increasing penetration and sales within existing markets, therefore not suffering from the perception of novelty which often inhibits new commercial development. For example, the average family expenditure on interior design items such as ornaments, pictures, indoor plants, and the like is generally based on shop presence or is sometimes catalogue driven. It is rare for the main decision makers in a family household to be together at other times to discuss purchases. The opportunity presented by a handheld channel of communication is that a targeted small screen catalogue, specifying items that have been identified as potentially of interest to a particular family (using historical customer expenditure data) can be transmitted at almost any time when the handheld devices owned by members of that family are switched on. (The selection of a family here is purely as an example – the points would be similar for other household groupings. Note also that this kind of communication needs to be carefully managed to avoid any perception of being 'spammed'.) So, the range of potential sales opportunities can increase almost exponentially – up to the point of saturation of course.

The point of this kind of example is to indicate that many of the key revenue growth opportunities lie not in dynamic new products and services, but in existing cash cows that are simply sold through different channels. The progressive entry of established companies into the e-business arena is likely to lead to a greater development of market development and market penetration activity than heretofore – when, in the first decade of its operation, the internet has been characterised by a development of a raft of new products and services. On the Diese *et al.* (2000) model, this emphasises the organisation's capabilities in extending its *reach* to customers, though also it gives a different interpretation to fulfilment time – the issue here, especially in the era of so-called 'time poor' consumers, is that of buying time, the whole spectrum form identification or presentation of potential sales items, through evaluation and making a decision to buy, agreeing a sale and then completing the transaction physically and receiving the goods of services. Partly, this is a matter of service, partly, a matter of looking more holistically at the customer experience of purchase.

Profit in e-business

A second financial side to e-business is the generation of profits. So far as profitability is concerned, this is always a complex issue, linking together costs with revenue models and margins, and with sales volumes. With physical goods and traditional services, the specific products and how they have been marketed in the past create a legacy sales pattern that has and will be a factor in determining how fast or how slowly the industry takes to the internet. The fortunes of dot.coms might suggest that internet-defined services have an intrinsic volatility. This is likely only to be the case due to the rapid rise and then stalling of the field as a whole. In time, the role of internet services will mature and show the same patterns of growth and decline of any other area of consumption.

Profitability is perhaps best illustrated by a hypothetical example of a clothing retailer, specialising in the ends of lines and seconds (garments with very slight flaws such as missing buttons, tiny breaks in the lining and so on) of major designer labels, that chooses to go online. The key features of this business model will be the purchase of garments from the manufacturers, distributors and wholesalers at the cost or near-to-cost price (which can be often less than 50 per cent of the standard sale price), the cataloguing and presentation of these via a web presence, a physical store for people to try on clothes and complete their purchase, the usual physical operations such as warehousing and, most important of all, a careful pricing policy that positions the goods as still of high-premium value, but representing a good bargain for the customer (especially in the light of the fact that these may become available at the end of a season, and therefore might not sell for several months).

Clearly, the profitability of such a business is already established, and the real issue is how far an internet operation will add to or subtract value for the owners. The implications of the Diese model are that, potentially in several areas, there are opportunities for improved owner value – such as a wider reach, an improved level of service and so on. However, all this is offset by the capital expenditure to set up and maintain a website. If the site is to function basically as an invitation to come to a store, then the increase in reach is negligible, and hence the potential revenue increase is not sufficient to justify the capital expenditure. If, on the other hand, there is a strategic choice to increase reach, then the site will be more of a catalogue, and may involve some purchasing without visiting a store (rather like mail order catalogues do). However, whilst this will increase reach, and doubtless the volume of enquiries, there will likely be a smaller enquiry to sale ratio (people tend to prefer to try on clothes physically before buying them) and doubtless the company will have to deal with a larger proportion of returns, order disputes and repudiations. Additionally, they may have to decide how much of the dispatch costs are to be passed on: some really large internet retailers, such as Amazon as it operates in the UK, have national centres where goods for customers in that country are dispatched by post using national or private third party carriers, for which an additional postage charge is made.

One could summarise this as follows:

- Enquiries: increase significantly.
- Sales volume: increase but on a smaller level.
- Cost of sales and after sales: increase significantly.

For a firm working on a reasonable margin this pattern may be a sound business proposition. It will turn on the pricing strategy – high enough to suggest high value, but low enough to suggest relative cheapness. Where exactly this mark up pricing lies will determine the profitability of the operation.

In this kind of example of a luxury good there is a significant degree of discretion over pricing. In the case of food supermarkets – the majority of which have now developed sophisticated internet operations – the prices are much more tight, as this is a highly competitive market. The websites themselves are highly complex, involving the listing of goods, the payment systems, some kind of well developed EDI systems for getting orders back to the warehouses, 'club' style customer loyalty schemes, and cross selling of additional services such as banking, or travel. An additional physical element here is the transportation of goods – the idea of the supermarket as a one stop shop for all food items was that the consumer took responsibility for transport, whereas if they order from home, the great benefit of this is to have it delivered to their door. So, there is a significant overhead here in terms of the website and physical infrastructure. But while the margins on any individual food items are probably less than those for a high class designer label dress, the volume of purchases is much higher. The average online supermarket shopper buys a family weekly shop – which can be anything from UK£80 to in excess of UK£200 depending on the family size. And, in addition, the supermarket is a national or international player, with very high customer numbers, and a major segment of highly loyal customers who will shop with them week in and week out. The real benefit for the customer value proposition here lies in services and order fulfilment time – or as we characterised this earlier, the customer purchase time (which includes the time taken to fill in an order as much as the delivery schedules).

There is yet another contrast here with more electronic services such as eBay, where the revenue element for each individual is relatively low – a small fee from the seller on completion of a sale. But the volume of sales here is vast indeed, and with an overhead that consists almost solely of the website and the cost processing mechanism, there is a narrow but healthy operating margin, offering ample scope for high profitability. This contrasts with a store such as Amazon, the legendary massive volume bookseller but still struggling to make any operating profit (let alone return for shareholders). The issue here[1] is that books are rarely bought in so many numbers. Often just a single text or maybe a couple

---

[1] We owe the discussion of this example to a former colleague, Jeremy Baker, of London Metropolitan University.

are ordered – maybe less than UK£25 in value, sometimes as little as UK£10. Although the postage itself is passed on, the cost of sales here includes the publisher's charge for the text (cost can be 50 per cent of the sale price), and all the physical operations of picking the book, packaging it, and dispatching it to the third party carrier. Secure packaging for transmission across a postal system is itself a major cost compared to the supermarket, where often the usual plastic bagging methods are used. Using the standard price/margin/volume analysis, it should be clear that a business like Amazon needs to generate quite an enormous amount of sales to recover its costs, because of the double aspect of a tight margin and significant overheads. The supermarket, on the other hand, has significantly better margins due to the size of each customer shopping event.

This should indicate that the issue of profit will remain a major problem for many internet firms for some time to come. Of particular concern here are just those services, such as Amazon, that promise greater reach and accessibility for standard retail items that sell for, say, less than UK£30. The larger the purchase, the less this is an issue.

We have focused almost entirely here on the B2C market. In practice, the issues for a B2B internet operation are more driven on price. Certainly, the development of practices such as reverse auctions and private industrial networks, especially in areas of manufacturing where there are large quantities of raw materials used or significant needs for MRO goods and services, means that price and conformance to specification become the most important drivers of sales. Because of the volumes of sales, and the greater elaboration of collaborative commerce, the B2B supplier can generally foresee greater opportunities for profit, due to the reduction in transaction and selling costs. This is certainly one reason why this sector has developed more quickly and with greater success than the consumer facing operations, where there are longer term issues retarding the development of strong profit lines.

Investment in e-business

The last area to consider here is that of the investment needs for successful e-business. As with all areas of e-business, the specific internet related aspects need always to be considered against a generic and physical backdrop of the practices that have evolved literally over centuries or more to facilitate commercial activity. Any sources that suggest that e-business will fundamentally rewrite the rule book are simply wrong – the rules may well have to be applied in novel ways and given new interpretations, but they stay the same, just as the invention of the airplane did not change the law of gravity, though it certainly changed the way we think about it.

In most respects, then, the issues surrounding investment in e-business are the same as those for physical only companies: amounts of initial capital required, costs of capital, costs of and time for developing new products and services, length of payback time, discounted returns measurements, degree of investment risk, hedging, and so on. There are one or two specific issues relating to this area.

The first of these is research questioning the level of return on computer related investments – as Brynjolfsson and Hitt (1998) have argued, IT investment against net company profit is not a straight line relationship: the quality of investment decisions is a more significant factor in determining profit than in physical only firms. Perhaps the reason for this is that the industry is still sufficiently young that there remains considerable lack of industry wisdom about the best areas to invest in. One way to evaluate this is to go back to value chain analysis and consider each step in the chain in terms of the potential impact on performance and profitability. Another is to use the Diese *et al.* (2000) model discussed and used earlier in this chapter.

Whatever specific way is used to identify investment opportunities, there are certain key issues that always need to be taken into account:

Threshold competences and resources: What is necessary simply to be in this business at all? This would include the possession of physical hardware – at the least a server and computing facilities sufficient to be able to upload web pages, as well as sufficient basic office resources, essential web design skills and related expertise (such as knowledge of the range of different online payment systems available).

USPs and core competences: What can give the business competitive advantage? This would include not simply the 'killer apps' of this world, which are few and far between, but also the capabilities that can generate a sustained and established position consistent with the e-business strategy and objectives. So, expertise focusing on the customer experience, for example, can be harnessed to provide a superior quality that maintains and consolidates a level of internet activity. High levels of sophistication in web design – not necessarily in visual terms, though that is always important, so much as in user-friendliness and navigability – are also potential core competences.

Efficient internal processes: These may come from physical efficiencies, or from smart thinking about the interface between the customer experience and the internal processing at electronic or physical level.

Technological dependencies: The more a service is dependent on a specific electronic platform, a specific kind of operating system or programming package, the greater the chance that it will at some point be rendered obsolete – overnight, in some cases. Hence, the greater the flexibility of a website, and the easier it is to convert from, say, e-commerce to M-commerce or T-commerce, or to private data networking such as EDI, the more resilient it is likely to be. Investment in this area is likely also to focus on linkages between the technology needed for an internet operation and the existing technology that is necessary for physical operations.

These illustrate the kinds of areas of investment focus, and will require different levels of evaluation and risk management at different points. Threshold competences just have to be there – just as a plane has to fly before you can run an airline. Issues such as technological flexibility are of a longer lead time – though they certainly are no less important for long-term survival.

The second point to be made is specifically in connection with the financing of internet firms, in particular the unprecedented levels of floatation of dot.coms in the late 1990s. There is a common presumption that dot.coms were to blame for the stock market slump from late 1999 to mid-2003. In practice, that is somewhat misleading, if only for the fact that investment happens because people have money to invest and choose to buy shares with it. In addition, there were other related areas of the economy that were irrationally booming at the time as well – pharmaceuticals, and mobile telephony in particular. Nevertheless, it is clear that there was a boom and bust cycle – some internet companies witnessed a soar in their price immediately after floatation only to see an enormous fall later (Ask Jeeves, for example, saw a fall from nearly US$200 per share to under US$1). The high share prices led to many dubious actions on the part of dot.com entrepreneurs, such as payment to staff in stock options rather than cash, which sounded great when the share prices were galloping upwards but became rapidly very hollow indeed.

This aspect has tarnished the image of the internet. But although there certainly were some bad investments and bad business models, almost of 'south sea bubble' dimensions at the time,[2] this is unlikely to be a continued feature of the growth of the internet, or of any further developments from it. The more substantial consolidation of the world wide web is going to come in the next few years, which promise to be altogether a more sober economic period, lacking the 'irrational exuberance' of which Alan Greenspan complained and which fuelled the dot.com boom. In addition, the prospects for growth in the late 1990s were quite unknown and were therefore subject to excessive intellectual speculation, that led to financial speculation. We are now in a period where the fundamental groundwork has been done. Although there are doubtless many developments which we can only guess at, there is less uncertainty about the basic potentialities of the infrastructure, and therefore less room for unconstrained speculation.

In this chapter, we have looked at the key aspects of finance and e-business. We have seen the range of payment systems and the opportunities that these present, the different challenges and opportunities for profit inherent in different types of e-business, and in the final section we have considered a few of the main issues relating to investment.

This concludes Part III of this book, which has been mainly concerned with operational issues. In Part IV, we shall turn to the future and the development of the internet in the wider context.

Questions for review and reflection

1 How would you evaluate the potential profitability of a small crystal shop deciding to develop a website as a basis for expanded retail operations?

---

[2] The authors take no great comfort from the fact that we gave our own warnings of the falls to come on our regular weekly comment column for CompuServe during 1999 and 2000.

2 What would you say are the key issues involved in using electronic tax collection? How far would you advise a government to press ahead with this development, and what risks would you point out?

Notes and references

Brynjolfsson, E. and Hitt, L. (1998) 'Beyond the productivity paradox', in *Communications of the ACM*, vol. 41, pp. 49ff.

Diese, M.V., Nowikow, C., King, P. and Wright, A. (2000) *Executive's Guide to e-Business: From Tactics to Strategy*. Chichester: John Wiley.

Laudon, K. and Traver, C. (2002) *E-Commerce: Business, Technology, Society*. Boston, MA: Addison Wesley.

Part IV

▼ The future of e-business

We have looked at the context of the development of the internet, the key application to marketing, some features of its application in operations and finance, as well as the structural and human implications of developing e-business.

In this final part, we look to the *emergent* properties of the internet – the manner in which communities develop, and how far an e-business can take steps to assist this process. Finally, we will look into the crystal ball, and speculate about future developments of the web itself and its social impact in the next few years.

⍁ 12 Developing user communities

Introduction

In this chapter, we examine user communities, their formation and relationship to online or virtual companies and organisations. The building of 'trusting' relationships between buyer and seller is far from new. Such activity can be traced back to the eighteenth century and earlier (Vaisey, 1998). However, here, a different medium is driving the relationship along. What becomes clear is that companies and organisations that are prepared to go beyond creating a 'light veneer' of personalisation have an opportunity to improve both market share and competitiveness. The key question is whether or not the company has the ability to build a truly interactive relationship with the user community.

Learning objectives

On the competition of this chapter you should be able to:

1 Explain the role of user communities within the wider internet environment;
2 Examine the potential value to internet providers of effective user communities;
3 Debate how online companies or organisations can enhance their alliances with user communities;
4 Consider how brands can be built (and dismantled) through virtual communities.

What is a user community?

A community can be defined as a group of people normally living and/or working within a specific locality or neighbourhood. For example, students within the business faculty of a university are a community. Similarly, those business faculty students who live in halls of residence can be considered another community. They share knowledge and similar experiences.

Communities, in one shape or another, have been with us since the dawn of humankind. What has changed, over time, has been their scale and the interrelationship between communities. The key factors in linking communities have been transportation and telecommunications. With transportation (for example, horse and cart) merchants were able to travel from one village to another marketing their wares. They were also able to disseminate news. The development of sea, land and later air transport improved links between nations, although not necessarily to everyone's betterment. With sea and air transportation came threats – invasion and occupation. Rather than linking communities, transportation was often used to enslave people and destroy communities. Sadly, this process continues to this very day.

Telecommunications, though, was probably the greater liberator. At first, the telephone was a luxury experienced by a few in power. With the development of satellite, microwave, and fibre optic technology, the telephone (whether fixed line or mobile) has become a liberating force; a force that not only allowed communication with both family and friends, but formed the linking device between the computer and the wider world. The 'simple' telephone line was the link between our home computer and the 'communities' beyond our physical location. Rather than being able to 'talk' to one person at a time, this allowed us to 'talk' to many simultaneously.

The idea of user groups or communities is not a new concept. Such communities have grown out of a group's interest or enthusiasm for an idea, concept, product or hobby. This can be seen, for example, with car enthusiasts who love caring for a particular make of car. Their enthusiasm spills over to every aspect from the history of a particular model to its very technical specifications. A classic (in many senses of the word) example is the Mini Cooper, made even more famous by the British caper movie *The Italian Job* (1969). As with the case of the Mini Cooper, these user communities of specialist automobile clubs enhanced the value of the brand.

Online communities

An online community can also be described as a virtual community or, indeed, a cyber community.[1] Schubert (1999) describes virtual communities as:

> the union between individuals or organizations who share common values and interests using electronic media to communicate within a shared semantic [meaning] space on a regular basis.

In Chapter 1, we described how scientists sought to enact their vision of being able to communicate with one another electronically. Their vision was the ability to share ideas to help create a better world. The work of Tim Berners-Lee in developing the world wide web greatly increased people's ability, whether scientist or layperson, to share knowledge, ideas and experiences.

---

[1] These terms are interchangeable and are used throughout this chapter.

The rise of the Usenet

In 1979 a group of American university science graduates created Usenet. Their objective was that, via a computer network, they, and others throughout the world, could work together to remove the flaws in the Unix computer operating system. Usenet has now become a forum or text based global bulletin board that consists of over 30 000 different newsgroups (McClellan, 1999 and Chaffey *et al.*, 2000). However, the term 'newsgroup' is somewhat misleading, for they usually have very little to do with 'news' as in terms of global events. These discussion nodes cover everything from the conspiracy theories associated with the highly-secretive US military research establishment known as Area 51 (officially known as Groom Lake Base) in the Nevada Desert, right through the whole range of subjects to who is the best garage music performer. As you can see, the diversity is beyond the imagination, such is the scope of the world wide web. Equally, the range of opinions shared within the 'newsgroups' can be both highly charged and diverse.

There are several key problems with newsgroups:

1   When a person posts a message, it can take some time before it reaches all within the newsgroup. That assumes that they have regularly logged on, which leads us onto the next item;
2   Newsgroups generate significant traffic such that internet service providers have to regularly purge material. Therefore, members of the newsgroup must log on regularly to grab information before it is deleted;
3   Whilst there is always a die-hard group of newsgroup members, the vast majority (90 per cent according to some sources) are lurkers[2] who view but do not participate (McClellan, 1999);
4   As we have seen above, there is a vast number of newsgroups operating. Whilst, perhaps, the vast majority cover subjects within both legal and ethical frameworks, unfortunately many do not. There will always be extremes of opinion (ultra right-wing political groups, for instance, or 'hacktivists') and human behaviour, and these are reflected in some of the newsgroups. Whilst law enforcement agencies work closely with internet service providers to eliminate this type of material, there is the complexity of legal jurisdiction that we have already encountered.

---

[2] A 'lurker' is net slang for a person who visits newsgroups and chat rooms, reads the views of other people but does not post anything themselves. This may be for several reasons: (1) They are seeking other people's views and thoughts on a particular subject in order to help formulate their own. Once they have formed a view they may share it with others but not necessarily within that particular newsgroup. It may be shared within the physical world rather than the virtual one; (2) They are shy and feel that any opinion that they express may create an aggressive response, a response that they clearly want to avoid. Evidence suggests that some participants can be extremely vocally aggressive (Groucutt, 2000). An approach that, while inexcusable, is driven by a particular passion or perspective. This is often clear within politically focused newsgroups.

Even with these negatives, newsgroups have a valuable role to play within the internet community. As well as sharing diverse views, they can be the centre of opinion forming.

Companies (and governments) would thus be wise to understand how newsgroups operate, and how they may affect them. Views, extreme or otherwise, do have a habit of being communicated 'downstream' and are thus affected by the swirling tide of knowledge and opinion. In other words, truths can become tangled amongst half-truths and falsehoods. Then they become myths and legends – though not always in the good light of King Arthur and his Round Table of valiant and honourable knights. For instance, let us reflect back for a moment on Groom Lake Base in the Nevada Desert. This is popularly known as Area 51. That, perhaps, portrays a much more 'sinister' connotation. In reality, apparently, it denotes a military grid-reference number that designates the expanse of the nuclear zone of the Nevada Desert. No big secret. For years, the base has been a test centre for advanced military aircraft, such as the stealth fighters. Again, now no big secret. However, since strange lights have been seen over the base, it has become a focal point of speculation as to what is actually now housed at the base. This speculation has lead to various conspiracy theories ranging from the US military's development of flying saucers to the testing of a flying saucer on 'loan' from mysterious aliens. Now, all this could be true – who really knows. However, the point is that numerous websites and discussion groups have formed to actively debate what really goes on at Area 51. Now, this probably does not really matter to either the US Government or its military. They may even view it with slight amusement. However, what it does show is that people, often very ordinary people, become highly charged, excited and involved in issues. This leads to the sharing of information and views. For companies, organisations, and to some extent governments, newsgroups and other types of user groups can become a very powerful 'opinion forming voice'. They can become a 'powerful' network that can lead to the support of a product, or indeed a boycott against it.

Therefore, companies and organisations must not believe that by creating a website glistening with features and benefits is the end of the matter. It is only one part of the complexity that is the internet and world wide web. Newsgroups and user communities as a whole are an important, often vital, part of the network process. Business is often won or lost on the 'buzz' of public opinion. As we will see later in this chapter, major companies have developed, and continue to develop, their own online communities. This can be an effective way of building longer-term relationships with their customers, and enabling customers to communicate with each other.

How are communities built?

Communities can emerge or be constructed around several different types of 'experiences', 'attitudes' or needs. For example, these can revolve around products (Tesco.com for online groceries), socio-demographic groups (iVillage.com and Avon.com for women), sports (F1.com for Formula 1 racing), and opinion formers (Greenpeace.com).

Table 12.1 Suggested framework for a transaction community

Level	Description
1	This is a straight transaction between the buyer and the seller. Whilst there may be an acknowledgement of the order, there is no interaction. This is the lowest level of transaction community.
2	Again, there is a transaction between the buyer and seller. However, there is an interaction between the buyer and seller beyond the pure acknowledgement of the order. The seller may engage in answering questions, for example, on the range of products or services on offer. For instance, a wine merchant may advise on the best types of wines to serve with particular types of food, or what are the best wines from a particular vineyard or region.
3	Here, the transaction is only one part of the overall experience. At this level, the interaction is wider than the buyer and seller, it encompasses a wider group. For instance, a specialist online CD store may incorporate a bulletin board and a chat room so that users can share both their knowledge and enthusiasm for the music. The online store can benefit in several ways: (1) they have regular returners who will 'pop' into the store to see what's new; (2) other users become the sales team for the online store by introducing new members; (3) members of the community will share 'recommendations', thus leading to potentially more orders from the online store; (4) the online music store can discover the various likes and dislikes of its community – thus there is the opportunity to produce a rich source of useable data. This may include CDs that are not readily available in one country but may be so in another.

Armstrong and Hagel (1996, 1997) suggested four types of developing communities – transaction, interest, fantasy and relationship. Of course, these are not mutually exclusive. Below, we consider the potential shape of these communities and how they may develop further in the future.

Transaction communities

Here, the community is based on the principle of 'transactions'. However, the involvement of the 'community' can vary significantly within this environment. Levels of involvement could emerge out of this community type. Table 12.1 presents a suggested framework.

Interest and information communities

This term can be expanded to include knowledge gathering; for instance, through a learning community. An example would be an online degree programme where students are involved in group work online (see the Case Study below).

▼ Case study   Online MBA programme

The Oxford Institute of International Finance is a strategic alliance between the Association of Chartered Certified Accountants (ACCA) and Oxford Brookes

University. In 2002, it launched an online-supported MBA programme specially designed for accounting and finance professionals. Through its Virtual Campus, it provides students with a range of facilities including Seminar Areas, Resource Centre, a General Notice Board and a Virtual Library.

The Seminar Area provides students with the opportunity to debate and discuss specific questions related to a Module topic with each other and the Module Tutor. The Student Common Room is an area where the students can develop a 'community' atmosphere. Here, everything can be discussed from coursework through to who supports which football or cricket team. As it is a 'virtual campus', students are attracted from all countries. Thus, the community has an international focus. Equally, as it is a non-competitive environment, the online community environment can provide a support network.

Source: www.oxfordinstitute.org

Fantasy communities

These are communities where individuals and groups can live out their fantasies. In general, these are harmless sites where people do battle in a range of computer games or take on roles of super heroes. However, we should not be so naïve as to think that every fantasy community is harmless. Yes, they do include pornography, and the laws governing such material vary from country to country. It is a question of personal taste and individual morality as to whether that which is deemed legal is acceptable or not. However, there is a much darker malevolent aspect to some extreme types of pornography, some of which is unequivocally illegal in almost all countries – especially that relating to children. These have been a focus of worldwide police and media activity leading to the arrest of countless individuals.

Relationship communities

Within a relationship community, the various parties involved seek a relationship (in the broadest sense) and an understanding. This can be seen, in particular, where groups come together because they have a core interest that they share. As such, the relationship community can be purely information or knowledge-led. However, the community may become an important opinion-forming body. As such, they are able to disseminate valuable information on behalf of a commercial entity. Equally, they can disseminate negative views. Bearing in mind the potential global reach of the internet, negative publicity can often create difficulties for the company concerned. An example of ongoing negative public relations can be realised in the case of the McLibel trial (see Chapter 7).

Personalisation: understanding the customer's requirements

Amazon's founder Jeff Bezos stated that their primary objective is to be customer-centric in three areas:

First and foremost, listen to the customers and figure out what they want and how to give it to them. Second, invent and innovate on behalf of your customers. Third, is the most unique definition for the internet – personalization, putting each customer at the centre of their own universe (Price, 2000).

As suggested throughout this book, the internet has provided an opportunity for increasing levels of personalisation. Yet, it must not be seen as personalisation *per se*, where the company garners information on the customer but the customer remains, in essence, passive. The aim must be to create an interactive relationship in which a two-way exchange can take place freely. By engaging in such activity, companies have an opportunity to understand both the individual and the user community in a more productive, and yes, profitable manner. Through 'narrow-casting', companies can offer customers products and services that they are 'more likely' to purchase. It is this ability to approach customers sympathetically that could be the key to a company's online competitive advantage (Willman, 1999).

The economist and sociologist Vilfredo Pareto (1848–1923) postulated the 80/20 rule as a means of understanding income distribution; that is, 80 per cent of a nation's income will benefit 20 per cent of the population. Since formulating this ratio, Pareto's Law has been extended to cover numerous business functions and activities. One such relationship is that between a company's customer base and the level of purchasing activity. On this basis, some 80 per cent of the business emanates from 20 per cent of the customers. Thus, repeat business is crucial to a company's existence. An example can be gleaned from Amazon, where repeat business supplies more than 60 per cent of its sales (Willman, 1999). Thus, the focus on building an 'interactive (long-term) relationship' is critical.

Schubert and Ginsburg (2000) suggest that there are three different levels of personalization on the internet: identical, categorised and individualised.

Identical presentation to all customers

This can be described as a 'standard' web page that is the same for every visitor, whether a past customer or not. Thus, the system makes no use of automatic email-address identifiers or user profiles. This is a very basic level of personalisation and one that, unless highly specialised or unique, may not generate repeat business.

Personalisation by categorisation

Customers are broadly segmented into different user groups (or groups of particular interests). This is 'tailoring' to groups rather than to individuals. None-theless, profiles do emerge that illustrate socio-economic, socio-demographic, group preferences and user community-related information. Companies can therefore tailor their products and/or services to the requirements of the interest group. If we reflect back to our example of the specialist online CD store (see Transaction communities) the store owners can tailor their 'stock' to the requirements of the group. Needless to say, the group's requirements will change over time, especially when new CDs are released and/or re-issued.

Individualisation – knowing your customer and forming an alliance

As the sub-heading states, the focus of individualisation is getting to know the customer and forming an alliance with that user to mutual benefit. The emphasis has to on the alliance – because if the user does not believe they are gaining any benefit they will, most likely – though not always, switch their allegiance.

When potential users first visit the website, they have to register (which is free). As part of this process, they input their preferences. This information is stored and is the basis for presenting web pages that are tailored to the interests of the individual customer. This is not a static process – it's dynamic in several ways. Firstly, every time the customer visits the website, the database can update the customer's profile, especially if they purchase a product or service. Secondly, the website can use this information to update the web pages it presents to the returning customer.

A very good example of individualisation is the online retailer www.amazon.co.uk. Key examples of personalisation are listed below:

1. The visitor is recognized, by the system through their email address as they enter the website. As the page opens, it displays the user's name;
2. The system makes recommendations based upon the user's profile (including previous purchases), items that belong to the same category or complimentary to the chosen one and buyers of similar tastes. This is updated live so as to reflect any 'current' purchases;
3. Users can be emailed with messages alerting them to new books or CDs that match their user profile or that they have specifically requested;
4. Buyers are invited to submit reviews and comments (positive and negative) that might help like-minded users make their decision to purchase. This can have the effect of creating a 'buzz' around the book or CD, leading to an increased exposure and resultant purchasing.

The matrix in Figure 12.1 illustrates the different recommendation techniques deployed by Amazon whether the user is 'individualised' or 'browsing'. The use of email alerts 'pushes' or drives information towards the established user. On the other hand, Instant Recommendations and Book Matcher (finding the required text, equally effective for CDs) has the effect of 'pulling' or drawing the user into that web page. For the occasional or first-time browser, Amazon also uses direct web page based recommendations and rating techniques, along with others with names such as *Customer Buzz, Mood Matching*, to draw or pull the browser further into the site. If the browser likes what they see, then there is the likelihood of a purchase and/or a return visit.

As Schubert and Ginsburg (2000) suggest, Amazon is a good example of a business where the user community is united in a community of common interests (and benefits). However, as they also point out, the user community

	Individualised	**Browsing-mode**
Push	e-mail recommendations	
Pull	Instant Recommendations Book or CD Matcher	Customer Buzz Mood Matcher Book/CD recommendations Reviews/Ratings

Figure 12.1 **Techniques of customer recommendation**
Source: Schubert and Ginsburg (2000)

has no control (selection or organisation) over the type and range of reviews posted by Amazon. Whether Schubert and Ginsburg's suggestion that a 'third-level architecture' between buyer and seller would certify buyer-seller information would work effectively or not is debateable. Another layer or intermediary may create additional tensions between the buyer and seller, leading to the loss of the mutually beneficial alliance.

Customer profiling

As Schubert and Ginsburg (2000) suggest, customer profiling is the core of any personalisation system. They categorise eight different types of profiles that allow systems to gather and track information. This categorisation is reflected in Table 12.2.

Table 12.2   Types of user profiles

Profile	Content
Identification	User name, contact information, personal browser settings, address and IP-address
System	User ID and system activities (login and log-off times)
Session	Session-related information (click stream – which areas or icons the user has click on and thus 'visited')
Socio-economic	The user's self categorisation into preferred groups (age, gender, income and interests)
Preference	The user self selects preferences (sub-sets of music, politics, sports, fashion, books)
Interaction	The recording of the user's interests
Transaction	This is the log of the user's transaction (for instance, purchases (when and at what time), payment and the system used (type of credit card) and types and frequency of enquiries
Community	The user's community profile which will be based on a template of categories

Source: Adapted from Schubert and Ginsburg (2000).

Online companies have tended to report the number of users or registered members as a basis for their high market valuations (Grande, 2000). This was particularly the case with the early dot.coms, many of which collapsed under a mountain of debt. The problem with this type of 'profile' is that there is no indication as to whether or not the website user will actually become a buyer. As Grande (2000) suggests, there is often a gap between the number of users defined as registered members and those that make a purchase. It is this gap that online companies have to bridge.

Already, we have seen the introduction of increasingly sophisticated customer profiling services. Companies are collecting and processing information. The critical issue though is, as we have seen, more than collecting data. It is about building truly interactive relationships.

Metcalf's Law

As with Moore's Law stated in Chapter 1, Metcalf's Law is significant to the development and understanding of the internet and clearly illustrates the power of networking. Robert Metcalf, founder of 3Com Corporation and a major designer of Ethernet, stated that the value of a network increases exponentially with each additional node (a person connected). On this basis, as the number of users doubles, the value of the network quadruples.

America Online (AOL) provides an interesting example of Metcalf's Law. Originally it had been a variable rate depending upon an individual's time online. The longer the individual spent online, the greater the charge, and this was not the only cost. In addition to the online subscription, there would also be the local telephone company charge. The combination of the subscription and telephone charges was prohibitive to individual's spending large parcels of time online. Perhaps this was significant where parents of children, who were increasingly devoting their life to the internet, were paying for the charges.

In late 1996, AOL in the USA (then later in the UK) changed their pricing structure. From then onwards, it was based on a flat monthly rate that allowed unlimited use of the service, and it would combine the local telephone charges. Four things happened as a result:

1 The number of new subscribers grew dramatically;
2 The average daily usage grew significantly, although it later levelled off;
3 As the number of users doubled, the value of the network quadrupled;
4 AOL became a dominate player within the market. The value of their user base made it difficult for other providers to gain significant marketshare. In terms of Porter's Five Forces model, AOL was able to leverage their locked in user base as a barrier to entry.

Building such a customer base is the dream of every company or organisation. However, where 'bricks and mortar' companies can build such customer bases steadily overtime (perhaps several years), the rapidity of the internet creates an additional burden. That is the risk of overloading the system.

Consider the following analogy. You invite a few friends to a party. Your friends know that your parties are always great fun. They then tell other friends how wonderful your parties are. Their friends, in turn, tell their other friends about your party. The door bell rings. You open the door in the expectation of seeing four or five people. Instead you are faced with 30! Whilst the value of your reputation for throwing 'great' parties has significantly increased, that is probably not the thought going through your mind. There are perhaps more pressing issues such as: 'We need more food and drink' and 'Will the floor take the weight?'

The same can be applied to websites that have experienced dramatic increased click-through rates over a very short period. In several cases, the system has not been able to handle the volume of traffic, and crashed. Although this was particularly the case in the mid- to late 1990s, cases still occur when events overwhelm the system. Just before and during the Second Gulf War (March/April 2003), several news websites were either slow in loading or unable to load altogether as people swamped the internet for information.

Where possible, companies using the latest software and increasingly more powerful servers and mainframes must seek to anticipate future demands. This, as always, is easier said than done. However, like any business, online companies are dependent upon their returning customer base. In the vast majority of cases, there are alternatives on the internet. Failure to connect successfully and conduct a transaction will drive the customer onto some else's website.

Communities and brand building

Various companies have embarked on creating web sites that encompass a range of user interests. These, in many respects, complement the products or perceived values of the company or organisation concerned. In 1996, Disney launched www.FamilyFun.com, a bulletin board aimed primarily at mothers. The site is essentially divided into seven main pages:

- Activities and Crafts
- Home and Garden
- Parties
- Raising Kids
- Recipes
- Travel
- Life with Kids

In addition to a library of articles, there is also the Parenting Message Boards, a Weekender Newsletter (requires registration) and the opportunity to subscribe to a paper-based magazine. The added value provided by such a site helps to reinforce the cross-selling opportunities afforded by the brand. For instance, there is the opportunity to cross-sell their vacation packages to the various Disney resorts and cruise line.

The Family Fun website underscores Disney's own personal statement on families and family values. Thus, there is strong linkage between the family.com web site and the Disney experience as a family-oriented experience. Thus, clear and strong links can be seen between the online community and the brand.

This relationship issue, as stated elsewhere in this chapter, is crucial. As McWilliam (2000) states:

> [The site] must offer members not only entertainment but also a sense of involvement and even ownership. Communities require a truly bottom-up view of brand building, whereby the customers create the content, and are in a sense, responsible for it. This view contrasts markedly with many brand strategists traditional top-down view of business, where products and services are created by organizations and sold to customers.

McWilliam's last sentence is particularly valid here. Whilst many aspects of marketing (as we have seen) remain the same – whether it is a virtual environment or 'bricks and mortar' or not – other aspects must adapt. In some cases, these adaptations are bold gestures; in other cases, not so. However, if companies are actively seeking the development of long-term online relationships, then they must be able to think proactively and strategically.

If we concede that business today operates both globally and within an increasingly highly competitive (dynamic and complex) environment, then companies must be prepared to think differently. But, of course, this is not a risk-free environment. Companies that take such bold steps (sometimes into the unknown) are placing their brand in the 'line of fire'. That is perhaps why many companies still exert an element of control (possibly 'filtering') of their online community.

However, some companies do believe in a more open approach. Petroleum companies have, over the years, received significant negative media coverage. On this basis, it could be argued that it is a brave company that seeks to create an open forum for debate on a range of topics, some of which can be contentious. This is, however, what the Anglo-Dutch oil company Shell has done. At www.shell.com/tellshell, Shell have created open forums that provide an 'area in which people are free to comment on any aspect of Shell's policies, practices and principles. Engaging our stakeholders is at the heart of our commitment to listening and responding ... We are committed to open and transparent dialogue with our stakeholders, so come in and join the debate' (Shell, 2003).

The Shell forums cover the following issues:

- Energy and technology, now and in the future
- The environment – issues and commitments
- How much freedom should we trade for our security?
- Society and multinationals.

According to McWillam (2000), this site has attracted a range of comments from staff and customers. For an oil company, for instance, to take an uncensored

Table 12.3 Managing a brand-based online community

Responsibilities and activities Total brand strategy	Online community strategy and management

Professional managers

• Set broad competitive goals for the brand • Plan how to develop the brand • Devise a marketing communications strategy for the brand. This will include a mixture of traditional communications as well as online. Must support an appropriate sales strategy	• Set broad goals for the community and implement development. • Attract visitors to the website (this may include links to other sites). • Develop a calendar and special events. (Disney's FamilyFun site links to school vacation periods and specific times such as Easter and Christmas.) • Train and supervise volunteer managers. • Administer archiving of content. (The FamilyFun site, for instance, has various article libraries linked to their various main contents pages.) • Monitor evolving areas of interest. (This can be a mixture of areas within the site that receive increasing volumes of traffic and external sites that can be emulated.) • Set editorial guidelines. (Whilst it may be an open forum, there remain basic codes of decency that should be adhered to. Companies need to state clearly that they will remove offensive and legally dubious material; for example, defamatory.) • Ensure site coherence. (The links within the site must work effectively. The site must also be able to handle volume traffic, otherwise the website becomes a focus of complain. Thus the original aims and objectives of the site are overshadowed.)

Volunteer managers (Could also be considered as moderators and chat room hosts)

	• Welcome new members. • Encourage participation (This can be one of the most difficult aspects, especially as the aim should be to achieve wide-ranging participation. Initially, it may only be a few who are particularly keen to debate and discuss issues. The remainder are lurkers (see earlier footnote). • Identify interesting new topics. (These may emanate from other community members.) • Nurture shared values (The objective here is develop a community that wants to have, overall, the same values. These may be, for instance, transparency of issues/concerns mixed with respect for the individual, whether you agree with their point or not.) • Arbitration (From time to time there will be disagreements over issues. As we have stated earlier, passions can run high. The volunteer manager must have sufficient diplomatic skill to foresee (not always possible) potential problems and diffuse them before they become a bigger issue than they really are.

Community members

	Mutual interaction and relationship building generating comments and stimulating repeat visits.

Source: Adapted from McWilliam (2000).

approach (except for the removal of obscenities) is a bold move. However, by openly allowing criticism within the forum, it is showing that it can be a transparent organisation (whether it agrees with the comments or not). It is providing a potentially valuable open discussion on issues that are important to everyone. That probably can only benefit the brand over the longer term. As implied in Chapter 4, such a move as Shell's might certainly take the steam out of some of the more ideological hackers who might be tempted to carry out DoS attacks on Shell, for example.

Whether a company or organisation creates an open forum or regulates content, the site has to be managed effectively so that mutual benefits can be gained. McWilliam (2000) suggests strategies for linking the brand to the roles and responsibilities within the online community. This is elaborated in Table 12.3.

Table 12.3 illustrates several functions and functional layers. Clearly, the various members of the community do not work in isolation. For a community to work effectively, to the benefit of all, there must be constant communication between all parties. But it does not stop there. If a company or organisation wants their online brand-based web community to be successful, it must be a component of their overall brand strategy. The two must work together in concert and this can only be achieved by a coherent integration strategy.

Summary

This chapter considered the role of the wider community within the e-environment. Since the early days of the internet and the world wide web, online communities, through various forums, have come together to discuss and debate a wide range of issues. Some of these forums have been, and remain, very esoteric, whilst others have been coherent and immensely practical and accessible by a wider populus.

Companies have sought to gain legitimate access to these burgeoning groups. For some organisations, the transparency of this approach carries its own in-built risks. However, by holding such forums, both the company and members of the community can perhaps gain a better understanding of the issues, even though they may not actually agree. Nonetheless, it can demonstrate that a company seeks to be inclusive of all stakeholders. However, where brands are concerned, it cannot be purely a 'talking shop'. The issues become much greater than that, as vividly pointed out by McWilliam (2000) when she says:

> once given a voice, the brand community will act as the living manifestation of the brand's personality and relationship with the consumers. The obligations inherent in a brand relationship, now vocalized by the online community participants, will have to be fulfilled.

The companies that can achieve the 'added value' of such fulfilment will most likely gain competitive advantage in the future. However, the added value will not be a one-off act – it must be an ongoing process, if companies seek to maintain any semblance of a longer-term advantage.

Questions for review and reflection

1   What are the key ethical problems affecting the development of user communities? What can an e-business do to avoid some of these?
2   Strategically, what would be the differences between the approach to developing user communities of a small and rapidly growing retail e-business, and that of a larger more established electronic marketplace?

Notes and references

Armstrong, A. and Hagel, J. (1996) 'The real value of online communities', *Harvard Business Review*, May–June, pp. 134–41.

Armstrong, A. and Hagel, J. (1997) *Net Gain: Expanding Markets Through Virtual Communities*. Boston: Harvard Business School Press.

Chaffey, D., Mayer, R., Johnston, K. and Ellis-Chadwick, F. (2000) *Internet Marketing*. Harlow: Financial Times/Prentice Hall. (They suggest that the figure is more in the order of 35 000 newsgroups.)

Grande, C. (2000) 'How dotcoms may learn to value customers', *Financial Times*, 11 May, p. 5.

Groucutt, J. (2000) In unpublished research, the co-author viewed several newsgroups to gauge the level of activity and online behaviour. For example, it was clear from one (to remain anonymous) music newsgroup that passions were inflamed over particular CDs. The resulting aggression lead several members of the newsgroup to resign in protest. Whilst others attempted to mend fences, the culprits remained adamant about their views, and anyone who disagreed with them!

McClellan, J. (1999) *The Guardian Guide to the Internet*. London: Fourth Estate.

McWilliam, G. (2000) 'Building stronger brands through online communities', *Sloan Management Review*, Spring, pp. 43–54.

Price, C. (2000) 'Obsessed with customer service and experience', Information Technology survey, *Financial Times*, 2 February, p. XV.

Schubert, P. (1999) 'Aufbau and management virtueller Geschäftsgemeinschaften', *Electronic Commerce Umgebungen*, St Gallen.

Schubert, P. and Ginsburg. M. (2000) 'Virtual communities of transaction: The role of personalization in electronic commerce', *Electronic Markets*, vol. 10, no. 1, pp. 45–55.

Shell (2003) This quote is from Shell's website where it explains the role of the tell Shell forums.

Vaisey, D. (ed.) (1998) *Thomas Turner: The Diary of a Village Shopkeeper 1754–1765*. London: The Folio Society.

Willman, J. (1999) 'Consumer profiles made to measure', *FT Guide to Digital Business*, Autumn, p. 10.

☑ 13 The future

> *There is always one moment in childhood*
> *when the door opens and lets the future in.*
>
> The Power and the Glory (1940)
>
> Graham Greene (1904–91)

Introduction

In this chapter, we consider the future e-world. Whilst much of the material within this chapter is based upon current research, there has had to be a degree of speculation. However, we feel that for the final chapter this is no bad thing. However, we also consider what can be learnt from history, especially in relation to dot.coms and their future. From this, we examine via a PESTLE several key elements in the development of future e-environments. It is very easy to let the imagination to run totally free and portray a world that would be at home in a Steven Spielberg movie. Hopefully, we have resisted such temptations and portrayed realistic (although, yes, speculative) issues.

Learning objectives

On the completion of this chapter you should be able to:

1 Debate the potential future of e-business and the internet within a regional and global context;
2 Consider what issues could be learnt from the past and applied to the future;
3 Examine the PESTLE factors in relation to the future e-environment;
4 Draw your own conclusions as to what you really believe the future will be and how you will interact with it.

Looking back into history to view the future

The late twentieth and early twenty-first centuries witnessed a boom in dot. com business, most especially in the UK and the USA. Venture capitalists and banks were 'quick' to jump on the bandwagon and fuel investment in the new generation of online businesses. However, ideas do not always translate themselves into successful (*read* 'profitable') business ventures. As well as seed money to start these dot.com businesses, many flocked to launch on the respective stock markets. Both small and large investor alike saw opportunities for long-term rewards and, of course, the 'quick killing'. The myriad of dot.coms helped to fuel a stock market boom. The dot.coms were viewed as the new world of business – this was to be the future.

However, there were fundamental problems with many of the dot.coms. They may have been great ideas but the business was built on 'shifting sands'. It was as if the basic principles of business had been exempted in relation to the dot.coms. For instance, was there an actual market for the product or service being offered by the dot.com? If so, how would the goods or services be delivered to the customer? And, how long would it take to deliver these goods or services to the customer? Many of these issues – the fundamentals of business – have been outlined throughout this text. Yet, under the grip of 'dot.com mania', these fundamentals seemed to have been cast aside, ignored.

The result was a slow but devastating meltdown. Dot.coms that, almost overnight, became multi-million dollar businesses were now haemorrhaging money. Company directors revised their plans to persuade investors to rescue their businesses. Stock values fell, rumours spread around the financial markets. The former 'darlings' of the City were now considered 'lepers' to be avoided. Investors were now pulling out of anything that marketed itself as a dot.com. The result was inevitable. Anyone who had not been able to build a real business was likely to collapse, further fuelling the growing reticence to invest in any business associated with the consumer side of the internet. The dot.com bubble had burst, and most people, directly and indirectly, were affected by the subsequent fall out.

However, this is not the end of the story. The collapse of the dot.com market was portrayed as the end of e-business, that there was no-way it could ever recover. But that is not the experience of new emerging businesses if we look back at history. By considering some aspects of the past we may be able to build a more successful future. Let us return to the railways example discussed earlier in this text.

The birth and early development of the railway industry in the UK is a very good example of volatile businesses. In 1825, the Stockton to Darlington railway line was opened. Following George Stephenson's success with his Rocket locomotive in 1829, the Liverpool to Manchester line was opened. What followed was a slow development in the railway system – that is, until 1844. From then until 1847, Parliament passed some 442 Railway Acts and more than 2000 miles of track was opened (Briggs, 1999). The growth in railway planning and construction provided both direct and indirect employment. Many other industries expanded to meet the demands of the burgeoning railway companies, most especially those associated with coal and iron production and engineering.

This 'railway mania' – bigger than anything previously seen – changed the British landscape through ambitious construction projects. The rapid expansion of the railways, which overshadowed everything else, created a booming economy.[1] Yet, the bubble was about to burst.

The railway companies had been financed in the form of joint stock enterprises. In order to finance construction, the railway companies relied upon the savings of thousands of small investors (Briggs, 1999). However, there was no protection for these investors. The railway companies had been sanctioned by Parliament, and thus were not covered by the 1844 Companies Act that sought to improve 'transparency' and reduce reckless speculation. According to Briggs (1999), any attempt to regulate the supposedly dubious methods of the railway companies was doomed from the outset. The problem was that the majority of the members of Parliament had either invested in the companies or were directors of the companies. Therefore, regulation was furthest from their mind, should it prevent them from reaping the rewards of their investment and power.

Many of the railway companies promoted lines between small towns. These were unlikely to reap reasonable, let alone substantial, profits and dividends for their shareholders. However, their stock was heavily promoted well in advance of construction. In effect, the lines were built on a promise, some might actually say 'a wing and a prayer'. Yet, this could not last. The construction of this vast railway system (though not a network) was avariciously consuming capital. Entrepreneurs such as George Hudson believed expansion was critical, as well as creating new companies, he amalgamated companies, thus reducing competitive forces. However, the 6 per cent to 10 per cent dividends promised were unrealistic. Increasingly, shareholders were being paid out of capital, a fraudulent act (even then!).

Hudson and others had not considered any of the potential risks from a recession or a slow down in the economy. After all, passenger rail traffic seemed buoyant, but that did not hide the fact that rail shares were now overpriced. By 1847, recession was beginning to set in, the overpriced rail stock began to slip in value, and soon afterwards there was a cascade and the market in rail stocks collapsed. Those who had invested in the rail companies faced massive losses, indeed, in many cases, financial ruin. It was only now that the real extent of the problem was revealed, everything from artificially inflating share prices in order to sell them, selling land the railway companies did not own and hiding the real financial state of the companies.

The future of the rail companies clearly looked bleak. Who would want to invest in such a fiasco now? After initial declines due to the recession, passenger numbers began to steady and slowly climb once more. By 1870, the railways were carrying 322 million passengers per year, more than four times the number at the time of the bursting railway bubble (Hof and Hamm, 2002).

In reality, the bursting of the bubble removed the highly speculative ventures and many of the fraudsters. Those that remained were stronger and able to

---

[1] Briggs (1999) believes that an improvement in export trade in 1842 and 1843 also helped to establish an expansionist economy. Other authors appear to place the focus purely on the railways. However, it is most likely a combination of factors with the railways providing the greatest impetus.

develop a solid railway infrastructure upon which to grow. The railways were to enter a period of both passenger and freight growth. Its subsequent impact upon the British landscape and society then became immeasurable. By 1914, the railway industry in the UK was substantial, covering 20 000 miles of track operated by the 600 000 employees of the 120 companies (Jeremy, 1998). The business landscape of the railway industry has since changed, sometimes for the better and sometimes for the worse.

So, what does this trip to the nineteenth century actually prove? Business historians believe that there are strong parallels between the rapidly emerging railway companies of the nineteenth century and those of the dot.coms of the twentieth and twenty-first centuries. Whilst the actual company may not have been a 'sound' investment, the overall industry is solid. The key, of course, is investing in companies that have a robust idea and the management expertise to support it. What is fascinating is that the vast majority of traditional companies – the 'bricks and mortar' businesses – did not rush into the dot.com marketplace. The view, at the time, was that such dinosaurs would die off just like their namesakes. In the vast majority of cases, the reverse is true. It was the young aggressive eager to market dot.coms that died away. It is now, after surveying the marketplace, that the more traditional 'bricks and mortar' companies (such as the grocery chain Tesco) have established a place for themselves in the e-world. Tesco has brought to bear its market research and logistics knowledge to establish itself as the world's most successful online grocery trader.

Learning from the past can provide some bearing on the future. If the industry's infrastructure is basically sound, then there is probably a future for the businesses involved within that industry. Of course, no one knows how long an industry may last within a particular country, a classic example of this being the British ship building industry. Britain was the number one large-scale ship builder until perhaps the 1960s, and then the industry gradually disintegrated. Large-scale shipbuilding as a global industry, however, dramatically increased. Taking this view suggests that the internet and dot.coms, in particular, are far from over. The internet as part of a wider Information Revolution may slowly, but significantly, build over the next ten years or so. As we will see later in this chapter, that build will coincide with societal changes and changing technological platforms. Whilst there will be business failures along the way, the industry is robust.

Where do we go from here?

The future is relative. It is relative to who we are and where we are. If you are living in a luxury apartment block overlooking the River Thames in London, you might be looking forward to another business revolution. On the other hand, if you are living on the banks of a polluted tributary in a developing nation your outlook may be on how to survive. These may be 'extremes' but they underscore a fundamental flaw regarding the future. There is an assumption that the present is based upon a level 'playing field', to use an archaic phrase. The world is not benchmarked, it is an unequal, dynamic, often disorganised environment. The view that the internet and the world wide web would somehow equalise the world is, at least, currently a myth. If the basic infrastructures are not in place and functional, then there cannot be equality in the accessing of the internet and the world wide web. At least, not now!

So, what of the future?

Here, we turn again to our old, tried and tested mnemonic PESTLE (on this occasion we shall consider just the Political, Economic, Social and Technological factors, however). This is generally used to consider what is happening now. We want to turn that on its head and use it as a format for considering the future – of where we could be in the future. To some extent, this chapter is based on a mixture of disciplines including science, sociology and politics. Equally, there is a great deal of speculation as to what could be the future. However, crystal ball gazing is no bad thing – at least it allows us to test ideas and worst-case scenarios. Some of what is discussed may become a reality within the next five years – but, equally, it may remain the work of science fiction, at least in our lifetime.

Political

The futures of e-business, the internet and the world wide web have many and varied political dimensions. Here, we consider some of the key issues that will most likely be debated over the coming years.

Competitive advantage of nations

Porter (1990) asked several questions, amongst them were: Why does a nation become the home base for successful international competitors in an industry? and Why is one nation often the home for so many of an industry's world leaders? In his work, Porter (1990) was attempting to single out the factors that lead to countries excelling in some fields of enterprise but not others. That is how nations gained competitive advantage in, for example, chemical manufacture. Now, we may argue that in a digital world that would not matter. That could not be further from the truth. Even within a truly globalised world (depending upon how you defined it), nations, if for only economic reasons, would still need to seek an advantage, if not a dominance, in some industries or businesses.

Equally, dominance within certain high-tech fields would also provide political leverage against other nations. Although we have entered the twenty-first century, countries still use the blunt instrument of the threat of trade embargoes, tariff and non-tariff barriers to exercise their power. Whatever the remainder of the twenty-first century brings the world, sadly, governments will still need to flex their muscles, even with nations that are meant to be partners.

Nations will seek to support and develop advanced technological platforms. In economic terms, success in developing such systems will greatly aid the balance of payments.

In terms of the UK, there are lessons to be learnt from history. In the 1960s, the Prime Minister Harold Wilson coined the phrase 'White Heat of Technology'.[2] The view was that Britain was leading the world in scientific developments. In many instances this was true – the supersonic passenger aircraft Concorde was one example. However, through a mixture of mis-management, lack of investment in projects and people, the 'white heat' soon cooled. Scientists went to live in other countries where increased resources were made available, and thus in many fields of high-tech research Britain lost its competitive edge.[3] This had a significant impact upon both the UK technological and economic power for decades. This is a lesson learnt and one that countries will seek to avoid.

Knowledge and privacy

Whilst individuals may cherish their privacy, governments are becoming increasingly concerned about the global transmission of information. In the vast majority of cases, this is harmless. However, for governments to track down material deemed harmful (terrorist activities, serious crimes and espionage), they seek the powers to 'invade' an individual's privacy. This is an issue that has tested libertarians and e-ethicists alike. In order for society to have a greater flexibility and agility in terms of virtual global communication, perhaps the *quid pro quo* is governmental oversight. Some may argue that there is a risk of Orwell's 'Big Brother' here.[4] However, governmental oversight of communica-tions is nothing new. In the 1980s, British Security monitored all faxes sent overseas. Sophisticated computer systems were programmed to scan for specific words or phrases. The aim was to thwart terrorist and espionage activities. The

---

[2] White heat is the temperature at which metal emits a white light. At the 1963 Labour Party Conference, Prime Minister Harold Wilson made reference to the 'White heat of technology'. He was referring to both the high technological skills that Britain possessed at the time, and those it could possess in the future. The research at the time was 'pushing the envelope' of the possible; for instance, supersonic passenger flight, advanced military aircraft (English Electric Lightening) and main-frame computers (ICL). His speechwriter, parliamentarian Tony Benn, was appointed Minister of Technology in 1966 and was a prime mover in the development of the supersonic passenger aircraft, Concorde.

[3] The exodus of academics, scientists and highly skilled technologists was to become colloquially known as 'the brain drain'. This had a severe impact upon Britain's competitive stature. In the early part of the twenty-first century there is talk of Brain Drain II. There is an increasing number of academics leaving for places like Australia and the USA, where they can command higher salaries and enhanced research facilities. The investment by the UK Government in vIRC, for instance, may be a means of stemming the flow of talented people to other countries.

[4] Big Brother is the all seeing, all knowing tyranny in George Orwell's pessimistic nightmarish vision *Nineteen Eighty-Four*. Written in 1948 (published 1949), it portrays a world divided into three super states, each of which is permanently at war. Big Brother oversees the country of Oceania, which is governed by the Thought Police. Its citizens are restricted as to what they can think and do. Orwell fashioned the book on Russia's Stalin and how the then NKVD, his secret police, purged the population.

vast majority of the British public were unaware of such activity and it did not affect their daily lives.

However, there has been much debate regarding oversight of individuals emails and internet activity. Finding the appropriate balance will perhaps be the most difficult of exercises for future governments. With the likely risk of increased terrorist activity in the foreseeable future, this is most likely going to be the case.

Internet software: freely available or available free

A critical issue that is both political and economic is the debate over whether source materials in computing generally – but the internet is perhaps its most acute manifestation – should be made available freely for all, or whether it can remain under the control of its providers. Everyone who buys an IBM compatible PC has a version of Microsoft Windows, and probably also a word processing package. But this is not something that is available free to them by right – it is a gift from the software and the hardware firms. (This is a gift that serves their purposes at least as much as it serves ours, for it creates huge critical mass for a particular operating system, and locks users into other Microsoft products). But upgrades to this cost significant amounts, and in any case you are not really buying the software coding itself, but only a licence to use it. If you read carefully the license agreements that accompany the installation of many software packages, you will see that you are not allowed to modify the code in any way. It is not yours, you are just buying or being given the opportunity to use it.

The alternative approach, as mentioned before, is especially exemplified by the dispersion of the Linux operating system and the invention of HTML and http. Anyone can download Linux and modify it to suit their needs – many do, and in turn disseminate their refinements on the web.

This is the sharpest manifestation of the general issue over whether the internet should be a resource for all to benefit from, or whether it needs to be treated as a commercial entity, with all the trappings of this – intellectual property laws, charges for access to software or to specific sections of the web and so on. The issue is likely to run for some years before a final resolution. Given the dominance of the internet by the USA, and the general trend of US legislation and political sentiment towards commercial interests before individual citizens, our own guess is that the eventual resolution will contain at the very least substantial advantages for large corporations, though it is likely that certain freedoms, such as academic exploitation of ideas, will be preserved. It is unlikely, however, that the individual consumer will ultimately benefit from any areas of free access available on the web – whether through political or economic means, the average user will probably end up committed to a charge based access.

UK funding

In April 2002, the UK Government announced that it would invest UK£40 million in new technologies and formed the Virtual Interdisciplinary Research

Centre (vIRC – www.nextwave.org.uk) (BBC, 2002). This is a Department of Trade and Industry (DTI) programme to ensure that British business is both structured and equipped to exploit the new information and communications technologies. The Research Centre and its partners will focus on the Next Wave of technological developments. These are also called pervasive technologies (see the Technology section of this chapter). They link to the embedded intelligent systems within non-PC products. The objective is that everyday appliances within electronic environments can communicate information both within the Intelligent House and to external suppliers (for example, repairs). vIRC is linking up with companies and various university research centres to develop such embedded intelligent products and systems. Clearly, the UK Government, from their original seed financing, consider it is an important opportunity for both universities and companies to develop, manufacture and market these systems. Britain has become a focal point of much of the work in cutting edge software design and development. As many countries, it sees Next Wave technologies as a vital part of the country's future economic development. Equally, other governments take the same view. In the longer term, it may be both politically expedient and sound economic sense for governments to merge their research and business developments in this field. This is a possibility, especially within the European Union, perhaps especially as the universities, often the original focus of such research, openly share their views and ideas.

Economic

The advancement of technology will have several potential impact points on the economy:

1 Companies that develop such technologies will aid the balance of trade by exporting their products and after-sales service internationally;
2 Wireless technologies have the potential for greatly improving supply chain management. This, if adopted, could greatly enhance efficiencies for companies involved in JIT operations and logistics;
3 Preventative systems using microchip and wireless technologies could reduce the number of machine breakdowns. This could improve overall efficiency, and thus productivity. It would reduce the number of missed orders and lost contracts;
4 Service providers are likely to witness increased consumer purchase and usage of appliances with embedded technologies. These will range from mobile phones and computers to household appliances such as intelligent refrigerators and washing machines. This will generate retail and online sales. This will have an effect throughout business from manufacturer to logisticians;
5 The knowledge management systems that will be inbuilt to websites will be able to anticipate customer orders and make 'close-fit' recommendations. This could, by its very nature, help to increase purchasing. There is, of course, the risk that it removes an element of consumer 'thinking' with everything presented before you. However, significantly more research needs

to be conducted before any firm conclusions can be drawn here. Overall, the consumer is not as gullible as some advertising executives think they might be!

Societal

When the internet and world wide web were first introduced, there was concern that language would be a major barrier to the development of e-business. As Singh *et al.* (2001) state, Europe, for instance, does not have a uniform language or homogenous cultural platform. With such diverse languages, Singh *et al.* (2001) suggest that companies operating within a B2B or B2C environment must be culturally sensitive to both language and local approaches to business. In other words, that whilst we are using a uniform electronic platform, we must not forget emotional elements that drive an individual's culture. Neither the internet nor the world wide web can be seen as an imperialist activity as one culture attempts to impose its will upon another. Several e-retailers have become culturally sensitive and developed sites specific to a particular country or region of the world. Equally, it provides them with the opportunity to deliver both products and services that match the demands and needs of that country or region. Such activity relates back to Ohmae (1990) and his view of 'Thinking globally and acting locally'. Even within our exceedingly globalised world, this remains a truism for any organisation, no matter what its operating platform may be.

Another factor that should be considered is risk avoidance. The Dutch social scientist Hofstede (1984, 1994) produced an analytical framework of national cultures. It is divided into four areas: Individualism, Power distance, Uncertainty avoidance and Masculinity (also considered as the level of competitiveness). In relation to the internet, Uncertainty avoidance is particularly apt. In essence, this is how different cultures perceive risk and the amount of risk that they should take. For example, in Hofstede's research, the USA displayed a culture that was prepared to take a greater level of risk compared to that of France. The net, perhaps by its very nature, is inherently risky. Take, for example, the possibility of online fraud. Thus, some cultures may be less enthusiastic in embracing web technologies and interfaces. That then begs the question as to how they will handle new, more pervasive technologies?

Society will be affected by the introduction of new technologies (see *pervasive computing* in the Technological section below). However, to what degree remains the unanswered question? Although the new technologies will most likely provide greater choice, flexibility, accessibility and 24-hour convenience (Stone, 2001), this does not necessarily mean that there will be overwhelming and immediate changes in societal behaviour. Any study of diffusion theory suggests that there are those that readily embrace new technologies and those that either are 'slow' (a relative term) or who do not embrace the product at all, no matter how much time elapses (see Rogers, 1990).

Of course, one of the issues with *pervasive computing* is that it is 'pervasive', permeating all aspects of our lives. It is already there, whether we like it or not. The key is encouraging people to use the systems that are linked to the pervasive computing. One approach is the use of *permission marketing*, where the consumer or customer states the level of involvement they will have. Equally, they can set the parameters by which their personal details can be used beyond any governmental data protection system (see Chapter 5 for *permission marketing*).

As intimated earlier, the world is not one homogenous group. Societies vary not just because of culture and established norms. They also vary due to the economic circumstances in which they find themselves. Whilst societies rarely remain static, some are more readily able to react to the changing technological world than others. If developing nations wish to be involved within the growing Information Revolution, then the developed nations must support them. In this context, 'support' does not mean dictated to. Developing nations must be free to choose the level of support that they require, and that suits their developing needs.

Successful e-businesses and related industries will be those that understand geodemographics and the lifestyle activities of their key audiences. Equally, companies should not take for granted that the world's most powerful economies are the ones that will adapt easily and most readily to mobile commerce. Research suggests that France, Italy and Finland currently outperform the USA and the UK in moving towards mobile technologies (Stone, 2001).

Whilst wireless technologies will be able to provide various benefits, they will not exist alone. In many cases, both companies and individuals will opt for *blended* solutions – that is, solutions that are a mixture of contemporary and traditional technologies. An example of this is the e-learning environment. Although there are many courses that are purely internet based, there are many that are a mixture of on-screen components and 'traditional' paper-based materials. With the development of enhanced mobile communication, the focus may shift within the next 15 years or so. Equally, it is the secondary school children of today, for whom the mobile phone and computer are 'second nature', who will be in the best position to harness the advantages offered by mobile communication.

As Kreitzman (1999) suggests in his book *The 24 Hour Society*, the 24-hour freedoms are much more than the time shops are open. In Britain, slowly at first, we have become increasing used to major supermarkets being open 24 hours, especially those situated near major city centres such as London. If you like, the new '24 hours' is beyond the physicality of the 'bricks and mortar' store. It is even beyond the fixed linkage to a telephone line (digital or broadband). The increasing development of mobile systems will enhance freedom of movement. Whilst Kreitzman's last paragraph in his book sums up the issues of a 'physical' 24-hour society, it can also be read as the basis for the wireless world. Whilst it will free many people, as Kreitzman (1999) suggests, it will require thought and understanding not only in terms of how we adapt to potentially radical changes but how others do:

> The 24 Hour Society is not an automatic panacea to our time problems. It requires thoughtful participation if it is to help in redefining temporal relationships. But most important of all, it enables us to have a more egalitarian society in terms of who works when, frees us from the vicissitudes of living under clock

time without losing the economic benefits, and a prospect of cities in the 21st Century in which people can work, relax and play (Kreitzman, 1999).

Technological

Research suggests that the emphasis on physical connectivity will continue as the wired world slowly gives way to a predominately wireless one from 2007 to 2010 (Gartner, 2002). The introduction of wireless technologies and embedded micro chips will present the greatest transformational changes over the coming decade. Both the home and the work environments will be provided with a new digital architecture in which to operate. This should add to greater flexibility, mobility and agility. However, as identified in the section above, not everyone nor every country will adapt rapidly to such technologies.

Pervasive computing and wireless technology

In Chapter 1, we referred to the development by BT of the communication components for intelligent refrigerators. The development of intelligent systems is only one element of what IBM call *pervasive computing*. This can be defined as 'any computing device that is not a personal computer and thus includes everything from the Intelligent Refrigerator to the mobile phone' (Pearce, 2003). Another perspective is that *pervasive computing* is 'the next generation computing environments with information and communication technology everywhere, for everyone, at all times' (CfPC, 2003).

By 2002, there were already 325 million pervasive computing devices in existence, the view is that this figure will exceed one billion by 2005 (Pearce, 2003).

In essence, these are non-traditional computing devices that have, and will, become an increasing part of the fabric of our digital world. Again, as illustrated in Chapter 1, the link between a diverse range of electronic technologies will be convergent tools such as Bluetooth.

As can be seen from the above statistics, *pervasive computing* has become part of our lives, whether we are aware of it or not. Clearly, technology is being integrated into every aspect of our lives. The intelligent home of the future will be more than having a dedicated system that switches lights on or off, lowers or raises the blinds. This was the prophecy of the 1950s and 1960s. It is already here.

We are already seeing larger flatter screened TVs – however, they still 'sit in the corner of the room'. In the future, all home entertainment will be linked to the internet, where the screen forms part of the wall. The screen will not only provide a myriad of television channels but also access to a range of information from banking to voting at local and national elections. There will be no remote control devices, the link between the individual and the system will be via voice activation, a wireless glove or finger print recognition on any part of the screen.

Already we can write on a palmtop and have that converted into a typed script. With a wireless glove, you will not need a palmtop. Simply writing your signature in the air can be translated to the screen for recognition. This could be used for signing your credit card as part of a virtual security validation. Smart cards will contain certain information including retina identity and photographs so as to verify your transaction immediately.

Sensors will be hidden throughout the house, communicating lighting and temperature information to digital agents. The role of the digital agent is to respond to the environmental demands of the individual. This leads us back to the intelligent refrigerator.

Microchips embedded in the packaging are scanned by the refrigerator, which then logs an array of information from what the food product is to its ideal temperature through to the weight of the product and by when it must be consumed. The intelligent refrigerator will monitor the level of food supplies. When they reach a prescribed level, it will automatically re-order through its internet connection with approved suppliers. The delivery date and time will match those input into its onboard calendar. Once the delivery is booked, the system will email or text a member of the household. It will also be displayed on a digital panel on the front of the intelligent refrigerator.

We can go beyond the intelligent refrigerator to appliances that have a state of self-awareness. Consider, for a moment, the various components of a washing machine linked to an array of small sensors. The sensors could not only be used to monitor the functionality of the machine (that is, the wash–spin cycle, water levels and so on) but could also monitor the performance of constitutant parts. Such monitoring by sensors may detect an impending component failure. Pre-empting a 'machine breakdown', the onboard computer could send a message to the manufacturer stating where the failure will occur. Having received this information, the manufacturer can send a repairer at an agreed time to replace the component and service the machine before it fails. Whilst it would prevent the inconvenience of breakdowns to a household washing machine, imagine its potential usefulness in an automated factory where machine downtime due to breakdown can be costly in terms of lost or delayed orders. This is especially so where customers operate to increasingly more time sensitive JIT methods.

Tags

Bar code technology has contributed significant benefits to supply chain management (B2B) and the ease of shopping (B2C). However, bar codes have their flaws. For instance, the are prone to damage, they require (normally) human intervention to operate the scanners and read them, and they provide limited information (usually only a product number). Overall bar coding is a passive technology.

In order to liberate supply chain management further, companies have sought a replacement for bar code technology. Radio frequency identification tags (RFID), using wireless technology, could provide companies and organisations with the ability to enhance supply chain processes significantly. RFID tags contain a semiconductor and a reader or a radio. These can provide opportunities to improve customer services. RFID tags can provide the following immediate benefits (Wolff, 2001):

- They are robust.
- They do not require line of sight (compare that against a bar code that must be lined up for the code reader to register the information).
- They are programmable, thus an array of information can be stored on the tags from product destination and contents to weight.
- They can be used as a tracking device. Customers will be able to track their parcel via information displayed on secure internet sites. This will further improve the services currently available, creating added value for the customer. As well as individual consumers tracking parcels that have been despatched to them, companies will be able to track large quantities of packages. Even with heightened security, post-9/11 baggage being transported by airlines still goes missing. If every bag was RFID tagged, then the bag should be loaded onto the right baggage trolley (which will be computer driven) and delivered to the right aircraft for uploading. Equally, it should be offloaded at the right destination if the aircraft has multiple stopovers. If the baggage was being offloaded at the wrong destination, an alarm would sound. There would either then be human intervention or the system would re-check status and redirect the baggage as instructed. Such operations would not only reduce the substantial compensation costs to airlines, they would improve security and the airline's reputation. Anyone who has had their luggage lost by an airline is unlikely to travel with it again. The use of RFID tags could eventually fully automate baggage handling.

Such technology would assist in simultaneously driving down costs and improve supply chain efficiencies. This provides an opportunity to improve overall competitive advantage by delivering products and services at a time when they are required by the customer.

The intelligent room (also known as the smart room)

The very title – *The Intelligent Room* – harks back to the opening sections of Chapter 1, where we considered three ground-breaking (in terms of reflecting on computers) movies. *The Intelligent Room* sounds as if it should, in reality, be a movie title. As far as we know, no one has used it. *The Intelligent Room* is the stuff of science-fiction movies, yet far beyond that created in Kubrick's *2001: A Space Odyssey*.

The Intelligent Room brings together some of the technologies we outlined earlier within this chapter. As in humans, there are degrees of intelligence, and therefore abilities. The intelligent refrigerator is only one component of the true *Intelligent Room*, for a complete architecture or infrastructure has to be created and embedded into the room and the system has to be efficiently managed (by computer, of course). So, what could the intelligent room look like in the future and what role will e-business play? Some of the ideas considered here are already in demonstration homes – but not yet widely available. However, the gap between ideas and commercial viability appears to be continuously shrinking. What we thought would take five to ten years is often a matter of two or three. So, do not be surprised if any of the following are available shortly. Then it will be an issue of cost. However, like so many technologies (the mobile phone is a classic example), the cost may well plummet over time.

Integrating sensors: The key to the *Intelligent House* is integrating the range of sensors and systems in operation. It is not just a question of whether we walk from one room to another and the sensor noting that. It is more of a question of the system recognising that there is more than one person in the house or room, who they are and what their preferences might be. A couple can happily live together but have different reactions to, say, heat and cold. The system must be able to tell the individuals apart and judge conditions such as temperature. Equally, it must react to voice commands to modify systems, as required.

Whilst ambient sensing is a key to an *Intelligent Room*, there are other factors that the system needs to analyse. For instance, monitoring the weight of the furniture on the floor structure. Heavy furniture can damage the floor boarding, especially in older houses. Equally the positioning of the furniture so that the room maximises the benefits from air conditioning systems.

Visual and audio systems: As stated earlier in this chapter, the television and audio systems that we use today will be significantly different in the future. The television, for instance, will not be a gigantic, often cumbersome, box in the corner of the room. Instead, the plasma screens will be embedded into the walls, as will audio systems. Thus, room space is maximised and size is not an issue. The screen will be as big or small as owner wants it to be – it could be the whole wall. The problem with the various large screens of the past has been the loss of picture quality. We have already seen, with the development of digital technologies, that this has become less of an issue. Audio systems will also physically change as new delivery systems become available.

Perhaps the key issue with both visual and audio systems is that the traditional hand controller will be replaced by voice activation, hand signals (the wireless glove) and an inbuilt knowledge of who is in the room and the type of music that they normally listen to. Equally, room sensors will be able to judge moods, and thus (if programmed) can select music to match the person's mood.

Floor, wall and ceiling sensors: As indicated above, the whole room can be covered in concealed sensors. These will be able to feed a variety of data to a central house computer that would allow the central computer to make specific decisions. Currently, a house may have one infrared sensor that informs the central heating system that the ambient temperature is falling below the prescribed limit. Thus, the boiler is fired up to increase ambient temperature. However, in a large house the individual room temperatures can vary. Individual room sensors would be able to regulate the flow of heat (from a central source) to the rooms that require it the most (in response to preset limits). Thus, individual room sensors, used to create the appropriate comfort zone, could control individual radiators.

Lighting and other systems: Currently, there are basic systems that can switch lights on when the exterior light fades. These are regimented systems that cannot be controlled by the householder outside the house environment. Wireless technology will change this significantly. If the householder is delayed returning home, say in the middle of winter, they will be able to use either their mobile computer or their mobile phone to dial up their central home computer to instruct it, via voice or text commands, to alter lighting patterns, adjust the blinds and room temperatures. Thus, on returning home the house is 'welcoming'.

Voice activation: Significant research has been conducted in the field of voice activation and artificial voicing. We can now dictate text to our computer and have it repeated back to us. However, it is not a perfect system – but it will develop. However, we have to switch on the computer, boot it up, wait for software loading before we can start any dictation. This is a keying-in process. However, wireless technologies and voice activation systems will allow voice commands to control this process – but not while sitting in front of the computer. The system will react to the voice command from anywhere – even away from the house.

Then, link these systems to diagnostic testing. Currently, we read on-screen instructions as to why the software programme has just bitten the dust. Often, they are written in language that 'non-tekkies' do not understand. In the future, the computer will tell you what the problem is and what it is doing to rectify it. That provides the user with the opportunity to use their time more effectively, rather than trying to diagnose a fault they do not understand.

In Chapter 1, we considered the scarier side of voiced computer systems. However, as more intelligent systems are developed, there is no reason why voiced computers cannot benefit how we live and work.

Personal security: Unfortunately there will always be crime, that appears to be part of the human condition. Technology has greatly assisted in combating and reducing incidents of crime. An example is the often underrated CCTV system. Within *The Intelligent House*, sensors will detect any movements outside the house and any attempt to gain unlawful entry. If a break-in is successful, the central house computer can immediately alert police with details – but not just that a robbery is in progress. Lights and digital cameras can be automatically activated, thus both recording the event and distracting the intruders.

These are some of the ideas in development for the *Intelligent Room*. However, that room does not need to be in a house. It could equally be in an office block or a factory. The combination of wireless technology, increasing computing power and new software developments will create a variety of *Intelligent Room* scenarios.

The link to e-business

E-business is involved in these technologies on several levels:

Level 1: Companies will be actively involved in the R&D processes and manufacturing of embedded systems. Component suppliers will communicate via e-business systems, as well as working with manufacturers to devise leading edge technologies;

Level 2: The marketing of these systems within the B2B and B2C environments;

Level 3: The ongoing maintenance of these embedded systems. This will include updating and further refinements;

Level 4: Companies will be deployed to monitor systems whilst, for example, the householders are away on vacation;

Level 5: Companies reacting to the demands of embedded and intelligent systems. For example, the intelligent refrigerator communicating with the online grocery store to replenish supplies or particular produce by a particular date.

In this brief glimpse of the PESTLE factors, there are both opportunities and concerns. The difficulty for both companies and individuals alike is finding the best way of exploiting the opportunities without increasing the potential side effects – namely societal disruption and disadvantage. This dilemma is far from a new experience. It has affected civilisations since the discovery of fire. However, the difference here is that technology and the impact of this technology is not gradual. As we have seen, it is exponential – something we have not seen before. How the global society copes with such potential transformation is the true unknown.

Summary

Figure 13.1 illustrates how we have moved from the mainframe computing environment of the 1960s to greater physical connectivity at the dawn of the twenty-first century. The vast majority of us have experienced that through the use of the internet and mobile phones. As this diagram suggests, the next 20 years will witness an increase in connectivity, that technology will be both all encompassing and an integral part of our lives – no matter what lifestyle we lead.

The introduction of wireless technology and associated hardware/software moves e-business away from a static model to an increasingly flexible one. In the future processes (for example, ordering and payments) and information will be available at any time and anywhere. Our ability to control information, whether on a personal or industry basis, will change radically. The use of voice and virtual touch systems will provide us with greater control over systems and provide the opportunity to improve our daily lives.

Some of the systems being developed and advocated may be in the realms of science fiction. However, the communicators portrayed in the 1960s TV series *Star Trek* were considered farfetched, ridiculous and just impossible! So, what do we consider the mobile phone to be? Today, we have small, highly portable videophones – what would have Captain Kirk made of them?

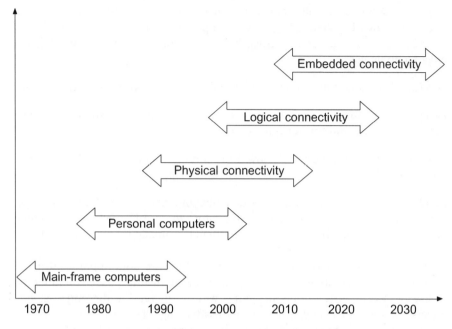

Figure 1 **From mainframes to embedded connectivity**
Source: Gartner (2002)

We opened Chapter 1 with a quote from the determined and ultimately brave scientist Marie Curie – 'Nothing is to be feared. It is simply to be understood'. That remains true, not only for today, but for the future.

Questions for review and reflection

1 The history of the internet to date has been technology driven – as certain facilities became functional they became available, and their role in the overall network emerged as users found applications for them. Social and political forces have trailed in the wake of technological development. How far do you think that will remain true in the next 20 years?

2 We gave an ambiguous, though tending to the pessimistic, view of the probable resolution of the tension between openness and commercial control regarding the internet. How do you think this (a) will; and (b) should be resolved in the future?

3 We have used the theory of intelligent buildings in several places in this text. What other aspects of our lives are likely to be changed to become more internet integrated over time?

Notes and references

Briggs, A. (1999) *England in the Age of Improvement 1783–1867*. London: Folio Society.

CfPC (2003) 'Concepts and technology for the future', Centre for Pervasive Computing, www.pervasive.dk

Gartner (2002) 'Key technology advances from 2003 to 2012', *Predicts Spotlight*, Gartner Group.

Hof, R. and Hamm, S. (2002) 'How e-biz rose, fell, and will rise anew', *Business Week Online*, 13 May.

Hofstede, G. (1984) *Culture's Consequences: International Differences in Work-Related Values* London: Sage Publications.

Hofstede, G. (1994) 'The business of international business is culture', *International Business Review*, vol. 3, no. 1, pp. 1–14.

Jeremy, D.J. (1998) *A Business History of Britain: 1900–1990s*. Oxford: Oxford University Press.

Kreitzman, L. (1999) *The 24 Hour Society*. London: Profile Books.

Ody, P. (1999) 'Online delights for the adventurous', Information Technology Survey, *Financial Times*, 1 December, p. v.

Ohmae, K. (1990) The *Borderless World*. London: Harper Business.

Pearce, J. (2003) 'IBM: Pervasive computing is the future', *Silicon.com.*, 30 January.

Porter, M.E. (1990) *The Competitive Advantage of Nations*. London: Macmillan.

Rogers, E. (1990) *Diffusion of Innovations*. New York: Free Press. (This remains the classic text on diffusion theory).

Singh, T., Jayashankar, J.V. and Singh, J. (2001) 'E-commerce in the US and Europe – is Europe ready to compete?', *Business Horizons*, vol. 44, no. 2, pp. 6–17.

Stone, M. (2001) 'Pervasive or invasive – managing the customer on the move', *IBM Global Services Report*.

Wolff, J.A., (2001) 'RFID tags – an intelligent bar code replacement', IBM Global Services Report.

⋈ Index of companies and organisations

Amazon 13, 21, 42, 115, 130, 138, 175, 200, 227ff, 242f
American Marketing Association (AMA) 92
AOL 21, 73, 244
Apple 3
Ask Jeeves 186, 230
Association of Chartered Certified Accountants (ACCA) 239f
AT & T 28

Barclays 41
Barnes & Noble 115
BASF 104
Bayer AG 103
BBC 129, 176
BBN 11, 27
Bell 6
Blackwell.co.uk 176
Bloomberg 42
BMW 103
Bookseller, The 176
BT 11, 18, 21, 28

CERN 12, 62
Chartered Institute of Marketing (CIM) 92
CIA 142
Cisco 13
CNN 129
Compuserve 230
Co-op Bank 41
Covisint 193

Daimler/Chrysler 193
Decca Classical Music 121, 147
Degussa 104
Dell 13, 95, 121, 138ff
Deutsche Telekom 104
Disney 245
DTI 257

easyjet 91, 107, 137
eBay 45, 227

Economist, The 134
Emagic 214
EMAP/DMAP 136
eMarketer 129
Eriksson 17ff
Ernst and Young 17
eUniversities Worldwide 39
Evening Standard 186
Expedia 138

Financial Times 129
Firstdirect 41, 186
Ford 193

General Motors 193
Giga Group 94
Glazxo-Wllcome 131

Heinz Foods 124f
Hoover 60
HSBC 41, 186

IAB 128, 136
IBM 4, 18, 256, 260
Infraserve Höchst 104
Institute of Public Relations 142
Intel 18
iVillage.com 103, 130, 131, 238

John Barry 147f
Johnson and Johnson 131
Jupiter 135, 136

Kazaa 44
Kimberley-Clarke 131

lastminute.com 118, 205, 216
Lee Jeans 147
Lloyds 41
Lucent 18

Marconi 6
Mastercard 222

McAfee   71
McDonald's   52, 145f
McKinsey   129, 135, 136
MediaGuardian   135, 136
MI5   142, 143f
Microsoft   12, 18, 26, 52, 61, 71, 79, 190, 221, 256
Midland Bank   186
MIT   6, 62
Motorola, 18
MSN/Hotmail   55, 73

Napster   44, 60, 61
Nokia   18
Norton   71

Oxford Brookes University   21, 239f
Oxford Institute of International Finance 239f

Peoplebank   39
Planet U   95
Pringles   127f
Procter & Gamble   131
Prudential   41
Prudential/Egg plc   141

Rand Corp   10, 11, 27
Royal Caribbean Int   125ff
Royal Mail   222

Sainsbury's   34, 176
SAPMarkets   104
Scotch Tape   43
Sellotape   43, 60
Shell   246, 248
Sony   52
Sunday Times   176

Tesco   34, 106, 107, 130, 137–8, 176, 238, 253
This is London   186
Toshiba   18
TSB   41

Unilever   131, 136
Université Catholique de Louvain   21
University College London   11
University of Southern California   11
University of Texas   155f

Verisign   86
Virtual Interdisciplinary Centre   257
Visa   131
Volkswagen   103

Wall Street Journal   129
Wal-Mart   106

Xerox   214

Yellow Pages   39

▣ ⍌ Index of web references

http://www.altavista.com   23
http://www.amazon.co.uk   21
http://www.amex.com   6
http://www.askjeeves.com   23
http://www.Avon.com   238

http://www.bayer.com   103ff
http://www.bbc.co.uk   129
http://www.bloomsbury.com/harrypotter
   175
http://www.bluetooth.com   18
http://www.brookes.ac.uk   21
http://www.bt.com   18

http://www.cnn.com   129
http://www.coolread   175

http://www.deccaclassics.com   121
http://www.dell.co.uk   121ff
http://www.dell.com   138ff
http://www.dfas.mil   22

http://www.easyjet.com   107
http://www.economist.com   134
http://www.eriksson.com   17
http://www.excite.com   23

http://www.F1.com   238
http://www.familyfun.com   245f
http://www.friendsreunited.co   33
http://www.ft.com   129

http://www.globalexchange.org   146
http://www.google.com   23
http://www.greenpeace.com   238

http://www.heinz.com   124f
http://www.hku.hk   22

http://www.infoseek.go.com   23
http://www.insf.org   22
http://www.ivillage.com   131

http://www.jamesbond.com   142f
http://www.jmm.com   135
http://www.jobs.ac.uk   36, 187

http://www.landsend.com   6
http://www.leejeans.com   147
http://www.libean.com   6
http://www.lycos.com   23

http://www.marketingpower.com   22
http://www.mastercard.com   6
http://www.mcspotlight.org/case/trial
   145–6
http://www.mi5.gov.uk   22, 143
http://www.monash.edu.au   21
http://www.monster.com   187

http://www.nextwave.org.uk   257

http://www.oxfordinstitute.org   240

http://www.pringles.com   127f
http://www.prudential.co.uk/plc   141

http://www.rand.org   10
http://www.royalcaribbean.com   125f

http://www.shell.com/tellshell   246

http://www.tesco.com   107

http://www.ucl.ac.bc   21
http://www.USP.com   6

http://www.virgin.net   22
http://www.visa.com   6

http://www.wsj.com   129

http://www.yahoo.com   23, 24

◪ Index of proprietary references

2001: A Space Odyssey   4, 262
ARPA, DARPA   10, 27
ARPANET   11

Billion Dollar Brain (film)   5
Biztalk   190
Bridget Jones Diary   115

Colossus computer   5, 9

Die Another Die (film)   142
Dove Nutrium Bar   136

eCount   222
ENIGMA   5, 9
Eternal Echoes (album)   147f

Flash   131

HAL (computer in film 2001)   4ff
Harry Potter, books and movies   174f

James Bond   142
JANET   36

Lotus Notes   207

Marketing News   20, 28
Microsoft Windows   256
MILNET   11
Mini Cooper   236
Mondex   222
MOSAIC   12

opodo   118

Passport system of payments   221
Paypal system of payments   222
Playing by Heart (album)   148

Star Trek (TV show)   265

The Antidote (publication)   13, 27
The Beyondness of Things (album)   148
The Italian Job (film)   236

USENET   12, 237

Virtual Campus and Library   240

■ ⌄ Name index

Aizu, I.   15, 27
Almquist, E.   158, 162, 163, 166, 166, 173
Andresson, M. and Bing, E.   12
Ansoff, I.   33, 36
Armstrong, A. and Hagel, J.   239, 249
Arnott, D. and Bridgewater, S.   172, 173

Babbage, C.   4
Baker, J.   227
Bamberger, P. and Meshoulam, I.   210ff, 215
Baran, P.   11
Barry, John   147f
Beaumont, J.   39, 46
Begley, E.   5
Berners-Lee, T.   11, 12, 27, 61, 236
Berry, L.   153, 173
Biro, K.   16, 27
Blackshaw, P.   146, 150
Bloomqvist   153, 173
Booms, B. and Bitner, M.   96
Bowman, C.   198, 215
Briggs, A.   251f, 266
Brynjolfsson, E. and Hitt, L.   229, 231
Bughin, J.   23, 27, 129, 135, 150
Burns, A.C. and Bush, R.F.   109
Byers, S.   144

Caine, M.   5
Cartellieri, C.   132, 150
Cartwright, R.   50
Castells, H.   27
Chaffey, D.   191, 197, 198, 215, 237
Chee, H. and Harris, R.   92, 93
Churchill, W.   9
Curie, Marie   3, 266

Day, G.   173
Day, G. & Montgomery, D.   119
Deighton, L.   5
Dell, M.   139, 150, 155
Dertouzous, M.   6, 27
Dibb, S.   112, 116, 119
Diese, M.V.   217, 218, 225f, 229, 231

Drucker, P.   93
Dutta, S. and Sergev, A.   96
Dye, R.   146, 151

Eisenhower, D.   10
Englehard, S.   136

Fanning, S.   44, 60
Ford, Henry   153
Forrester Research   66, 103
Furash, E.   172, 173

Gartner Group   20, 260, 266
Gates, B.   26, 27
Gavin, D.   163, 173
Godin, S.   167, 173
Gormsson, H.   17
Grande, C.   244, 249
Greene, Graham   250
Greenspan, A.   230
Greiner, R.   205f
Grönross, C.   154, 173
Groucutt, J.   237, 249
Guptara, A.   93

Handy, C.   205, 215
Hodges, A.   5, 11
Hof, R.   94
Hof, R. and Hamm, S.   252, 267
Hofstede, G.   258, 267
Hudson, G.   252
Hunt, S. and Morgan, R.   154, 173

IDG   68, 87
Innis, H.   14

Jeremy, D.   253, 267
Johnson, G. and Scholes, K.   46
Joscher, C.   5, 9, 12, 13, 27

Kelly, S.   169, 170, 174
Khermouch, G.   151
Kinkin, E.   94, 152
Kotler, P.   112, 119
Kreitzman, L.   259f, 267

Kubrick, S. 4
Kung, H. 16, 28
Laudon, K. and Traver, C. 68, 87, 191f, 197, 224, 231
Lerer, L. 111, 115, 119
Lewis, D. and Bridger, D. 34, 46
Longworth, D. 94
Louvier, P. and Driver, J. 112, 113, 117/8, 119

MacIver, K. 102
Madden, R. 5, 28
Masood, S. 103, 104, 105
Mattelart, A. and Mattelart, M. 14, 27
McCarthy, Joseph 10, 96
Mcfarlan, F. 16, 27
McLellan, J. 13, 27, 237, 249
McLuhan, M. 14, 15
McWilliam, G. 246f, 249
Metcalfe, R. 244
Mintel 101
Mintzberg, H. 201ff, 215
Moore, G. 13
Moore, Jo 144
Morris, D. 145

Naughton, J. 27
Nicolle, L. 167, 174
Nielsen/NET 7, 28, 96, 98, 101
Nonaka, I. 165, 174

O'Donahue, J. 148
Ody, P. 267
Ohmae, K. 6, 28, 258, 267
Orwell, G. 255

Pareto,V. 241
Pearce, J. 260, 267
Peattie, K. and Peters, L. 172, 174
Peppers, D. 154, 169, 171, 174
Percival-Straunik, L.L. 66, 87
Perreault, W. 114f, 119, 121
Pettinger, R. 46

Porter, M. 36, 40, 46, 244, 254, 267
Price, C. 241, 249
Princess Margaret 144

Rapp, S. and Collins, T. 153, 154, 174
Rayport and Sviokla 16
Reichheld, F. 154, 174
Ries, A and Trout, J. 116, 119
Rimmington, S. 143
Ritzer, G. 145, 151
Rowling, J.K. 174f
Ruello, A. and Renault, E. 18, 28
Ryan, C. 94, 174

Schmidt, C. 7, 17, 28
Schubert, P. 236, 249
Schubert, P. and Ginsberg, M. 241, 243, 249
Sculley, J. 3
Shrut, B. 126
Singh, T., Jayashankar, L. & Singh, L. 28, 258, 267
Stalin, J. 255
Steel, H. 145
Stephenson, George 251
Stone, M. 258, 267

Turban, E. and King, D. 184f, 197
Turing, A. 5, 9
Twentyman, J. 105

Vaisey, D. 235, 249
Varianini, V. and Vaturia, D. 93, 99, 154, 174

Walsh, J. and Godfrey, S. 172, 174
Ward, R. 160, 174
Wedgwood, Josiah 105
Willman, J. 138, 151, 241, 249
Wison, H. 255
Wolff, J. 261, 267
Wunderman, L. 105

Yelkur, R. and DaCosta, M. 91, 112

⩔ Subject index

24 hour society 259f
24/7 society, advantages and potential problems 57, 58
Abba, hit singles websites 54
academic community and influence on internet tradition of freedom 61
acceleration of global competition 3
access to internet 34, 55
acquisition of customers 157
ActiveMedia 8
adhocracy 203
advertising driven revenue model 224
advertising on the internet – ethics of 63
affiliate revenue model 224
Afghanistan 59
'airport' technology 73
aligning organisational elements 167
allegiance, political in internet era 53
Altavista 23
ambient sensing 263
Ansoff matrix 32ff
anti-advertising movement 137
anti-competitive behaviour 105
anti-virus or anti-malware software 71
applets, bad 70
Area 51 (US military base) – subject of newsgroups 237
Asia 8, 137
AskJeeves 23, 40
asymmetric encryption *see public key*

B2B (Business to Business) 16, 20, 24, 40, 42, 93, 102, 105, 121, 140, 180, 190, 196, 219, 222, 261
B2C (Business to Customer) 16, 22, 24, 40, 42, 102, 121, 130, 180, 219, 222, 228, 261
B2E (Business to Employee) 17
BACS system 221
banking online 114
banner advertising, animated 128, 131
barriers to industry entry 34
behaviour-based segmentation 113
Belgium 58
Big Brother in Orwell's 1984 255
Big Brother state, fear of 50–51

billing and invoicing 25
Biztalk 190
Bjork, website 59
black hat hackers 80
Bletchley Park 5, 9
bluetooth 17, 28, 260
Bombay 6
book matcher 242f
bookmark moment 45
bookselling – profit margins 227f
bookshops 56
brand based online communities 247
brain drain 255
brand awareness and marketing communications 121, 122–3
brand names – registration of by unrelated individuals 78
bricks and mortar 114, 130, 163
broadband 28
brokers 183
bulk purchasing 36
bundling of software 61
business models 200
button advertising 131ff
buy-side procurement 191
buzz 237
buzz marketing *see viral marketing*

C2B (Customer to Business) 16, 17
C2C (Customer to Customer) 16, 180, 190, 222
call centres 39
campus networks 29
'car radio' style tests of web pages 77
cartels 105
categorised web personalisation 241
cc-Chemplorer 104
cc-markets 104
CD-ROMs 43
CDs 114
CERN 12, 62
chat rooms 133
chat rooms – liability for content 60
chat rooms used for market research 99
Chemplorer marketplace 104

chess on the internet   53
'chicklit' genre   115
China   6
Christianity   59
Classifications of e-business   16ff
classified website advertising   131ff
click through rates – increases and
    operational implications   245
clicks and mortar concept   199
click-through tracking of customers   133
client/server system   29
clothing retail firm as hypothetical example
    of physical/internet business   226
collaborative commerce   41, 194f, 228
collaborative planning forecasting and
    replenishment (CPFR)   195
commercially confidential information   75
Companies Act 1844   252
competence and management of resources
    213
concept virus   71
Concorde   255
connectivity, levels of   266
consortium exchanges   103
consumer exchange model   23
consumer packaged goods (CPG) brands
    136
contagion marketing   see viral marketing
content service provider model   23, 40, 130
continuous replenishment of supplies   182
contract risk   184
contractual commitments made via
    email   76
control over suppliers   183, 188
cookies   29, 44, 63, 133
core competencies and capabilities   213f
core competencies   229
cost of capital – internet having little direct
    influence on   218
cost of standard PCs   55
crackers – criminal hackers   80
credit worthiness   223
crop circles websites   54
CSS (Cascading Style Sheets)   22
cult of the dead cow hackers community
    79
customer buzz   242f
customer cycle   157
customer data collection   161
customer groups on internet   96
customer groups on internet compared by
    gender   96
customer profiling   243
customer relationship management
    (CRM)   152, 158
customer service   37

customer service quality   208
customer value analysis   164f
customer value proposition   217
customer values   158
customers on the internet compared by
    age   96
customers wishing to see/touch goods
    pre-sale   34–5
cyber communities   see virtual
    communities

data mining   44, 95, 102, 118, 168f
data protection   74
data theft from databases   81
data warehouse development   170
data warehouses   95, 102, 118, 168f
data warehouses, ethics of   102
death of distance   xiii, 39
decline and termination of customers
    157
delay times, reduced with
    cyber-segmentation   117
delegation of managerial responsibilities
    204
demogrphic segmentation   113
denial of service (DoS) attacks   81f, 248
Denmark   17
designators   22
developed vs. developing nations and
    e-businesses   3
development of customers   157, 163
development of internet   9–13ff
Diana, Princess, death of   52
Diese model adapted for local
    councils   219f
Diese model intended for PLCs essentially
    219
digital cash   221f
digital certificates   86
digital envelopes   85
digital signatures   86
digital wallet   221
digitisation   42
direct marketing   105, 137
disabled and immobile members of society,
    use of internet   57
disaggregation   170
discussion groups on internet   54
disintermediation   170, 184, 187
distributed HR services   39
distributors   183
diversification   36
divisionalised   202
domain name regeneration   30
domain names   21, 30
dot.com 'bubble'   251

dot.coms   xiii, 106, 163, 199, 216, 250f
dot.coms and stock market slump   230
downstream supply chain   181f
DSL   28

e-procurement and operating margin   218
e-advertising   128f
ease of payment as a source of competitive
    advantage   223
e-auctions   41
e-business defined   19
e-business models   43ff
e-cards   148
e-commerce defined   19
economic implications of the internet   55ff,
    257
e-distribution   106
e-distributor   192
education online   52
e-focus groups   99
elderly people, use of internet   57
e-learning   39
electronic letters of credit   223
electric pen and screen facility   225
electricity consumption of the internet   62
electronic billing presentment and payment
    (EBPP)   223
Electronic Commerce Directive (EU 2002)
    60
electronic consortia   192
electronic data interchange (EDI)   189, 190,
    195, 227, 229
electronic exchange   192
electronic surveillance and telemetric
    devices   17
e-logistics   106
email alerts   168
email wiretraps   81
email, potential negative impact on
    marketing communications   120ff
email, unsolicited   82
e-marketing   95
e-marketing programme stages   171
e-marketplaces   102f, 140
e-marketplaces – collapse of many in
    2000   104
encryption   75, 85   (see also private key,
    public key, symmetric, assmmetric)
English, use of on the internet   53
enterprise application software   189
entry barriers to industries   42, 43
environmental implications of the
    internet   62
e-observation   100
e-pricing   96
e-procurement   19, 25, 36, 40, 102f, 180

e-procurement – forms   191
e-questionnaires   99
e-tailers   23, 130
ethical implications of internet   63
Europe   8, 105, 137
European Union   60
Excite   23
exclusion   54ff
extended mark-up language (XML)
    22, 189f
extranets   189

fantasy communities   240
financial fraud on internet   68
financial risks in international transactions
    223
Finland   53, 258
firewalling   71, 72f, 75, 82   (see also proxy
    server)
firm infrastructure   38
first mover advantage   60
first time buyers   156
five forces model   40ff, 244
floor, wall and ceiling sensors   263
Florida, disputed election result   51
four 'e's' of internet marketing   94
four/seven 'P's' of traditional
    marketing   96, 97
Framework for Global Electronic Commerce
    (USA 1997)   60
France   258, 259
freedom vs. control debate for internet   61
FTP (File Transfer Protocol)   31

G2B (Government to Business)   17
G2C (Government to Customer or
    Citizen)   16, 17, 50ff, 180, 219
garage music   237
GCHQ   9
geodemographic segmentation   114
geographic segmentation   113
Germany   39
global online advertising   137
global sourcing   62
global village concept   14ff
Google   23
government service delivery online   51
grey hat hackers   80
growth of homes in UK with internet   34
growth of online population   20
Gulf War, Second   245
Gutenberg   3, 6

hackers   63, 74, 78ff
hackers – types of   80
hacking – people's reason for   78–9

hactivists and hacktivism 79, 237
heterogeneity in market segments 115
holographs on internet, potential for 59
home use of internet 7, 96
homogeneity in market segments 114
Hong Kong 8, 51
horizontal marketplaces 194
HR business model 211
HR strategy 198, 210ff
HTML (HyperText Markup Language) 12, 20, 22, 24, 189, 256
HTTP (Hyper Text Transfer Protocol) 12, 21, 31, 256
hub marketplaces 193
hubs 29
human factors in internet security 71, 75f, 83
Human Resources (HR) 38, 39

identical presentation style 241
identity misrepresentation 81, 85
IMAP (Internet Mail Access Protocol) 31
impact of e-business on culture and society vxi
impact of www on lifestyles 13
increase in tracking platforms 34
India 6, 8, 39, 53
individualism, cultural dimension 258
individually customised web presentation 242
industry analysis 33
infomediaries 184
information as raw material 16
Information Revolution 253
information sharing in government – relative lack of 50
Infoseek 23
infrastructure necessary for internet 15
innovation 211f
innovative assemblage of competences 213f
instant recommendations 242f
integrated marketing communications (IMC) 120, 122f
integrating sensors 263
integration of internet and customer activity 155
intellectual property 59
intelligent fridges 18, 261
intelligent house concept 18, 42, 261, 263
intelligent room concept 262f
interactivity 138
intermediaries in the supply chain 183f
internal efficiencies in internet operations 229
internal; secondary research under-

utilised 100f
internet 2 31
internet advertising – impact so far 135
internet advertising spend 128–9
internet advertising – types 131ff
internet and world wide web 19
internet backbone 28
internet based EDI 223
internet cafes 55
internet communities 45
internet deprivation 15
internet personalisation styles 241
internet recruitment 36
internet services provider (ISP) 21
INTERNIC 30
interest communities 239f
interstitials see pop-up advertising
intranets 120f
investment in e-business 228f
IP (Internet Protocol) 30
IP address 30
iris recognition software 75
irrational exuberance 230
Islam 59
ISP model 23, 29
Italy 59, 259

Java 189
job applications, pre- and post-internet compared 186f
job design 209
junk mail and/or faxes 116
just-in-time (JIT) 261

killer applications 43, 60, 61, 212
knowledge management 207f
knowledge workers 201
Kuala Lumpur 6

labour rates, effect of global operations in driving down 62
land registration by local authorities 52
languges used on the internet 15, 53, 258
learning organisation 163
learning relationship and marketing 154
legal implications of internet 59ff
legal jurisdiction over web sies 76
legal protections of internet security 83
libel laws 60
life time value (LTV) of customers 156f
lines of credit 223
Linus operating system 12, 256
Liverpool to Manchester railway line 251
local area networks (LANs) 29
logic – role in development of computing 4
logistics 37, 42

logistics   181
London   253
lurker and browser customers   133
lurkers on newsgroups   237
Lycos   23

machine bureaucracy   202
maintenance, repairs and operations (MRO)
    goods   180, 193, 228
malware   69ff
managerial commitment to learning   166
Manchester University   9
market segmentation   44, 111–19
market segmentation – criteria for   113
marketing communications   120–51
marketing research   99
marketing, definition of   92
marketing, traditional and electronic
    compared   93
marketing/sales   37
marketplace procurement   191, 192f
masculinity – cultural dimension   258
mass customisation   170
Mclibel trial   121, 145f, 240
m-commerce/m-business   18–19, 225
Metcalfe's law   244
micropayments   221
middlemen   see intermediaries   188
mobile phone text polling   225
mood matcher   242f
Moore's Law   13, 58
MOSAIC   12
MP3 file format   44, 60

national service providers   28
Netscape   13
Netscape Navigator   13
new customer concept   34
news internet sites   129
newsgroups   133
newsgroups   237f
Next Wave technologies   257
non governmental organisations (NGOs)
    122
non internet B2B electronic interaction
    188f
non-repudiation   68
non-tariff trade barriers   39
North America   8, 105
not-for-profit business   xiv

online marketing   25
online payment   25
online supermarket malls   185
Open e-book standard   190
open source debate   12

operating margin   218
operational use of market segments   115
operations   37
order disputes   222
organisation structure for internet
    operations   203
organisation structure and growth via
    crises   205f, 212
organisational cultures   214f
organisational structure   123, 198f

P2P – person to person internet transactions
    222
Packet switching technology   11, 30
palmtops   260
parenting message boards (Disney)   245
Pareto's law   241
Parliament   251
passowrd protection – potential
    shortcomings   74f, 85
Pentagon   59
Pentium II   13
permission marketing   105, 111, 167f, 258
pervasive computing   258, 260f
PESTLE analysis   xv, 49, 105, 250, 253f
point of sale (POS)   106
political action, direct   53–4
political implications of the internet   50ff,
    254
pollution   62
POP (Post Office Protocol)   31
pop-up advertising   131ff
portals   23, 40, 129
positioning   116
postnationalism   52
power distance   258
pricing efficiencies   184
pricing, effect of internet on global prices
    56, 62
primary marketing research   99
primary value chain   37ff
printing press and growth of reading   3
privacy in transactions   184
private exchanges   103
private key encryption   85
private networks   194f
problem child – internet B2C market
    originally   224
procurement   180
production supply chain (example)   182
professional bureaucracy   202
profit in e-business   226
profitability and non-profit organisations
    154
proprietrary information, scale of theft of via
    internet   68

prospects   156
Protocols   30–1
proxy server   73
psychographic segmentation   114
public exchanges   103
public key encryption   85
public relations   142
public relations – government use of   143
publicity – risk of bad   77
purchasing   180
purchasing patterns e.g. food, clothing   227

qwerty style text messaging   225

radio frequency indentification tags (RFIDs)
   261f
Railway Acts   251
railway bubble   251f
railways – parallel with growth of internet
   205f, 251f
reach extended via internet   225
'real time' segmentation   115
regulation – corporations subverting via
   global operations   62
regulation of marketplaces   191
regulation of individuals and organisations
   in internet era   53
regulation of internet as a whole   60
re-intermediation   187f, 221
relationship communities   240
relationship marketing fatigue   169
relationship marketing   see customer
   relations management
remote working and security   73
repeat purchasers, short, medium and long
   term   156
repudiation of service   222
reputational damage   150
resistance to change   123
retail customer power vs. purchasing of
   corporations   41
retailers   183
retention of customers   157
reticence of public to buy on internet   34
return on investment with computer based
   investments   229
revenue collection   221
revenue management   220f
revenue models and growth   224
rising star of internet sales in recent years
   224
Risk in market strategies   33
risk on internet   66ff
river Thames   253
Rocket, railway engine   251
routing   30

sales based revenue model   224
sales direct from websites   185
sales promotions   139f
'script kiddies'   78–9
search costs for products   184
Search engines – use of   25–6
secondary marketing research   100
secret shopper   100
Secure Electronic Transaction (SET)   86
Secure Sockets Layer (SSL)   86, 221
Security in trading   34
security on internet, general issue   66ff
security risks, types   68f
self-employed, patterns of work   57
sell-side procurement   191
server downtime   209
service marketing   96
service relationship building   159f
service supply chain (example)   182
sexual abuse – protection in English law   77
shared information between supplier and
   customer   183, 188
shipbuilding, rapid decline in UK   253
simple structure   202
Singapore   6, 8
skyscraper advertising   131ff
smart cards   222
SMEs – restrictions on IMC   123
SMEs, low level of malware protection
   70–1
SMTP (Simple Mail Transfer Protocol)   31
sniffing   81   (see also email wiretrap)
social dumping   62
social implications of internet   56ff, 258
software/hardware leapfrogging   13
sources of external market research   101
sourcing of suppliers   180
South Korea   8
spam emails   44, 63, 82, 116
spam filters   45, 82
specialisation, growth of with internet
   staff   204
'spectacles' model of external environment
   50
speed of technological change   xv
spin doctors   121
sponsorship of web pages   141
spoofing   see identity misrepresentation
sputnik   10
stakeholder groups and performance
   measurement   218f
Stockton and Darlington Railway   251
stored value payment methods   222
STP (segmentation, targeting, positioning)
   models   116
subscription revenue model   224

substantiality of market segments   115
supply chain   180
supply chain management   181, 262
supply chain network   181
surveillance, ethics of   100
suspects   156
symmetric encryption   *see* private key

tags   189f
targeting   115f
tax returns online   51
T-Commerce/T-Business   225, 229
TCP (Transmission Control Protocol)   30
TCP/IP   30–1
technological convergence   17
technological convergence, financial
    implications   225
technological dependencies   229
technological implications of internet   58f,
    260f
telecommunications and its impact on
    communities   236
TELNET   31
text messaging   56
theft of websites and domain names   77, 85
third party marketplaces   193
threshold competences and resources   229
thumb and thumb text messaging styles
    225
tiger teams of authorised hackers   80
time poor customers   225f
time, manner of handling in physical and
    internet businesses   209f
trade regulated by government   53
transaction communities   239
transaction fee revenue models   224
transferring customers from physical to
    non-physical environments   185
transport   62
transport and impact on communities   236
Transport Layer Security (TLS)   *see* Secure
    Sockets Layer
Trojan Horses   69, 70, 81
trust, question of re suppliers   183, 188
TV advertising   128
twin towers disaster Sept 11, 2001   144
types of net marketplace   192

UK   51, 53, 55, 60, 101, 244, 250, 253, 256f
uncertainty avoidance   258

universities as highly risky internet
    environments   83
University College London   11
University of Southern California   11
upstream supply chain   181f
URL (Uniform Resource Locator)   30
USA   8, 39, 51, 53, 55, 60, 113, 129, 135, 137,
    244, 250, 256, 258
user communities   235–49
USPs   229

value added networks (VANs)   189
value based management   217
value chain analysis   xv, 33, 36ff
value chain support activities   38ff
value drivers in Diese model   218
value exchange   170
vertical marketplaces   194
viral marketing   146
virtual communities   236
virtual currency   221f
virtual private networks (VPNs)   189
virtualisation of organisations   206
viruses   44, 63, 69, 70, 81
visual and audio systems of the future
    263
voice activated software and appliances
    260, 264
voice recognition software   75
voting online, prospect of   51
vulnerabilities – sources of on the internet
    67f

w3 consortium   22
WAP   19, 28, 59
weaknesses in land telephony systems   39
web addresses   21
web dating   58
webcams   75
white hat hackers   80
wholesalers   183
wireless and mobile technology   259,
    260f
wireless connectivity   18
Wisconsin   6
women using internet   96, 98
world wide web   20
worms   69, 70

Yahoo!   23, 24